MAXIMIZING
SCHOOL LIBRARIAN
LEADERSHIP

JUDI MOREILLON

MAXIMIZING
SCHOOL LIBRARIAN
LEADERSHIP

Building Connections
for Learning *and* Advocacy

ALA
Editions

CHICAGO 2018

JUDI MOREILLON is a literacies and libraries consultant and a staunch advocate for the leader and instructional partner roles of school librarians. Currently a mentor for the Lilead Project, Moreillon served for thirteen years as a coteaching school librarian at all three instructional levels and taught graduate students in library science for twenty-one years, most recently as an associate professor at Texas Woman's University. She earned both an MLS in library science and a PhD in education at the University of Arizona. She has written three other books published by the American Library Association: *Collaborative Strategies for Teaching Reading Comprehension: Maximizing Your Impact* (2007), *Coteaching Reading Comprehension Strategies in Elementary School Libraries: Maximizing Your Impact* (2013), and *Coteaching Reading Comprehension Strategies in Secondary School Libraries: Maximizing Your Impact* (2012). Her home page is http://storytrail.com. She blogs at http://schoollibrarianleadership.com and tweets @CactusWoman with #schoollibrarianleadership and #buildingconnections4learning.

© 2018 by the American Library Association

Extensive effort has gone into ensuring the reliability of the information in this book; however, the publisher makes no warranty, express or implied, with respect to the material contained herein.

ISBN: 978-0-8389-1525-7 (paper)

Library of Congress Cataloging in Publication Control Number: 2018003534

Book design by Alejandra Diaz in the FreightText Pro and Gotham typefaces.

♾ This paper meets the requirements of ANSI/NISO Z39.48–1992 (Permanence of Paper).

Printed in the United States of America

22 21 20   5 4 3 2

CONTENTS

FIGURES

PREFACE

I BELIEVE THAT STUDENTS, EDUCATORS, ADMINISTRATORS, AND school communities who are teaching and learning within a culture of collaboration can and will succeed in educating today's students for the present and their futures. This core belief is why I wrote this book. In partnership with principals and as instructional partners with classroom teachers and specialists, school librarians can play an instrumental role in building connections that develop and sustain an effective learning culture. I have had firsthand experience serving as a school librarian in collaborative culture schools. In these schools, I have had the opportunity to teach where everyone on the team is a learner, and everyone has opportunities to lead. Serving as a school librarian in a collaborative culture school supported me in maximizing my role as a leader who built connections for effective teaching and successful learning.

A collaborative teaching environment also serves as an optimal setting for school library advocacy. When the library serves as a hub for collaboration, stakeholders become invested in having a professional school librarian on their teaching teams. They understand the need for an expert school librarian leader who codevelops and integrates library resources and tools, coplans with classroom teachers, coteaches future ready students, and co-leads professional learning with administrators and colleagues. I have written *Maximizing School Librarian Leadership: Building Connections for Learning and Advocacy* for all library stakeholders. School librarians, in particular, can use the information in this book to increase their knowledge and hone their skills in building a future ready learning culture in their schools.

During the 1990s, I served as a school librarian during the exciting days of the National Library Power Project. From 1988 to 1998, the Dewitt Wallace-Reader's Digest Fund provided over $45 million in grant funds to 700 schools in 19 school districts across the United States. These districts worked with public education foundations in their communities and funded full-time, state-certified school librarians in Library Power schools. All Library Power school library programs in the Tucson Unified School District (TUSD) were required to operate with flexible scheduling based on classroom-library collaboration for instruction. The grants included funds for purchasing new print and electronic resources and renovating the physical spaces of the libraries. Perhaps most importantly, Library Power districts provided professional development (PD) for classroom teachers, school librarians, and principals, and the National Library Power Project offered PD for district-level library supervisors and Library Power directors.

School librarians involved with TUSD's project participated in Cooperative Program Planning, a weeklong training provided by Ken Haycock. In our district, we launched a follow-up series of PD opportunities for which Library Power school librarians were required to bring a classroom teacher colleague to learn and practice coplanning strategies. Together, we prepared to coteach in the classroom or library. In our school, the collaboration that began while writing our Library Power grant developed through collaboration-focused PD and coteaching in a learning culture in which the principal, classroom teachers, specialists, and I worked as a team to meet students' needs.

The Library Power model for classroom-library coteaching, integrating the resources of the library into the classroom curriculum, and educator PD have a great deal in common with today's "learning commons" model, the Lilead Fellows Project, and the Future Ready Librarians initiative. School librarians who codevelop a learning commons create a collaborative, flexible, and results-oriented learning, teaching, and PD space in the physical and virtual library. The Lilead Fellows Program, led by Ann Carlson Weeks, who coordinated the National Library Power Project from 1992 to 1996, is building a peer community among district-level school library supervisors that builds upon the work of Library Power. Follett's Project Connect and the Alliance for Excellent Education launched the Future Ready (School) Librarians Framework in June 2016, which positions school librarians at the center of educational transformation (see figure 6.2).

The conditions are right and ripe for school librarians to maximize their leadership roles in building collaborative school cultures. There is an urgent need for students, educators, administrators, and communities to work together to create dynamic learning environments. In a learning-centered school library, relationships are strengthened, ideas are explored, and risks are taken—together. Through "competitive collaboration," "educators push and help one another to become better" (Couros 2015, 73). The result is improved student learning and continuous improvement in educators' instructional practices. In *Maximizing School Librarian Leadership*, I provide school librarians, district-level school library supervisors, principals, and other leaders and educators with strategies based on research and firsthand experience to make future ready library programs a reality. With these strategies in place, school librarians and library stakeholders can cocreate optimal conditions for teaching and learning that result in ongoing, systemic advocacy for professional school librarians and exemplary school library programs.

JUDI MOREILLON
November 17, 2017

ACKNOWLEDGMENTS

THIS BOOK WOULD NOT HAVE BEEN POSSIBLE WITHOUT THE support and expert guidance of my editor, Jamie Santoro. Jamie and the entire ALA Editions team worked tirelessly to make this book the best it could be. I am in their debt.

I would also like to acknowledge the collaborating classroom teachers and administrators with whom I served during my tenure as a practicing school librarian. They helped shape my thinking and guided my practice of coteaching. The school librarian graduate students in the courses I taught over a 21-year period have also influenced my thinking, as have the Cohort 2 Lilead Fellows. Their knowledge, strengths, and challenges are represented in these chapters. Alongside these educators, I continue to develop and refine strategies for maximizing school librarian leadership. Together we strive to position school librarians and school library programs in their rightful place—at the center of teaching and learning in our schools.

INTRODUCTION

FUTURE READY LEARNING IS COMPLEX. IT REQUIRES ALL EDUCATION stakeholders to collaborate in order to prepare students to learn, work, and participate in a global society. School librarians lead by building connections. They position their work at the center of learning through coteaching future ready learning; that is, the multiple literacies, skills, and dispositions that are essential for student success (see figure 1.1). School librarians can serve as models for continuous learning while they engage in professional development (PD) with colleagues. School librarians help all library stakeholders reach their capacity. School librarians' leadership builds and sustains future ready education and enlists library stakeholders as advocates who ensure the central role of the librarian and the library program in their schools.

For school leaders, the first step on this pathway to leadership is understanding *systems thinking*. Systems thinking involves taking stock of the whole system before attempting to change any part of it. Systems thinkers closely examine the interdependent relationships among people and practices within the system, and they search for patterns. They use this reality check to determine the places in the system that support their vision, mission, or goals. They also note what currently hampers progress toward achieving their aspirations. In collaborative culture schools, systems thinkers use their shared commitment and individual talents to meet challenges head-on and collectively solve the dilemmas that keep students from achieving success.

"Taking stock of the whole system" is not a new practice for effective school librarians. The job of the school librarian requires a broad understanding at both the building and the district levels. It necessitates seeking insights into and alignment with the classroom curriculum, and knowing how the library program connects to and supports the many components that make up the whole. School librarians work with all administrators, educators, and students in their buildings. They also reach out beyond the school walls to work with families and other community members. This gives school librarians a natural vantage point for systems thinking. Along with principals, school librarians share a global view of the learning community.

A collaborative learning culture provides a foundation for taking a systems thinking approach to educational transformation. Systems thinking involves people engaged in learning together—as a team. Team learning "is a discipline of group interaction. Through such techniques as dialogue and skillful discussion, small groups of people transform their collective thinking, learn to mobilize their energies and actions to achieve common goals, and draw forth an intelligence greater than the sum of individual members' talents" (Senge et al. 2012, 8). Systems thinking has the potential to revolutionize the way school librarians interact with administrators and classroom teacher colleagues. With a systems thinking approach, school librarians can serve as "big picture" leaders and change aides who work with administrators and others to build connections that transform teaching and learning (see figure 1.5).

While this whole-school approach is developing, team learning can be honed at the classroom, grade level, or disciplinary department level. When classroom teachers, specialists, and school librarians coplan and coimplement instruction, their lessons and units of instruction are better constructed and more creative and successful for students. With two or more educators to guide students, learners can go deeper. Their learning can be more personalized, and therefore, more personally meaningful to each student. While this model provides choice and learning support for students, coteaching also provides job-embedded PD for educators. Figure 0.1 shows some of the challenges that future ready school librarians can solve alongside their classroom teacher and specialist colleagues. (This figure is also available as a downloadable Web Extra.)

One approach to teaching and learning that aligns well with student-led learning, a collaborative culture, and systems thinking is Guided Inquiry Design (GID). This is a learning process that requires expertise and guidance by an inquiry learning team. The purpose of this team is "to take full advantage of the varied expertise in the school and community," and the team is organized around students' specific learning goals and needs (Kuhlthau, Maniotes, and Caspari 2012, 11). A culture of collaboration supports inquiry-based learning, and inquiry-based learning strengthens a culture of collaboration.

The goal of GID is for students to learn how to learn. With the guidance of a team of educators, GID requires students to grapple with the learning process and gradually internalize it so they can take full responsibility for their own learning. Through the inquiry process, students learn from a variety of resources and use problem solving, critical thinking, and decision-making. In the process, they

FIGURE 0.1

The Future Ready School Librarian (with apologies to outstanding future ready male school librarians)

WHO CAN HELP? -BY JMOREILLON

apply additional skills, such as creativity and innovation, and develop dispositions including persistence and self-direction. GID puts students and their learning at the center. As Senge and his colleagues suggest, this can help the school "reestablish its place as a social institution by making children's lives, not the classroom, once again the center of their learning" (Senge et al. 2012, 66).

Educators collaboratively plan, teach, and assess student learning outcomes in order to facilitate GID. School librarians cannot effectively implement inquiry learning without the involvement of classroom teachers and specialists. Classroom teachers and specialists benefit from collaborating with a school library professional to facilitate deeper and more personalized inquiry learning for students. Creating an inquiry-centered learning community begins with building relationships and providing systemic support for student and educator success. When school principals and librarians partner to develop strong library programs built on coteaching future ready learning, they create programs that serve as hubs for building connections. In this model, school librarians demonstrate the unique, high-impact contributions they make to the learning community. They can document the measurable difference their teaching makes in student learning outcomes and educator instructional practices.

Maximizing School Librarian Leadership is intended to provide educators with instructional and cultural interventions that can "help create new norms that foster experimentation, collaboration, and continuous improvement" (Guskey 2000, x). School librarians who build connections transform school cultures, curricula, and teaching practices. I wrote this book to support school librarians as they build these connections, sustain, and advocate for their central role in future ready learning. In the chapters that follow, preservice and practicing school librarians, district-level library supervisors, school librarian educators, school principals and administrators, and others will find strategies to position school librarians as leaders. In their leadership and instructional partner roles, school librarians make essential connections that build and sustain a culture of learning and engender advocates among library stakeholders.

HOW TO USE THIS BOOK

Maximizing School Librarian Leadership gives all members of the school community a foundation on which to build a shared vision within a collaborative culture of learning. It describes a future ready culture and pedagogy that meet the needs of today's students and educators. It also provides tools to sustain and advocate for effective future ready learning and collaborative teaching practices. To support the book study potential of this text, there are nine chapters that can be read one per month during the academic school year. Each chapter offers a study guide for individual, small-group, or whole-group work, and sample reflection prompts. The book can be read and the study guide can be used by individual educators as well.

The reader of this book will frequently encounter words that are in **boldface** type. These words are bolded the first time they appear in the text and are defined in the Glossary section near the end of this book. Be sure to consult the Glossary when you come upon unfamiliar words and terms that are in **boldface** type.

As noted, this text can be used as a book study selection at the school or district level. To support a professional book study approach to using this text, each chapter includes three discussion questions and three reflection prompts. The discussion questions are designed to help readers connect the information in each chapter with their own background knowledge, experience, and teaching environment. Educators can use these discussion questions with partners or in small or large groups. They can also respond individually to the questions—either orally or in writing, on paper or electronically.

Although they can be conducted by individuals, the three activities at the end of each chapter are intended for small or large group work. The activities require various kinds of teamwork. Some of the activities are repeated in different ways in various chapters. Some activities lead readers to resources beyond this book. Downloadable Web Extras are offered online to make reproducing and sharing some of the figures in this book easy. The book also includes a glossary of terms.

In the following chapters, principals and school librarians, in particular, will find support for their shared leadership roles in building connections for learning in collaborative culture schools. Building and sustaining an effective school culture are an ongoing process of nurturing relationships and collectively developing, reaching, and revising agreements. This book can provide inspiration, strategies, and guideposts for these efforts. Individuals, cadres of librarians, whole schools, or districts can use this book to guide their path toward the goal of a school community that learns together. It can help them build capacity in order to transform teaching and learning. For information beyond these covers, see the "Next Steps" section found at the end of this book.

Web Extras
can be found at
alaeditions.org/webextras

CHAPTER ONE

Building Connections for Learning

In a school that learns, people . . . recognize their common stake in each other's future and the future of the community.

PETER SENGE

◇◇◇◇

EDUCATORS AND EDUCATIONAL RESEARCHERS AND decision-makers are making informed predictions about what today's students will need to be successful both in their education and in their future social, economic, and civic lives. There are two facts on which they all agree. Literacy expectations are rising, and technological innovations are reshaping our daily lives. Schools must respond to these societal transformations or students will be left behind. In these dynamic times, educators are charged with creating empowered learning environments that are engaging, challenging, and relevant for students. These environments must be equally empowering for educators. By pooling their knowledge and skills in a **culture** of **collaboration**, all learners, young and older, can meet the learning needs of the present and prepare for the possibilities of the future.

In this evolving environment, school librarians have a unique, urgent role and an unparalleled opportunity to build connections for learning. School librarians who create and sustain a **future ready learning** culture in their schools position themselves as leaders. One could argue that educators have always been focused on preparing students for their futures. However, in this age of innovation, the "unknowable" nature of even the near future presents educators with an urgency that may not have been felt by previous generations. Every thought leader and education-focused organization cited in this book have an idea of the **literacies, skills,** and **dispositions** that students need in order to be successful.

Educating future ready students for **college, career, and community readiness** (CCCR) is a complex proposition. Figure 1.1 shows the pieces of the future ready learning puzzle. (This figure is also available as a downloadable Web Extra.) Discipline-specific **content literacies** combined with **cultural, digital and media,**

BEFORE READING

How does the culture in your school support your professional growth? How does it support you in individual and collective risk-taking, problem solving, and innovation?

1

and information literacies comprise the knowledge base that students need to be future ready. Students must learn and practice skills as they apply literacies in order to create new knowledge. They must also practice the dispositions—traits, behaviors, and mindset—that learners need to be successful in school and in life. With a focus on these essential pieces of the puzzle, educators can facilitate learning opportunities in which empowered students can thrive.

FIGURE 1.1

Future Ready Learning

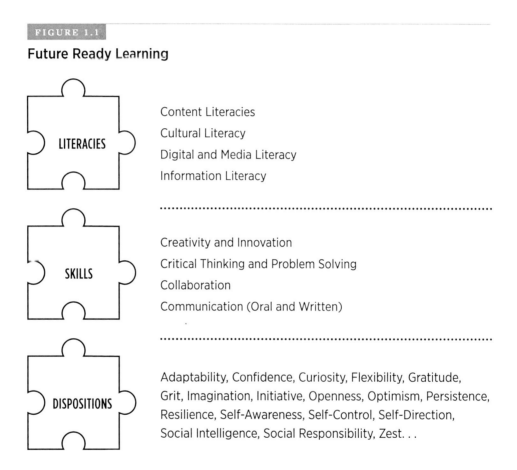

LITERACIES

Content Literacies
Cultural Literacy
Digital and Media Literacy
Information Literacy

SKILLS

Creativity and Innovation
Critical Thinking and Problem Solving
Collaboration
Communication (Oral and Written)

DISPOSITIONS

Adaptability, Confidence, Curiosity, Flexibility, Gratitude, Grit, Imagination, Initiative, Openness, Optimism, Persistence, Resilience, Self-Awareness, Self-Control, Self-Direction, Social Intelligence, Social Responsibility, Zest. . .

There are many aspects of preK–12 education that educators and school administrators do not currently control. External forces such as state and federal mandates, changes in funding levels, and the social, political, and economic conditions in our communities, state, nation, and world all affect individual schools and school districts. Being mindful of and making their voices heard in these larger systems in which schools function is important work for educators. Yet, it is in their immediate school buildings, classrooms, and libraries where educators can respond with urgency to students' needs for future ready learning. It is at the school and district levels where educators have the greatest opportunity and the most pressing responsibility to enact the transformation they want to see in the larger education environment.

VISIONS FOR SCHOOLING

As educators analyze and assess their current learning and teaching environment, it is important to look outward to learn what thought leaders are writing and saying about effective practices in education. A school faculty can use these leaders' ideas to engage in discussions around the issues they raise. Educators can use this information as a lens to closely examine their school culture and teaching practices. They can collaborate to build a shared vision that focuses on high aspirations for all students and educators alike.

In the United States, there are a growing number of organizations and individuals that have presented their frameworks for the present and future of learning and teaching. The thought leaders' and organizations' visions discussed in this chapter are the product of years of experience, study, and research. While these individuals and organizations currently publish much of their professional development material online, the print resources cited here present their foundational work.

School librarians can play an essential role in actualizing the strategies for transforming learning and teaching proposed by these thought leaders. In any school-based change movement, school librarians are "insiders" who know stakeholders' values, prior knowledge, and experiences. They are in a position to know their colleagues' various levels of commitment and openness to change and risk-taking. School librarians create a shared space in the library and a collaborative model for the school library program. This allows them to facilitate learning in a whole-school network that transcends grade levels and disciplines. They can extend that network to include families, experts in the field, and community members at large. Through the library program, school librarians build connections for transforming teaching and learning in their schools and communities.

Through the library program, school librarians build connections for transforming teaching and learning in their schools and communities.

#schoollibrarianleadership

BERNIE TRILLING AND CHARLES FADEL
❯ 21st-Century Skills

The Partnership for 21st Century Learning (http://p21.org) encourages educators to use "the learning and thinking power tools of our times" to engage students in the kinds of learning experiences that are most needed to develop twenty-first-century skills: "inquiry, design, and **collaborative learning** projects that deal with real-world problems, issues, questions, and challenges" (Trilling and Fadel 2012, 142). In relation to learning and "innovation skills," the Partnership asks educators to focus on the 4Cs: (1) creativity and **innovation**, (2) **critical thinking** and problem solving, (3) communication, and (4) collaboration. These skills apply equally to educators who must effectively model and teach the 4Cs.

In their book *21st Century Skills: Learning for Life in Our Times,* Bernie Trilling and Charles Fadel describe the characteristics of "expert" educators who have the necessary skills to teach today's learners. These educators must exhibit passion for their discipline and for the teaching profession. They must use and apply the power of learning tools and technologies. They must use digital thinking tools to expand, organize, and deepen their expertise, and they must apply their knowledge and skills to new and more complex challenges. They must share motivations, values, attitudes, and beliefs with others in their **professional learning community** (PLC), and they must care about issues and dilemmas that challenge their profession (Trilling and Fadel 2012, 146–47).

KEN ROBINSON AND LOU ARONICA
❯ Creative Schools

In *Creative Schools: The Grassroots Revolution That's Transforming Education*, Ken Robinson and Lou Aronica (2015) use a gardening metaphor to illustrate the power of teaching. They note that gardeners prepare the soil, plant seeds, tend their gardens, and have faith that their efforts will lead to a bountiful harvest even though they know they don't control all of the variables, such as weather, that affect their gardens. Likewise, educators who are not in control of all the conditions in which they teach, must persist in their four main roles: to engage, enable, expect, and empower learners (104). By nourishing the conditions, "the soil," with their knowledge and passion, educators create an environment where students will want to learn, persist when learning is difficult, learn from missteps, and continue to strive for success.

The curriculum is a critical ingredient in creating fertile conditions for learning. Robinson and Aronica outline three principles of curriculum: diversity, depth, and dynamism. Diversity in the curriculum allows learners to discover and develop personal strengths and interests. Educators guide students and provide them with choices to pursue their interests to a proper depth that can lead to mastery. Dynamism, the third principle, develops from collaboration and interaction between students in the same grade level and of different ages, between students and educators with varying specialties, and between students and experts in the field. A dynamic curriculum is constantly evolving and developing. In the process, it creates bridges between in-school and out-of-school learning and between the school and the wider community.

MILTON CHEN
❯ Education Nation

Milton Chen, senior fellow and executive director emeritus of the George Lucas Education Foundation, is the author of *Education Nation: Six Leading Edges of Innovation in Our Schools* (2012). In his book, Chen describes six innovations that he believes help educators facilitate exciting learning experiences for students: the thinking edge, the curriculum edge, the technology edge, the time/place edge, the *coteaching* edge, and the youth edge. While all of these are important, the **coteaching** edge may be the most relevant innovation in regard to the content of this book. In society today, many endeavors require that people organize their work in teams in which each member brings her or his areas of expertise to the collaboration table. Educators who adopt this model break down the isolation that can keep school learning communities from diffusing and integrating instructional and technological innovations. The ability to collaborate with other adults, both within the school community and with experts in the field, is an essential skill for all educators.

Working in collaborative teams, educators can pool their resources and strategies for making learning more relevant to students. When educators take student learning beyond memorization to transferrable skills, such as information-seeking and reading comprehension strategies, they create a learning environment that helps students reach long-term goals for college, career, and community readiness. In addition, collaborating educators develop their communication skills and can better model and teach these skills to students. With a honed curriculum comprised of fewer **standards** that allow for more in-depth study, educators coplan and coteach in order to focus instruction on helping youth *learn how to learn*, which is the most transferrable skill of all (see the "Curriculum Edge" chapter in Chen's book).

CAROL KUHLTHAU, LESLIE MANIOTES, AND ANN CASPARI
❯ *Guided Inquiry Design*

In *Guided Inquiry Design: A Framework for Inquiry in Your School*, Carol Kuhlthau, Leslie Maniotes, and Ann Caspari (2012) apply a **constructivist approach** to learning and teaching. Their work is based on Kuhlthau's information search process research, which describes students' interconnected thoughts, feelings, and actions in a series of information-seeking stages: initiation, selection, collection, formation, presentation, and assessment (Kuhlthau, Maniotes, and Caspari 2012, 18). "An environment of inquiry enables students to learn the difference between simple and complex questions and what type of research addresses their questions. Through inquiry, students learn the whole range of research and media skills and develop their own research process, leading to deep understanding and production of media to share their learning" (Kuhlthau 2013, 6–7).

Inquiry learning helps prepare **future ready students** for schooling, daily life, and citizenship in an information-rich, real-world learning environment. **Guided Inquiry Design** (GID) requires expertise and guidance on the part of adults to support students as they grapple with this dynamic process and develop literacies, skills, and dispositions. This support depends on the involvement and collaboration of school librarians, classroom teachers, specialists, administrators, parents, and experts in the community. An inquiry mindset can change the way students, educators, and communities conceive of teaching and learning. "Guided Inquiry is a way of thinking, learning, and teaching that changes the culture of the school into a collaborative inquiry community" (Kuhlthau, Maniotes, and Caspari 2012, xiii).

An inquiry mindset can change the way students, educators, and communities conceive of teaching and learning.
#buildingconnections4learning

ANDY HARGREAVES AND MICHAEL FULLAN
❯ Professional Capital

Andy Hargreaves and Michael Fullan (2012), coauthors of *Professional Capital: Transforming Teaching in Every School,* offer strategies for enacting change in schools. They define "professional capital" as the human, social, and decisional components that are necessary to transform learning environments. Human capital refers to the "talent," or the credentials, experience, and teaching ability of the faculty. Hargreaves and Fullan note that "groups, teams, and communities are far more powerful than individuals when it comes to developing human capital" (2012, 3). Social capital is comprised of networks built on trust and based on shared conversations and interactions related to instruction. When social capital is present, educators become "socialized" into a culture that builds their confidence, knowledge, and skill levels.

Decisional capital acknowledges that schools are complex environments in which educators must make informed decisions in order for schools to reach their full capacity. As with human and social capital, decisional capital is best exercised in a collaborative culture. Shared decision-making leads to collective responsibility and the confidence to take calculated risks and learn from missteps. When these three "capitals" are combined, transformation can be built on "shared experiences, trusting relationships, and personal and social responsibility, as well as transparency. What pulls people in, teachers all the more so, is doing important work with committed and excited colleagues and leaders engaged in activities that require creativity to solve complex problems and that make a real difference" (Hargreaves and Fullan 2012, 151).

PETER SENGE ET AL.
❯ *Schools That Learn* and Systems Thinking

While there are many connecting themes among the ideas championed by these education thought leaders, there is one strategy they all have in common; all require **systems thinking**. Their visions for today and tomorrow require that educators understand the interdependent relationships and behavior patterns in the whole system in which they serve. Systems thinking provides a reality-based view that illuminates those aspects of the system that are functioning optimally and those that are not yet doing so. With these understandings honed at the school site level, a faculty can identify both its strengths and the challenges it faces. They can collaborate to modify and adjust or transform the school's system in order to achieve their desired outcomes.

In *Schools That Learn: A Fifth Discipline Fieldbook for Educators, Parents, and Everyone Who Cares about Education,* Peter Senge and his colleagues describe "team learning" in which all members of the learning community exhibit a willingness "to think and act together as a living system" (2012, 115). Members of the team make a conscious effort to transform their communication skills in the classroom, at faculty meetings, and during staff development. They develop respect for one another and "establish some common mental models about reality" (Senge et al. 2012, 116). This helps build a team of educators who are community-minded and who value and seek collective as well as individual learning. They develop a web of **interdependence** that supports all members of the community. In this model, learning is embedded in relationships in the school and greater community and includes students, educators, administrators, families, and the community at large. "In this discipline [systems thinking], people learn to better understand interdependency and change and thereby are able to deal more effectively with the forces that shape the consequences of their actions" (Senge et al. 2012, 8).

Figure 1.2 summarizes these thought leaders' visions for schooling.

FIGURE 1.2

21st-Century Visions for Schooling

Publication	Authors/Organizations	Main Thrust of Vision
21st Century Skills: Learning for Life in Our Times (2012)	Bernie Trilling and Charles Fadel/Partnership for 21st Century Learning	Identifying skills for a "knowledge society": learning and innovation skills, digital literacy skills, and career and life skills
Creative Schools: The Grassroots Revolution That Is Transforming Education (2015)	Ken Robinson and Lou Aronica	Revolutionizing education from the ground up: creating motivating and effective learning environments through teacher facilitation, principal leadership/school culture, and policy-makers creating necessary conditions for the grassroots revolution
Education Nation: Six Leading Edges of Innovation in Our Schools (2012)	Milton Chen/Edutopia	Describing innovative classroom practices that use technology tools for transformation
Guided Inquiry Design: A Framework for Inquiry in Your School (2012)	Carol C. Kuhlthau, Leslie K. Maniotes, and Ann K. Caspari	Defining a framework for a student-centered, educator-guided inquiry process for deep meaningful learning supported by a collaborative culture
Professional Capital: Transforming Teaching in Every School (2012)	Andy Hargreaves and Michael Fullan	Focusing on teachers, improving professional development within a collaborative environment
Schools That Learn: A Fifth Discipline Fieldbook for Educators, Parents, and Everyone Who Cares about Education (2012)	Peter Senge, Nelda Cambron-McCabe, Timothy Lucas, Bryan Smith, Janis Dutton, and Art Kleiner	Developing processes to support "schools that learn" as incubation sites for continuous change and growth in order to meet the needs of 21st-century students

As Shelley Burgess and Beth Houf (2017) proclaim, when school leaders strive for excellence, there is one factor that can make it happen: culture, culture, culture. Educating future ready students requires a flexible, open, continuously learning school culture. Educators must be trusting and trustworthy adults who communicate effectively, listen to one another with empathy, and develop shared values. They must enlist critical thinking and problem solving skills to creatively address the pressing challenges in their schools and neighborhoods. If a culture of excellence is to succeed throughout the school community, then all of the faculty (and staff) must engage in effective collaboration and commit to change processes that result in improved student learning. As Peter Senge and his colleagues note: "In a school that learns, people . . . recognize their common stake in each other's future and the future of the community" (2012, 5).

DEFINING CLASSROOM-LIBRARY COLLABORATION

Collaboration is required if the library program is to achieve its place as the school's hub of academic and personal learning.

#buildingconnections4learning

Collaboration is required if the library program is to achieve its place as the school's hub of academic and personal learning. In their role as instructional partners, school librarians can serve as "culture builders," faculty members who build positive energy and reinvigorate the school culture (Gruenert and Whittaker 2017). The American Association of School Librarians (AASL) recently adopted new national school library standards. One of the common beliefs is that "qualified school librarians lead effective school libraries" (AASL 2018, 11). AASL also recently published the "Definition for an Effective School Library Program," which states that an effective program requires a certified school librarian who is an instructional leader and teacher. "Collaboration" is one of the definitions included in that position statement: collaboration entails "working with a member of the teaching team to plan, implement, and evaluate a specialized instructional plan" (AASL 2016a). This definition also frames the collaborative practices specified in the "Instructional Role of the School Librarian" position statement (2016b). For school librarians, collaboration is essential in order to enact their leader and instructional partner roles and make measurable contributions to students' learning grounded in the classroom curriculum.

Integrating the expertise of the school librarian and the resources of the library into the classroom curriculum through instructional partnerships is not a new concept. Since the 1960s, AASL has recommended a team approach to library instruction (AASL 1960, 1969). More recently, the association has used the terms "instructional consultant" (AASL and AECT 1988) and "instructional partner" (AASL and AECT 1998; AASL 2009a; AASL 2018). These terms further emphasize the collaborative role of the school librarian as a teaching partner rather than as an educator who works in isolation from classroom teacher colleagues.

School librarians' work includes cooperation, coordination, and collaboration. In contrast to collaboration, cooperation and coordination involve less intensity (AASL 2006). Cooperation tends to be more informal, short-term, and often lacks a focused planning effort. In cooperative activities, each individual maintains authority, and there is no joint mission or shared structure. Coordination requires more communication over a longer duration. The relationships in coordinated activities are a bit more formal, and they have an understood mission or goal. With a specific focus, coordination requires some amount of communication or some measure of planning. Often one person will take the lead in coordination and the other (or others) will simply follow along in supporting roles. While there is more intensity in coordination than in cooperation, authority is still maintained by each individual.

Collaboration is a more sophisticated and complex level of work. It requires true *interdependence*. Collaboration is a way of working in which team members work together as equal partners to achieve a particular outcome or goal. Collaboration requires effective ongoing communication, joint planning, individual and collective action, and commitment to a shared outcome. Collaboration takes time and investment from all team members. Collaboratively planned lessons and units of instruction tend to be more creative, effective, and engaging for students.

During the school day and throughout the year, effective school librarians will serve in cooperative, coordinated, and collaborative roles as their various responsibilities require. When administrators and faculty have a shared understanding of the differences between these three types of library work, they can best maximize the expertise of the school librarian and assess the effectiveness of the library program. School librarians collaborate in order to ensure their impact on student learning outcomes. Collaboration reaps rewards far beyond what any one individual can achieve. As the African proverb says: "To go fast, go alone. To go far, go together."

CHARACTERISTICS OF A COLLABORATIVE SCHOOL

The Association for Supervision and Curriculum Development (ASCD) notes that a school's climate and culture are important foundations for students' learning and educators' teaching, and shape a community's perception of school quality. "School climate refers to the school's effects on students, including teaching practices; diversity; and the relationships among administrators, teachers, parents, and students. School culture refers to the way teachers and other staff members work together and the set of beliefs, values, and assumptions they share" (www.ascd.org/research-a-topic/school-culture-and-climate-resources.aspx).

A positive school climate is one in which all school stakeholders work together to create and maintain a welcoming, respectful, and caring environment. From the moment students, educators, staff, families, or community members arrive on the school grounds or enter the school building, they experience a tangible sense of feeling "at home." They are greeted with friendly faces and kind words. The cheerful school secretary who answers the phone or welcomes office visitors, the friendly cafeteria workers who make sure no one goes hungry, and the helpful custodian who retrieves and returns lost items to their rightful owners—everyone in this school contributes to this positive climate and feels good about being part of this community.

School culture is enhanced by a positive school climate. A school's culture is supported by the entire learning community, but administrators and educators have a larger part to play in agreeing upon and sustaining the beliefs, values, and assumptions that are related to learning and teaching. The school culture projects what is important to educators. When a school faculty has shared beliefs about the purpose of schooling and their roles in helping students and families succeed, their school's vision and mission statements will reflect their collective commitments. In a collaborative learning culture school, faculty communicate their beliefs and values in every communication and action they undertake. A strong, consistent culture ensures that all school stakeholders have a firsthand experience of the vision and mission of the school.

Schools that build a collaborative culture of learning based on systems thinking require effective **distributed leadership**. Principals in these schools develop and encourage formal and informal leaders who engage in planning, initiative implementation, and system-nurturing in order to sustain the necessary environment for what Senge and his colleagues call "schools that learn." These schools are "places where everyone, young and old, would continuously develop and grow in each other's company; they would be incubation sites for continuous change and growth. If we want the world to improve, in other words, then we need schools that learn" (Senge et al. 2012, 4–5).

Administrators and educators who collectively build and sustain a collaborative school culture share common motivations; they care about other people's children and want the youth they serve to succeed in school and in life. They express these values in the ways they communicate with students, families, and with one another. They show respect for others; they are kind. In a collaborative school culture, educators will share many attitudes and beliefs with others in their professional learning community. They will also have different opinions. When conflict arises, they have the skills and commitment to listen to one another and respectfully work through their differences. These educators care deeply about issues and dilemmas that challenge the teaching profession, and they strive to improve their individual and collective instructional practices. They know they can accomplish more by working together in a system that supports their efforts.

In a school that learns, an openness to a shared sense of risk-taking is essential to all learners—students as well as educators and administrators. The principals in this learning community plan for and provide professional learning that is driven by real problems that need immediate solutions. In-services or workshops that address actual school problems include active, hands-on learning, follow-up, and assessment. Such staff development is generative and directly supports the school's vision.

Both formal and informal leaders are needed to shepherd a collaborative culture of learning. In his book *Every Child, Every Day* (2014), the award-winning superintendent Mark Edwards described how school culture and vision mattered in the Mooresville (North Carolina) Graded School District's successful "digital conversion." Four of the six ingredients in the Mooresville district's initiative did not involve technology per se: building the culture, building capacity through ongoing professional development, an "all in!" attitude, and ubiquitous leadership.

While the technology tools were important, Superintendent Edwards placed a greater emphasis on the idea of "all in!" In the school culture he helped create, everyone is invested in and is committed to providing students with the most engaging, collaborative, real-world learning experiences that lead to student (and educator) success. In this model, every stakeholder has "the opportunity to lead and is expected to lead—and that leadership is not solely reserved for those at the top" (Edwards 2015, 2).

Figure 1.3 captures the key attributes and school stakeholders in a collaborative culture school.

FIGURE 1.3

A Schoolwide Culture of Collaboration

In a collaborative culture school, educators have a shared vision and mission. They have invested in relationships and have developed trust. They are committed to individual and joint success. These educators are open to new ideas and to learning with and from one another; they have a **growth mindset**. They are led by formal and informal leaders who take a systems thinking approach and rise to the challenges they face. Together, they develop a culture of collaboration and continuous learning in their schools.

RESPONSIBILITIES OF LEADERS

Principals and school librarians can be leaders at the forefront of building a collaborative culture of learning in their schools. While district-level administrators develop policies that affect every student and educator in the system, the building-level principal has the responsibility to guide faculty in developing a site-based vision and mission. These fundamental policies must be aligned with the district's initiatives. They must also reflect the unique characteristics of the school's students, educators, and curriculum, as well as meet the needs of the surrounding community. "One of the most difficult things to address in schools these days is the development of a shared vision. Vision statements abound on paper, but the key to the success of any vision is goals and objectives to be shared and grounded in practice. There is only one way to accomplish this, and that is to have leaders at all levels working, interacting, examining impact, and learning from implementation" (Edwards 2015, ix).

Shaping a school's vision and building a collaborative learning culture can only occur in an atmosphere of trust. Building relationships and trust among the various stakeholders is an ongoing process. As the faculty is working toward a shared vision, it is essential that the principal prepare the school culture for collaborative work. "Without culture, there is no culture of innovation. It all starts by creating an environment where people feel cared for, supported, and nurtured—the very things we know that impact learning for students in the classroom" (Couros 2015, 79). With the goal of infusing trust throughout the system, the leader creates a space in which people can build collaborative relationships, develop their strengths, and meet challenges head-on.

As the instructional leader for the school, the principal sets the tone for learning. The principal must be the "lead teacher and lead learner and steward of the learning process as a whole" (Senge et al. 2012, 20). In short, the principal must possess and model what Carol Dweck (2006) calls a "growth mindset." Dweck, who studies motivation, has found that people who believe that intelligence and talent are fixed will accept their fate. They will not take a proactive stance toward their own learning. If, on the other hand, people believe that intelligence and talent can be "grown," they will be open to learning new strategies and will commit to the task of developing their capacity. While people have both fixed and growth mindsets in various contexts, principals can lead learning by modeling a continuous openness to growth.

BUILDING CONNECTIONS FOR LEARNING

School librarians must directly support and meet their principal's need to help every member of the learning community reach his or her full capacity. Ideally, school librarians possess and develop complementary strengths and serve as coleaders alongside their principals. In *National School Library Standards for Learners, School Librarians, and School Libraries,* AASL reaffirmed and expanded the roles for qualified school librarians: as instructional leaders, program administrators, educators, collaborative partners, and information specialists (2018, 12). Major national initiatives, such as the Every Student Succeeds Act (U.S. Department of Education 2015), Future Ready Librarians (2016), and the Lilead Project (2011) have also noted opportunities for school librarians to increase their influence and the impact of their teaching.

AASL's position statements published in 2016 clarified school librarians' responsibilities in learning and teaching. Figure 1.4 highlights these responsibilities and specifies the potential impact of the school librarian's work in the learning community.

FIGURE 1.4

Responsibilities of School Librarians

Document	Summary
Every Student Succeeds Act (U.S. Department of Education 2015)	School librarians and effective school library programs "positively impact: • student achievement; • digital literacy skills; • and school climate and culture" (Title I). School librarians "support • rigorous personalized learning experiences supported by technology; • and ensure equitable access to resources for all students" (Title IV, Part A). School librarians are responsible for: • "sharing professional learning for colleagues; • and disseminating the benefits of new techniques, strategies, and technologies throughout the district" (Title IV, Part A).
Position Statement on the Definition for an Effective School Library Program (American Association of School Librarians 2016)	The effective school library program has a "state-certified school librarian who • is an instructional leader and teacher; • supports the development of digital learning, participatory learning, inquiry learning, technology literacies, and information literacy; • supports, supplements, and elevates the literacy experience through guidance and motivational reading initiatives; • provides up-to-date digital and print materials and technology, including curation of openly licensed educational resources; • and provides regular professional development and collaboration between classroom teachers and school librarians."
Position Statement on the Instructional Role of School Librarian (American Association of School Librarians 2016)	School librarian instruction results in: • "students who read and utilize print and digital resources for curricular and personalized learning needs; • inquiring learners who evaluate and use both print and digital resources efficiently, effectively, and ethically." School librarians are "educators and instructional partners who are critical to teaching and learning in the school community."
Future Ready Librarians (Alliance for Excellent Education 2016)	Future Ready Librarians "partner with educators to design and implement evidence-based curricula and assessments that integrate • elements of deeper learning; • critical thinking; • information literacy; • digital citizenship; • creativity; • innovation; • and the active use of technology."

FIGURE 1.5

Building Connections for Learning and Leading

Connecting Professional
Development to Practice

Connecting Resources
and Tools with Curriculum

Connecting Library
and Classrooms
through Coteaching

Connecting Inquiry
Learning across Disciplines

Connecting Future Ready
Learning to
College, Career,
and Community

With a focus
on professional
development for
colleagues as well
as on student
learning, school
librarians reap
the benefits of
being both leaders
and instructional
partners.

#schoollibrarianleadership

These responsibilities result in **job-embedded professional development** for school librarians, classroom teachers, and specialists. "All aspects of teaching and learning are built on collaborative partnerships. . . . These partnerships require creativity, an openness to trying new approaches, and a willingness to take risks . . . All members of the learning community now share the roles of teacher, learner, and collaborative partners . . . By modeling such collaborative relationships, the school librarian helps change the culture of the learning community to reflect the kind of relationships that comprise the 21st-century work environment" (AASL 2009a, 20–21).

When asked whom they serve, "most [school librarians] would answer students, yet the primary clientele in terms of power, impact, and effect would be teachers" (Haycock 2017, 3). With a focus on professional development for colleagues as well as on student learning, school librarians reap the benefits of being both leaders and instructional partners. They are able to document the impact of their coteaching on student learning and on classroom teachers' teaching. School librarians are charged with collecting, curating, and integrating the resources needed to support the curriculum. When coteaching, they have firsthand knowledge of how those resources are being used, and they learn how to improve library collections in order to meet students' and classroom teachers' needs. They have daily and hourly opportunities to learn with and from their colleagues, and they can improve their own teaching proficiency through **reciprocal mentorship** (see chapter 2, "Job-Embedded Professional Development").

Future ready school librarians collaborate with classroom teachers to connect resources and tools with the classroom curriculum. When they coplan and coteach lessons and units of instruction, they connect the library program with classrooms and advocate for student choice and voice. With their global view of the learning community, school librarians can connect inquiry learning across grade levels and disciplines. They collaborate to ensure that students have opportunities to learn and apply inquiry in multiple disciplines. School librarians ensure that future ready learning supports students in developing the literacies, skills, and dispositions for college, career, and community readiness. Figure 1.5 shows five ways that school librarians build connections to maximize their role as learning leaders. (This figure is also available as a downloadable Web Extra.)

WHAT TO DO WHILE YOUR SCHOOL IS BUILDING A SHARED VISION

"Educational leaders are tasked with establishing a collective vision for school improvement and initiating change to spur innovation, ensure student learning, and increase achievement" (Sheninger and Murray 2017, 24). Building a shared vision that is embraced and actively supported by all members of school learning communities will take time to plan, implement, and institutionalize. An organization's vision is based on a shared set of values or purposes. There are many books written on vision-building, and there are no shortcuts. However, building relationships in a trusting collaborative culture is necessary to prepare a fertile ground for that process. "In any human endeavor, the quality of relationships determines outcomes" (Senge et al. 2012, 403).

A collaborative culture is needed in order to build, implement, and sustain a shared vision and a **community of practice** (Wenger 1998). A collaborative culture based on trust can also ensure that while a vision is being formulated, the social, emotional, and academic needs of students, classroom teachers, librarians, specialists, administrators, families, and the community are being addressed. "Only when individuals can trust the culture or organization will they take personal risks in order to advance that culture or organization as a whole" (Sinek 2009, 104).

Educators will find further support for using a systems thinking approach to building a collaborative culture in the chapters that follow. The first paragraph of each chapter in this book states why that piece is an essential component of an empowered collaborative learning culture puzzle. Readers will gain knowledge and strategies for enacting distributed, **strengths-based leadership** and job-embedded professional development through coteaching. They will learn strategies for coteaching inquiry learning, information literacy, reading comprehension and writing, and deeper and digital learning. Educators will also learn strategies for assessment and will come to understand the interdependence of assessment and **advocacy**.

By putting these pieces of a collaborative culture into action, educators will have the tools they need to codevelop a dynamic learning culture. Along the way, school librarians will build support to help them lead and advocate for future ready learning. Each chapter offers specific ideas for administrators, for classroom teachers and specialists, and for school librarians, in particular, to connect the essential pieces of an empowered collaborative culture. These chapters also provide school librarians with strategies for advocating for their own professional development as a place to begin.

BOOK STUDY GUIDE

I. Discussion Questions

QUESTION #1: Use systems thinking to explain how your school is helping students prepare for their futures. Map or list the various and interconnected ways that students and educators engage in the 4Cs; that is, the skills set out by the Partnership for 21st Century Learning: (1) creativity and innovation, (2) critical thinking and problem solving, (3) communication, and (4) collaboration. How can you build on your strengths? Where can your school sharpen its focus?

QUESTION #2: Make a list of the stakeholders in your immediate learning community. The list may include students, classroom teachers, specialists, librarians, administrators, families, and more. Discuss which stakeholders' needs you are currently meeting and which of their needs could be more effectively addressed. How could schoolwide collaboration increase your impact as you strive to meet more stakeholders' needs?

QUESTION #3: Using AASL's definition, how would you characterize your school's culture in terms of classroom-library collaboration?

- *Individual Thinking*: Compose individual responses to the questions asked above.
- *Partner Sharing*: Share your individual responses to these questions with a colleague in your own school or another school.
- *Group Sharing*: As a small or whole group, discuss the feelings, ideas, hopes, and challenges that occurred to you as you responded to the questions or listened to your colleagues' responses.

II. Activities

Although these activities can be undertaken by individuals, they are designed for group work.

Activity 1

Systems Thinking Tool: The Mind Map

Mind maps are one way to explore the big picture of how the various components of your learning organization fit together and support the whole endeavor. In *Schools That Learn*, Senge and his colleagues provide a sample map that puts the classroom, school, and district within larger interactions in the community and society (2012, 23). While their map shows the complexity of the education landscape, in this exercise your team will focus its lens on the interactions of those directly responsible for teaching and learning within your school building. It is within this sphere of influence that you and your colleagues will initially endeavor to build a culture of collaboration.

Use the mind mapping tips at www.mindmapping.com. Draw your school's map on paper or electronically. This activity can be done individually or with a partner, grade-level or departmental team, or as a whole faculty or staff. One strategy is to ask various groups within the school to compose maps and then compare them. After sharing all of the maps, create a "final" map that represents the interdependency of all stakeholders and instructional activities in your school. (District-level mapping can also be done by a cadre of school librarians.)

Activity 2

Divide the group into four or eight smaller groups. Ask each group to compose a list related to Discussion Question #1 above. If using four groups, one for each of the 4Cs, each group will list both student *and* educator opportunities to practice learning and innovation. If using eight groups, the groups will examine opportunities for students *or* for educators.

Exchange lists at least one time so another group can add to each list. Post the lists and then assess each list through discussion. Determine if there are one or more areas of strength on which the school learning community can focus its immediate efforts. Brainstorm possible ways to provide students and educators with more opportunities to practice the identified skill or strategy.

Note: This could evolve into a whole-school inquiry project (see chapter 3, "Inquiry Learning").

Activity 3

Write a job description for a future ready student. This could be a student at a particular grade level, in a particular course, or it could be generalized for all students in the school. Then rewrite a job description for yourself in your particular role in the school, or for other educators, administrators, staff, parents and caregivers, or other members of your learning community. Make sure that the adults' job descriptions support student success as you have defined it in the student job description. Which traditional and which new characteristics, behaviors, and skills do these job descriptions include?

III. Reflection Prompts

Choose from these possible reflection prompts or compose one of your own.

1. Reflect on your thoughts, feelings, and next steps as you read this chapter and/or engaged in the discussion questions or activities.

2. Reflect on previous instructional innovations that have occurred during your career as an educator. Think about how you responded to one of these initiatives. What about it worked well and why? What could have worked better?

3. Especially for school librarians: Reflect on your role as a leader who builds connections and a collaborative culture of learning in your school. In what activities are you currently engaged that develop your leadership skills and build connections? What new leadership opportunities are you seeking? How will you measure your individual progress toward increasing your capacity to lead and connect?

CHAPTER TWO

Job-Embedded Professional Development

The best strategy for improving schools and districts is developing the collective capacity of educators to function as members of a professional learning community—a concept based on the premise that if students are to learn at higher levels, processes must be in place to ensure the ongoing, job-embedded learning of the adults who serve them.

RICHARD DUFOUR AND ROBERT MARZANO

◇◇◇◇

UPON ENTERING A FUTURE READY SCHOOL WHERE learning is the central focus, every student, educator, administrator, staff member, and community member will sense excitement; there's electricity in the air. Similar to the atmospheric pressure change before an impending storm, there is a sense of anticipation—something is happening or is about to happen—and that something is change. Trusting relationships and an openness to change are essential ingredients in innovative teaching and learning. They are essential for results-oriented job-embedded professional development (PD).

Educators in this school are a team. "A team is not a group of people who work together. A team is a group of people who trust each other" (Sinek, Mead, and Docker 2017, 104). Trust is the foundation on which they build connections in a "culture of learning." Future ready learning schools require leaders who collaborate to nurture and sustain relationships and a culture of collaboration. These schools require leaders who can co-facilitate PD in order to diffuse innovations throughout their buildings and districts. Professional learning embedded in the everyday practice of educators is an effective way to transform teaching and learning.

Learning implies change. When people learn, they add new **schemas** to their understanding of themselves, others, and the world. People must also replace, modify, or eliminate established patterns of behavior, beliefs, or knowledge. Learning is not about reaching a specific target and then resting on one's laurels. Rather, it is about a continuous process of building and tearing down and building up again. Transforming a learning culture requires change with a capital "C."

Peter Senge (1990) has long made the case for twenty-first-century organizations to create new and flexible methods to assist people as they develop their

BEFORE READING

Who are the colleagues in your face-to-face or virtual professional learning network who have propelled your development as an effective educator? Think about how you have worked with others to help them grow as well.

capacity for change. Adults can be more enthusiastic risk-takers when they have the support of someone who is willing to risk alongside them. Just as young people do, educators can grow and develop more fully and more quickly by learning with and from their peers. School-based, peer-to-peer, job-embedded PD is an ideal strategy for diffusing innovations.

The change process requires risk-taking on the parts of all learners—students and educators alike. The possibility of failure is inherent in risk-taking. The psychologist Carol Dweck (2006) notes that learners who have a growth mindset understand that failure can lead to personal growth. These learners believe that they can apply hard work to develop their talents and abilities, and they can learn from their mistakes. With an understanding of the individual person's power to improve, people with growth mindsets are more likely to explore new ideas. This can also be true of a school or an organization. With a growth mindset, all stakeholders understand that every team member should be supported in taking risks, trying new strategies, learning from missteps, and improving their own and the team's performance the next time.

"The best strategy for improving schools and districts is developing the collective capacity of educators to function as members of a professional learning community (PLC)—a concept based on the premise that if students are to learn at higher levels, processes must be in place to ensure the ongoing, job-embedded learning of the adults who serve them" (DuFour and Marzano 2011, 21). Traditional PD strategies distance adult learners from their daily practice and are misaligned with **andragogy**, or adult learning theory (Knowles 1980). In contrast, job-embedded PD meets the criteria for effective adult learning. In this model, adult learners determine what they want to learn and how they will learn it. To summarize, adult learners:

1. are self-directed and take responsibility for their own learning;
2. have prior experiences that can be a positive or negative influence on learning;
3. are motivated by an internal need to know;
4. have a problem-solving orientation to learning (Knowles 1990).

As Bernie Trilling and Charles Fadel note, successful professional development tends to be "grounded in a teacher's own questions, problems, issues, and challenges, as well as what professional research has to offer" (2012, 138). A school that develops a culture of collaboration is primed for effective PD practices. Educators who collaborate with one another have shared commitments and agreements. They are taking a learning and teaching journey together as a team.

"Collaborative cultures create and sustain more satisfying and productive work environments. By empowering teachers and reducing the uncertainties of the job that must otherwise be faced in isolation, collaborative cultures also raise student achievement. Collaborative cultures facilitate commitment to change and improvement" (Fullan and Hargreaves 1996, 49). Professional learning communities (PLCs) and coteaching are two effective collaborative job-embedded strategies for faculty learning.

PROFESSIONAL LEARNING COMMUNITIES

PLCs are one way to organize more effective faculty development. PLCs are comprised of grade-level teams, vertical teams that span grade levels, discipline-focused teams, or interdisciplinary teams. PLC members collaborate to use data, including observations, in order to set specific objectives for learning outcomes. They collaborate to clarify teaching in terms of student learning and are able to measure their success relative to the performance of other students whose teachers are on their PLC team. The team works together to provide a guaranteed (for all students) and viable (developmentally appropriate) curriculum, one of the school-level factors that improves student achievement (Marzano 2003).

The PLC whole-school approach places the emphasis on working together as a collective to improve student learning (DuFour and Marzano 2009; Fullan 2010). When educators share ideas, they strengthen their practice as well as build trust in their professional relationships. Charles Feltman writes that "trust is defined as choosing to risk making something you value vulnerable to another person's actions" (2009, 7). When educators coplan and coteach, they open themselves to both positive and negative feedback. Feltman also notes that before people trust one another, they will assess each other's sincerity, reliability, competence, and care. Colleagues will take the measure of each other's trustworthiness. Effective school librarians who expect to position themselves as "centralized" instructional partners will continually monitor their own trustworthiness to ensure they measure up.

PLC teams may share lesson plans. They may develop a common assignment and a shared assessment instrument. Team members may visit each other's classrooms to observe student learning in progress. They may engage in lesson study, in which educators teach the same lesson and are observed by their peers who provide them with feedback. They may even team teach, with two educators in the same room working with the same group of students (see figure 2.1). They may also coassess student learning outcomes and the effectiveness of their collaborative instruction. PLC members learn from their missteps and modify their teaching with input and support from their colleagues. PLC members also celebrate when the team achieves a particular benchmark.

PLC TEAM LEADERS

Selecting team leaders for PLCs is an important consideration for school principals. In their book *Leaders of Learning* (2011), Richard DuFour and Robert Marzano set out criteria for PLC team leaders. Among these considerations is the influence a potential leader has on others. These faculty members are what Everett Rogers (1995) calls "opinion leaders." They may also be early adopters who, according to Rogers, are positioned to have a great deal of influence on the **diffusion of innovations**. In fact, Rogers states that the acceptance or rejection of an idea often depends less on the merits of the idea itself than on the person who is proposing it. School librarians can be trusted leaders who inspire their colleagues to action and support their schools in the change process.

With the school librarian's leadership, the library has the potential to serve as the hub for all of the school's PLC activities. It is often the largest, most comfortable room for adults in the school building. With room to spread out and work in small groups and ready access to resources, including technology tools, the library is often used for faculty meetings. Classroom teachers, who are experienced in using the library, will be comfortable holding their PLC meetings in the physical or virtual library. Using the library for PLC teams'-work can be a natural extension of the ways the library and school librarian have been used to support professional development.

"Successful change requires multiple layers of leadership roles. Formal and informal leaders, at the classroom, school, and community levels, each provide different resources to the organizational learning effort" (Senge et al. 2012, 323). Allison Zmuda and Violet Harada also point out that since librarians fill a special niche between classroom teachers and administrators, they can be referred to as "'informal leaders," and in a "distributed leadership model [they] create an additional layer of leadership within the school" (2008, 24). With this model, principals and librarians join forces to further develop educators' skill sets and elevate teaching and learning in their schools.

RECIPROCAL MENTORSHIP

Educators practice reciprocal mentorship in the library learning commons.

#schoollibrarianleadership

The **learning commons** is one model for creating a collaborative learning space in the library. The knowledge-building focus of the learning commons is its core mission. In this model, educators place the emphasis on how the physical and virtual resources of the library are used by students, faculty, and community members. A schoolwide team, including the school librarian, principal, faculty members, parents, and, in the best examples, students, guide the development and use of the learning commons. Involving multiple stakeholders helps ensure that the ways students and educators interact with the library's resources and with one another lead to learning. This model for the use of the library's physical and virtual spaces, resources, and the expertise of the school librarian results in professional development for adults as well as learning opportunities for youth.

Educators practice reciprocal mentorship in the library learning commons. Peer-to-peer coaching can be a "tool for professional learning, focused on developing a vision of effective instruction, creating a common language of practice, constructing an avenue for building competence in specific domains, and, in the process of doing this, generating norms of continuous improvement within a culture committed to fostering the learning for every one of its members" (Robbins 2015, 15). In these ways, effective PD is tied to school improvement, reform, or transformation initiatives that are underway in the school building or district.

Collaboration in the learning commons involves educators in **coplanning**, **coteaching**, and coassessing student learning. Through collaboration, educators work together to transform the curriculum, instructional practices, and learning. Through practicing reciprocal mentorship, "school librarians and classroom teachers have the opportunity to learn alongside each other while planning, implementing, and assessing student learning and the effectiveness of the lesson or unit of instruction" (Moreillon 2017b, 24). Coteaching educators facilitate **differentiated professional development** for one another.

In schools with **flexible scheduling** in the library, school librarians have the opportunity to coplan and coteach with classroom teachers and specialist colleagues at the point of need. They arrange coplanning time to fit classroom teachers' schedules. Together, coteachers determine time in the library, classroom, lab, on the athletic field, or in the community as necessary to meet the student learning objectives. In these schools, the schedule is based on students' and classroom teachers' needs for the librarian's expertise and for access to the library facility and resources. Since these school librarians don't have a specific group of students for which they are regularly responsible, time for classroom-library coteaching does not require more staffing to cover another teacher's classroom, and other educators' teaching is not disrupted by classroom-library coplanning and coteaching.

COTEACHING AS JOB-EMBEDDED PROFESSIONAL DEVELOPMENT

"Collaboration is integral to school librarians' work as educators. Being skilled in collaboration and practicing coteaching positively affect learners' learning" (AASL 2018, 148). Marilyn Friend and Lynne Cook, researchers in the special education field, identified five *coteaching approaches*. Figure 2.1 provides a summary of each approach. The "one teaching, one supporting" approach may be most useful in the context of special education. When applied to classroom teacher–school librarian collaboration for instruction, the other four approaches have the greatest potential to improve student learning and increase educator proficiency.

By applying these approaches in classroom-library collaborative instruction, school librarians can develop their own expertise as instructional partners and can play an essential role in developing classroom teachers and specialists as effective coteachers as well.

In the library setting, team teaching may be the most effective of all of these coteaching models. In this approach, both educators are in the same room at the same time taking responsibility for all students. This gives them the benefit of two heads, two perspectives, four eyes, and four hands as they coteach the lesson. Using the **think-aloud strategy**, educators can demonstrate collaborative learning, discussion and debate techniques, and other strategies so students can see exactly what is expected of them in the lesson. Educators can authentically share divergent responses or strategies that draw the same or different conclusions. They can jointly monitor students' individual, partner, or small group work.

The greatest benefit for the coteachers is that they experience another educator's instructional methods, teaching style, and behaviors in an authentic context. A

FIGURE 2.1

Coteaching Approaches

Team Teaching	After collaborative planning, educators coteach by assuming different roles during instruction, such as reader or recorder or questioner and responder, modeling partner work, role playing or debating, and more.
Parallel Teaching	Each educator works with a portion of the class to teach the same or similar content using the same or different modalities. Groups may switch and/or reconvene as a whole class to share, debrief, and/or reflect.
Station or Center Teaching	After determining curriculum content for multiple learning stations, each educator takes responsibility for facilitating one or more learning centers while in other centers, students work independently of adult support.
Alternative Teaching	One educator pre-teaches or re-teaches concepts to a small group while the other educator teaches a different lesson to the larger group. (Pre-teaching vocabulary or other lesson components can be especially valuable for English language learners or special needs students.)
One Teaching, One Supporting	One educator is responsible for teaching the lesson while the other observes the lesson, monitors particular students, and/or provides assistance as needed. In the library setting, this approach may be best applied with special education teachers.

Adapted from Friend and Cook (2012)

"personal approach" is "needed to shift instructional pedagogy" (Sheninger and Murray 2017, 26). Through coplanning and coteaching, school librarians and classroom teachers expand and refine their teaching toolkits. They analyze and reflect on their instructional practices. Coteachers develop their craft alongside each other as equal partners, and together they improve student learning outcomes.

Parallel teaching has the distinct advantage of lowering the student-to-teacher ratio at the point of the instructional intervention. After collaborative planning, the educators may divide the class in half or in some other grouping that best meets the students' needs. Each educator facilitates instruction targeted to the same objectives. They teach the same or similar content using the same or different modalities. Parallel teaching allows for more student-to-educator interaction. With more opportunities for student participation, educators can more effectively monitor students' thinking. Educators may also decide to bring both groups together to share, compare their learning, and reflect as a whole class.

Station or center teaching can be especially effective in the larger physical space of the library. Stations can be set up so that learners can access resources and technology tools and have some distance from students working in other centers. Each educator can take primary responsibility for one of the teacher-facilitated centers, or she can be a roamer who monitors progress and answers questions in all centers. The library's paraprofessional staff, student aides, or volunteers may also help with one or more stations.

With alternative teaching, one educator works with students who need an intervention to help them build vocabulary or acquire background information. The other educator works with the larger group in some way that positions these students in a holding pattern until the smaller group of students is prepared to rejoin the instruction. This organization for instruction can be of particular benefit to students who have special needs, such as English language learners who may need extra **frontloading** with academic vocabulary before a lesson begins. Alternative teaching may also be necessary for students who missed previous instruction for a variety of reasons, such as music or dance group rehearsals. When all students are prepared to move forward, the groups are rejoined and the cotaught lesson begins.

To be effective, all of these coteaching approaches require coplanning. Through coplanning, educators clarify the goals and objectives for cotaught lessons. In planning sessions, they bounce ideas off one another. They determine the most effective strategies and engaging resources, and they codesign learning activities for student success. Coplanning graphic organizers can guide educators' lesson and unit design. Through coplanning, educators are intentional in their design of a relevant and engaging curriculum. Sample coplanning forms for elementary educators are available on the ALA Editions Web Extras site at http://tinyurl.com/impact13-g-o. Forms for secondary educators are available at http://tinyurl.com/impact12-g-o.

Through coplanning, educators are intentional in their design of a relevant and engaging curriculum.
#buildingconnections4learning

EVIDENCE-BASED PRACTICE

Since the No Child Left Behind Act of 2001, U.S. educators have increasingly focused on using research-based instructional practices and collecting, analyzing, and applying data for decision-making. Various states have enacted policies, including rewards and consequences, related to student performance on standardized tests. In addition to the many literacy curriculum standards that relate directly to learning through the school library program, the Every Student Succeeds Act of 2015 provides school librarians with specific areas in which they can help support student achievement, including digital literacy skills and personalized learning supported by technology. Educators, including school librarians, are required to systematically collect data related to their teaching effectiveness.

Evidence-based practice (EBP) is one way to improve instructional effectiveness. EBP centers on "three integrated dimensions of evidence: evidence *for* practice, evidence *in* practice, and evidence *of* practice" (Todd 2009). Evidence *for* practice is derived from systematic scholarly research studies. School librarians build their practice on this foundation. This evidence could be related to flexible scheduling, coplanning and coteaching, inquiry learning and teaching, access to information or integrating technology tools, or any other aspect of teaching or librarianship that has been studied and reported by researchers. For school librarians, these research-based practices may come from the fields of education and technology, as well as library science.

Using this research-based evidence, school librarians make informed decisions about which of these practices to enact in their school library program. This results in evidence *in* practice. Librarians and coteachers test, gather, and document evidence of the effectiveness of that particular practice in their local learning environment. If the results are positive, they share this evidence *of* practice with library program stakeholders and decision-makers and continue to build their practice on a solid foundation of local as well as scholarly research-based evidence. If the evidence *in* practice does not reach the aimed-for target, school librarians and classroom teachers may review the research-based practice and further modify, adapt, or completely revise that particular practice. When they achieve positive student learning outcomes, they can make informed decisions about their teaching.

The evidence *of* practice component, in particular, helps school librarians build credibility with administrators, colleagues, families, and community members. School librarians must share evidence of student learning outcomes. Applying evidence *for, in,* and *of* practice through classroom library coteaching can help ensure that effective instructional practices are diffused throughout the school. Classroom teachers, specialists, students, and administrators who have had first-hand experience with classroom-library collaboration efforts and results will take up the role of advocates for the library program. This is the most effective kind of library advocacy—when stakeholders speak from personal knowledge about the effectiveness of the school librarian's contribution to student learning.

RESEARCH SUPPORTING CLASSROOM-LIBRARY INSTRUCTIONAL PARTNERSHIPS

The research base for instructional partnerships and coteaching is found in both the education and library science literature. The evidence cited here is from the library literature in order to provide school librarians with evidence on which to build their instructional practices. Two recently published articles provide comprehensive summaries of school library research (Johnston and Green 2018; Lance and Kachel 2018). This research may also be beneficial to principals, as well as to classroom teachers who may not be aware of the potential contribution of the school librarian to the school's academic program.

State-level studies, known at the School Library Impact Studies, have consistently shown a correlation between improvements in students' standardized test reading scores and having a full-time, state-certified school librarian on the faculty and a well-resourced school library collection (Lance 2017; Library Research Service 2017). Debra Kachel and library science master's degree students at Mansfield University (2011) summarized the research findings of these studies and identified a positive correlation between classroom-library collaboration for instruction and increased student achievement in fifteen out of the twenty-one studies they reviewed. In the South Carolina Study published in 2014, 55 percent of administrators noted that it is "essential that librarians and teachers design and teach instructional units together" (Scholastic 2016, 13). These same principals were more likely to view their librarians' teaching of writing and English language arts standards as excellent.

Additional studies further suggest the relationship between the collaborative work of the school librarian and student learning outcomes. According to the results of Phase Two of the New Jersey Study, in collaborative culture schools the instructional partner role of the school librarian is highly respected and prized by administrators and fellow educators because of the school librarian's positive impact on student learning outcomes (Todd, Gordon, and Lu 2011, 26). In another study focused on the perceptions of classroom teachers who had experience coteaching with their school librarian, teachers reported that compared to when they taught alone, student learning outcomes improved between 20 and 50 percent when they cotaught with their school librarian (Loertscher 2014, 11). The school librarians in this study also reported they were more effective when they cotaught with classroom teachers.

COPLANNING AND COTEACHING BENEFITS

"The librarian's role in school-wide curriculum integration and literacy . . . bring[s] a unique expertise to providing services to students" (Ewbank 2010, 9). There are many benefits for students when classroom teachers and school librarians coteach. Students have access to the complementary and distinctive skill sets of two (or more) educators who facilitate their learning. Learners have access to library materials and technology tools when they need to use these resources to accomplish a task. Two educators can provide more individualized attention, can respond to students' questions faster, and can facilitate **differentiated instruction** more effectively than one classroom teacher or school librarian working alone can do.

Figure 2.2 shows a progression from cooperation in providing library services to collaborative instructional partnerships. This chart shows various levels of communication and planning as well as examples of cooperation, coordination, and collaboration based on four types of coteaching approaches. (This figure is also available as a downloadable Web Extra.)

Coplanning can ignite "creativity among teachers," and this "creative fire" can spread to students (Robert Grover cited in Haycock 2007, 25). One of the school librarian's roles in coplanning with classroom teachers and specialists is building connections between the curriculum and the library's resources. The school library collection includes a wide selection of resources at various reading proficiency levels and in various formats. School librarians who are charged with developing and maintaining a collection to support the curriculum have knowledge of materials that can help classroom teachers and specialists more effectively support students' learning. Sue Kimmel found that "the school librarian was particularly key in connecting resources to unit objectives. . . . The librarian also made connections with other grade levels or with school-wide events such as assemblies, author visits to the school, or a Poetry Day" (2012, 11).

Educators typically have some content areas that they feel more comfortable with than others; it is extremely difficult to have an in-depth understanding of all topics and materials that interest students (Parrott and Keith 2015, 14). By pooling their expertise, coteachers can codesign and support more engaging curricula. In their graduate school education, school librarians gain expertise in integrating information literacy skills into subject-area content. In their preservice education,

By pooling their expertise, coteachers can codesign and support more engaging curricula.
#buildingconnections4learning

FIGURE 2.2

Levels of Library Services and Instructional Partnerships

Planning		Service/Partnership	Subtype	Examples
Collaboration	**Coplanning Required** Coplanning occurs when equal partners work together to design instruction. Educators begin with the end in mind—students' performance of learning objectives that show what students will know and will be able to do at the end of the learning activity. During coplanning, educators codesign assessment instruments and align students' learning tasks with objectives and assessments.	**Collaboration** The school librarian and the classroom teacher schedule formal planning time. Together, they design a lesson or unit of instruction to achieve shared goals and specific student learning outcomes. They coimplement the lesson or unit using one or more coteaching approaches. Collaborators co-monitor student progress and share responsibility for assessing and analyzing student learning outcomes.	**Team Teaching**	After collaborative planning, educators coteach by assuming different roles during instruction, such as reader or recorder or questioner and responder, modeling partner work, role playing or debating, and more.
			Parallel Teaching	Each educator works with a portion of the class to teach the same or similar content using the same or different modalities. Groups may switch and/or reconvene as a whole class to share, debrief, and/or reflect.
			Station Teaching	After determining curriculum content for multiple learning stations, each educator takes responsibility for facilitating one or more learning centers while in other centers, students work independently of adult support.
			Alternative Teaching	One educator pre-teaches or re-teaches concepts to a small group while the other educator teaches a different lesson to the larger group.
Coordination	**Coplanning Required** (Will not be as in-depth as above) A brief conversation about a lesson topic or objective.	**Coordination** Coordination requires more communication than cooperation. It includes a shared mission and may include planning and can be supported over a longer time period. Often one person will take the lead in coordinating activities and the other (or others) follow along in supporting roles. While there is more intensity in coordination than in cooperation, authority is still maintained by each individual.		The school librarian aligns library instruction with the topic or learning objectives the classroom teacher is addressing in the classroom. *or* The school librarian may support classroom teachers by helping them implement a new strategy, tool, or resource in the role of an extra set of hands in the room.
Cooperation	A brief conversation about a lesson topic or objective.	**Cooperation** Compared with collaboration, cooperation tends to be more informal, short term, and often lacks a focused planning effort. People who cooperate maintain their individual authority. They may not have a shared mission, but rather provide pieces of a puzzle without a commitment to the whole picture.		The school librarian provides print, digital, or technical resources for students' and classroom teacher's use in the classroom or in the library. The school librarian is not involved in instruction.

Codeveloped with Misti Werle, Library Media Systems Innovator, Bismarck (North Dakota) Public Schools classroom teachers are not typically taught how to teach information literacy skills such as identifying resources to answer inquiry questions, using databases effectively, evaluating the authority and accuracy of information, making notes, and organizing information so it is useful.

When classroom teachers coplan with school librarians, these skills can be integrated into the classroom curriculum so that students learn and practice these skills at the point of need. In addition, classroom teachers further develop their own ability to teach these skills and will apply them in their classroom instruction even when they are not coteaching with the school librarian. Educators who coplan and coteach experience the adage that "two (or more) heads are better than one." Bouncing ideas off of a peer while coplanning helps educators clarify their shared goals and objectives for student learning. Together, instructional partners can codevelop **graphic organizers**, checklists, and rubrics to measure learning outcomes and use these measures to coassess the effectiveness of their teaching.

In a study conducted with both primary and secondary school principals, South Carolina principals rated collaboration with teachers to build students' information literacy and integrate the library program into the school's curriculum in the top five of nineteen competencies, with over 90 percent assigning it the highest value of "very important" (Shannon 2009, 7–8). In an open-ended section of the survey, principals noted that they value the school librarian's personality, interpersonal skills, and ability to work well with others more highly than the librarian's knowledge-based skills. Perhaps this is because these "interpersonal and communication skills are important factors in facilitating collaborative planning, innovative instructional approaches, and implementation of resource-based learning" (Shannon 2009, 16). Principals' experiences and perspectives support the efficacy of classroom-library collaboration for instruction.

Principals, as "lead learners," can build capacity in their schools by setting the expectation that school librarians and classroom teachers will coplan and coteach. School librarians are responsible for keeping their principals informed of their collaborative activities. Principals should see evidence of classroom-library coteaching in the librarian's newsletters and in her monthly and annual reports. Principals should also see lesson and unit plans that document collaborative planning, coteaching, and the resulting student learning outcomes. Principals should also provide sufficient paraprofessional support staff to manage clerical work and the library facility so that the school librarian is free to "devote more time to making a major difference [in student learning] alongside the faculty" (Loertscher 2014, 14).

THE DIFFUSION OF INNOVATIONS

In addition to their coteaching role, school librarians can be partners with principals in providing formal on-site staff development. In a study conducted in Virginia, more than 86 percent of the elementary school principals surveyed agreed or strongly agreed that building the capacity of the adult members of the learning environment in the use of technology, intellectual property and copyright, effective web searching, and the use of databases is important work for school librarians (Church 2008, 13). One benefit to this strategy for formal PD is that the school librarian can then follow up and coteach with classroom teachers to apply new strategies and tools with students. In this way, school librarians help ensure that instructional innovations, resources, and tools are integrated into classroom teachers' teaching and are diffused throughout the building.

A collaborative culture of learning is an enabling factor in making positive changes to a system. Still, it is often challenging to get new initiatives adopted even when a new idea has obvious advantages. Everett Rogers (1995) identified the factors, the beliefs, and the behaviors that underlie the rate at which new ideas and practices are adopted by individuals and subsequently by organizations. Understanding and applying Rogers's theory can support organizing the learning environment for effective job-embedded PD. Research conducted on the diffusion of innovations asserts that high-risk innovations are adopted more slowly than ideas with low-level risks. Some would argue that breaking down the isolation of the classroom teacher or the school librarian could be perceived as a high-risk proposition. At the same time, Rogers's research also shows that innovations which can be field-tested on a small scale have a greater probability of being adopted. If a few educators in a building are willing to experiment with classroom-library instructional partnerships, they can serve as "early adopters" who share their first-hand experience and lead other members of the faculty as they test the coteaching waters (see Activity 1 at the end of this chapter).

Rogers describes various roles for participants in the diffusion of innovations model. Figure 2.3 shows the various roles and the paths their influence can take.

FIGURE 2.3

Roles and Influences in the Diffusion of Innovations Model

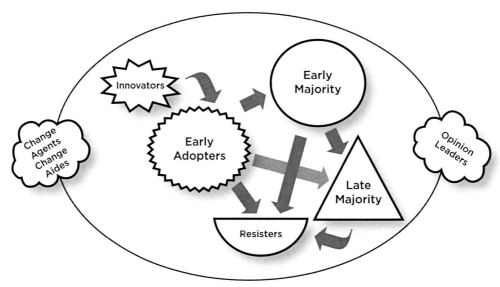

Caption: *The Diffusion of Innovations* by Everett Rogers (1995) illustrated by Judi Moreillon

Innovators are self-motivated people who easily understand and apply knowledge. They have a global perspective and think in terms of the future. Innovators may exist within a school system; they may also be leaders in the field who exert influence from outside of the system. One of the strengths of innovators is that they can tolerate uncertainty and take an experimental approach to the innovation. They may operate on the fringes of a social system. To others, they appear "different," which can negatively impact their effectiveness in spreading the innovation.

Early adopters, on the other hand, are respected by their peers and are considered to be "one of us." They are known among their peers as "successful but discrete" in their use of new tools, methods, or ideas (Harris 1998). They serve the system by being good role models. School librarians and teacher leaders are perfectly positioned to serve as early adopters. "The vision and charisma of the leader are enough to attract the innovators and the early adopters" (Sinek 2009, 139). The innovators and early adopters in any school form alliances with the principal and each other to enact the principal's vision and move the system forward in a positive direction.

While they are "willing," early majority people are those who do not tend to hold leadership positions in the organization. It takes them much longer to decide to implement a new idea or use a new tool. Late majority people are skeptical of new ideas and adopt innovations only after strong pressure. Once the use of the innovation is the "norm," they will go along. Providing early and late majority people with assurances of administrative or technical support can help them overcome their uncertainty. Finally, laggards are resisters. They are the most traditional or conservative members in the system; their reference point is the past. Laggards serve an important function in any system; they remember history and provide continuity. Laggards accept change "only when their survival depends upon it" (Harris 1998, 15).

Rogers describes two additional roles in the diffusion of innovations: opinion leaders and change agents. Opinion leaders are people who have informal influence over the behavior of their coworkers. They often have a higher social status outside the organization and are perceived as competent by their colleagues. According to Rogers, opinion leaders are more likely to uphold the "norms" of the system. Change agents, innovators, and early adopters should identify the most influential opinion leaders and make extra efforts to ensure that they become advocates for the change that is under way.

Change agents are people who mediate between the change and the system. They diagnose and develop the need for change for individuals, small groups, or the system as a whole. Change agents monitor the rate of change and slow down or terminate the diffusion of an innovation if the system cannot tolerate it, or if the innovation turns out to be undesirable. While individual educators in a school can serve as change agents, the principal's position is best suited for this role.

Change agents, however, do not work alone; they need change aides. These are people who promote the goals of the change agent. Change aides have respect from other members in the organization. They are able to influence outcomes because they have direct and frequent interaction with others. Ideally, school librarians

School librarians are coleaders alongside their principals in implementing change.
#schoollibrarianleadership

FIGURE 2.4

Coplanning and Coteaching Assessment

COTEACHERS: _____

LESSON TOPIC/OBJECTIVES: _____

DATE(S): _____

Collaborative Planning: Coteachers:	Assessment				
• Collaboratively design standards-based learning plans that are inquiry based and/or address information literacy, reading literacy, and technology skills.	0	1	2	3	4
• Collaborate to identify and curate differentiated resources in multiple formats and/or with multiple perspectives.	0	1	2	3	4
• Plan for differentiated instruction.	0	1	2	3	4
• Share responsibility for creating assessments.	0	1	2	3	4
Implementation: Coteachers:	**Assessment**				
• Coteach in the most appropriate environment to support student learning.	0	1	2	3	4
• Enact one or more coteaching strategies:					
– team teaching;	0	1	2	3	4
– parallel teaching;	0	1	2	3	4
– center or station teaching;	0	1	2	3	4
– alternative teaching.	0	1	2	3	4
• Share responsibility for teaching assessment tools.	0	1	2	3	4
• Comonitor student learning and adjust instruction as needed.	0	1	2	3	4
• Provide feedback to students throughout the lesson(s).	0	1	2	3	4
Outcomes Assessment: Coteachers:	**Assessment**				
• Share responsibility for assessing and analyzing student learning outcomes.	0	1	2	3	4
• Provide self-assessment opportunities for students.	0	1	2	3	4
Collaboration Assessment: Coteachers:	**Assessment**				
• Reflect on their collaborative process and effectiveness of instruction.	0	1	2	3	4
• Identify instructional improvements for subsequent lesson(s).	0	1	2	3	4
• Share the process and results of their coteaching with administrators and colleagues.	0	1	2	3	4

RATING SCALE:

0=No evidence   1=Emerging   2=Advancing   3=Advanced   4=Exemplary serve as both change aides and early adopters. In supporting their administrators' initiatives, school librarians are coleaders alongside their principals in implementing change.

BUILDING CONNECTIONS FOR TRANSFORMATION

Principals who take a systems thinking approach to professional learning will seek support from other members of the faculty in order to effect change. The principal, in the role of learning leader, can structure a change effort in such a way as to acknowledge the various needs and strengths of faculty members. School librarians can partner with the principal in order to map the learning community in terms of how innovations can best be tested, adopted, and diffused within the school. School librarians can also help principals who are new to a building understand the various roles that faculty have played in previous improvement efforts (see Activity 2 at the end of this chapter).

When school librarians coteach with classroom teachers and specialists, they support their principals' initiatives for change and improvement, and they support their colleagues' and their own professional learning. Together, educators can practice the most effective kind of professional development—job-embedded—when they "coteach actual students in real time, with the taught curriculum, available resources and tools, and within the supports and constraints of their particular learning environments" (Moreillon 2012b, 142).

School librarians, classroom teachers, specialists, and administrators can use figure 2.4 to determine the coplanning and coteaching proficiency level of any given lesson or unit of instruction. This tool can help educators assess their development as effective coteachers. It can also can help administrators or other observers of cotaught lessons understand the depth of professional learning in which coteachers are engaged. (This figure is also available as a downloadable Web Extra; it includes an additional field to record evidence.)

When school librarians are involved in school-wide coteaching and serve as leaders in job-embedded professional development, they help diffuse innovations and effective teaching practices throughout the school. By building connections and instructional partnerships, school librarians help ready the faculty for a culture of innovation. They support the change process that leads to institutionalizing future ready learning. One instructional innovation that meets the needs of future ready students—inquiry learning—can be successfully achieved in a culture of collaboration.

BOOK STUDY GUIDE

I. Discussion Questions

QUESTION #1: Have you participated in a PLC since becoming a professional educator? How were you supported in your professional growth? Describe your experiences.

QUESTION #2: What prior experiences have you had with coteaching? When you were a K–12 or college student, did you observe educators coteaching? Did you coteach during your student teaching experience or during a practicum/internship? Describe your experiences.

QUESTION #3: What is your highest hope or greatest reservation about coteaching or PLCs?

- *Individual Thinking*: Compose individual responses to the questions asked above.
- *Partner Sharing*: Share your individual responses to these questions with a colleague in your own school or another school.
- *Group Sharing*: As a small or whole group, discuss the feelings, ideas, hopes, and challenges that occurred to you as you responded to these questions or listened to your colleagues' responses.

II. Activities

Although these activities can be undertaken by individuals, they are designed for group work.

Activity 1

Force Field Analysis

A force field analysis is a decision-making process. It can involve individuals or groups in considering an issue that involves making a change and then identifying the internal and external forces that are driving the change forward and the internal and external forces that are restraining the change.

Begin by working as a group to describe the decision or change under consideration. In the context of this chapter, this could be classroom-library coteaching. Provide participants with four different marker or sticky note colors and a key for the colors:

GREEN—Internal Driving Forces	**YELLOW**—Internal Restraining Forces
BLUE—External Driving Forces	**RED**—External Restraining Forces

Ask participants to brainstorm as many ideas as possible in each area. The facilitator will want to help participants organize their ideas in some fashion. (The person who explains and leads this activity may want to search the Web for examples of how the analysis can be mapped.)

After organizing participants' input, analyze the force field map and reflect as a group on which are the most powerful driving and restraining forces. Discuss these results and consider how to act on them. If, for example, one of the most significant restraining forces holding the faculty back from coteaching is coplanning time, faculty and school administrators can then work together to remove this barrier.

For more information about force field analysis and for some examples, see "MindTools: Essential Skills for an Excellent Career" (https://www.mindtools .com/pages/article/newTED_06.htm).

Activity 2

Faculty Roles and Strategies for Success in the Diffusion of Innovations

Focus on a particular initiative recently enacted in the school, or one that is under way or planned for the future. Using figure 2.3 as a graphic organizer, identify members of the faculty who may serve in each of the diffusion of innovations roles as defined by Everett Rogers: innovators, early adopters, early majority, late majority, laggards, change agents and aides, and opinion leaders. Depending on the size of the faculty, the graphic organizer can include the whole faculty or it can be organized by grade levels or disciplines.

Chart the progress of a recent initiative or speculate on the necessary levers that will need to be in place in order for it or a future initiative to be successful.

There are many possible stakeholders who may be involved in this process. The principal and the school librarian can engage in this activity together. A leadership team responsible for the initiative, such as instituting the learning commons model in the library, may also benefit from this activity. Working with a high level of trust, the entire faculty may complete this chart and discuss it as a whole group.

Activity 3

Coplanning and Coteaching Self-Assessment

Along with a coteacher, use figure 2.4, "Coplanning and Coteaching Self-Assessment," to analyze and reflect upon a coplanned and cotaught lesson or unit of instruction. Coteachers can complete this form individually and then compare their assessments, or they can complete it together and discuss the various criteria on the form. A lesson observer or evaluator can also use this assessment tool in a pre-observation or post-observation conference to further clarify the depth of coteachers' collaborative work.

III. Reflection Prompts

Choose from these possible reflection prompts or compose one of your own.

1. Reflect on your thoughts, feelings, and next steps as you read this chapter and/or engaged in the discussion questions or activities.
2. Individual educators can reflect on what knowledge, skills, and talents they bring to the collaboration table. In addition, record some ideas related to what you can learn more about with and from your colleagues during coplanning and coteaching.
3. Especially for school librarians: Reflect on your role as a coteacher who supports your colleagues' growth as well as pursuing your own professional growth. In what areas of the curriculum do you see particular benefits from implementing coteaching? How will you take action in this/these areas? How will you measure your individual progress in coteaching?

CHAPTER THREE

Inquiry Learning

The crucial task of education is to teach kids how to learn.
To lead them to want to learn. To nurture curiosity, to encourage wonder,
and to instill confidence so that later on they'll have the tools for finding answers
to many questions we don't yet know how to ask.

SALMAN KHAN

◇◇◇◇

ONCEPTS LIKE "LEARNING HOW TO LEARN" AND "learn by doing" have been used in education for several decades. Beyond the fundamentals of core subjects, "the crucial task of education is to teach kids *how* to learn. To lead them to *want* to learn. To nurture curiosity, to encourage wonder, and to instill confidence so that later on they'll have the tools for finding answers to many questions we don't yet know how to ask" (Khan 2012, 180). Yet, "very rarely do students have the opportunity to follow passions, explore their interests, and engage in relevant opportunities that break down traditional classroom silos" (Sheninger and Murray 2017, 25). All of the thought leaders cited in this book would agree that future ready students must have multiple opportunities to engage their curiosity and pursue real-world projects. They would agree that hands-on, minds-on experiences help students learn how to learn and build their confidence. These types of learning experiences also help prepare students to problem solve when confronted with the inevitable learning and living challenges they will encounter in their futures.

In fact, in his most frequently viewed TED Talk, Ken Robinson (2006) proclaims that systems of schooling in the United States and around the world are robbing students of their innate curiosity. With more than 48 million views (at the time of this writing), Robinson's video "Do Schools Kill Creativity?" is a wake-up call for educators everywhere to transform teaching and learning in order to nurture creativity rather than undermine it. Robinson proposes that educators rethink their conception of the "richness of human capacity" and "cultivate the diversity of human intelligence" to develop the whole person—body and mind (and not just the math and language parts of the brain).

BEFORE READING

What do the phrases "learning how to learn" and "learn by doing" mean to you? How are these concepts manifested in your personal life, classroom, library, or school?

In his book *The One World School House: Education Reimagined* (2012), Salman Khan, founder of the Khan Academy, takes a critical view of the factory model of education still implemented in many U.S. schools today, and lays out his vision for an education system. He calls for flexible, not fixed, environments (in terms of time and place) that capitalize on technology to support learning based on students' mastery of content. In Khan's vision, all students would engage in personalized learning and have access to information via technology and mentorship from educators and experts at the point of need. Students would be allowed the necessary time to learn, to be creative, and to be innovative. Khan writes, "More creativity would emerge because it would be *allowed* to emerge and because there would be *time* for this to happen" (2012, 250).

"Inquire" is one of the shared foundations in AASL's *National School Library Standards for Learners, School Librarians, and School Libraries* (2018). When learners inquire, they "build new knowledge by inquiring, thinking critically, identifying programs, and developing strategies for solving problems" (AASL 2018, 34). Figure 3.1 offers a recipe for exemplary learning opportunities through inquiry learning. (This figure is also available as a downloadable Web Extra.)

FIGURE 3.1

Recipe for Inquiry Learning

From the Recipe Book of
Future Ready Educators and Students

Ingredients

- Curiosity
- Connections
- Motivation
- Content Knowledge
- Literacies
- Skills
- Dispositions

Directions

Beginning: Igniting Curiosity + Sparking Interest → Making Connections = Motivation

Preparing: Immersing in Content Knowledge + Real-World Issues + Student-Developed, Personally Meaningful Questions = Relevance Ready

Mixing: Interacting with Multimodal Information + Human Resources + Applying Skills and Dispositions = Rich Learning Environment

Cooking: Making Inferences + Interpreting Information → Synthesizing = New Knowledge

Sharing: Deep Understanding + Creativity + Authentic Audience(s) = Empowered Presentations

Ending: Process/Product Reflection + Assessment → Learning That Sticks = Transferrable Knowledge, Literacies, Skills, and Dispositions

Beginning Again: Repeat Often

IMPORTANT: Add sufficient time in each of these steps for maximum results.

Serves: All Future Ready Learners

38

By adopting inquiry learning, educators can provide students with the necessary time and a framework to follow their curiosity, explore ideas, develop meaningful questions and personal perspectives, practice problem solving, and express their creativity. Inquiry learning also supports content literacy. It provides students with opportunities to build upon core subject content in order to acquire new knowledge. It also gives them authentic reasons to apply content-specific literacy skills, such as reading graphs in math or maps in geography, in order to master content literacy.

In the Guided Inquiry Design (GID) framework, learning is supported by a process. "Inquiry is learning-centered, not product-driven" (Maniotes and Kuhlthau 2014, 14). Unlike **project-based learning**, which by its very name suggests a focus on a final project, a focus on the learning process is what distinguishes the GID framework. Inquiry may have more in common with **problem-based learning** or challenge-based learning, in which educators pose a problem or present a challenge for students to explore and solve. Hands-on experiential learning results in a **performance task**, which begins with a real-world scenario, problem, or question. While pursuing the task, students are involved in a complex learning process that requires them to apply critical thinking. The students' learning process as well as their final products or performances relate to real-world applications of the content and skills involved.

"School librarians collaboratively partner with fellow educators to facilitate learning in the school library, classroom, and within a variety of physical and virtual educational environments" (AASL 2018, 54). Through coplanning and coteaching with classroom teachers and specialists, future ready school librarians can be leaders in ensuring that inquiry is systematically integrated into school curricula. As Ross Todd, Carol Gordon, and Ya-Ling Lu found in Phase Two of the New Jersey Study, "The school library offers a learning environment that is not based on 'the right answer' prompted by rote learning, but on a more complex model of teaching and learning that is exploratory and highly motivational" (2011, 27). To be effective, these library learning environments must be guided by professional state-certified school librarians (AASL 2016a). These librarians must be capable instructional partners who coplan and coteach with classroom teachers and specialist colleagues. They must identify and **curate** an array of print and digital resources and tools, and they must be experts at integrating these into standards-based instruction. School librarians must know how to cofacilitate learning experiences that nurture students' curiosity and creativity.

Future ready school librarians can be leaders in ensuring that inquiry is systematically integrated into school curricula.
#buildingconnections4learning

NURTURING CURIOSITY AND CREATIVITY THROUGH INQUIRY-BASED LEARNING

"Curiosity is the tool that sparks creativity. Curiosity is the technique that gets to innovation" (Grazer and Fishman 2015, 62). Learners need to be challenged; they must master skills and develop dispositions that can support them in activating their curiosity, in taking risks, in expressing creativity, and in innovating. As the pace of change in our society continues to accelerate, today's students need foundational skills and strategies that transcend content, devices, and formats. Now more than ever before, empowered learners need to be curious, flexible, and creative people who know how to learn, how to teach themselves, and how to collaborate with others.

Inquiry-based learning is one way that educators can create opportunities for learners to use and develop their innate curiosity, express their creativity, and reach toward innovation. As a place to begin, the scientific method has a long and honored tradition in the preK–12 curriculum. In fact, the Next Generation Science Standards are described as a set of behaviors that "scientists engage in as they investigate and build models and theories about the natural world" (www .nextgenscience.org). Inquiry in science requires applying a range of cognitive, social, and physical skills. In science investigations, students may be provided with teacher-presented questions or hypotheses or they may need to develop hypotheses of their own. Students may be given a specific set of procedures, or they may be required to design procedures of their own. Finally, students are expected to draw conclusions and relate their findings to scientific principles. In all cases, students' inquiry learning is based on achieving specific outcomes required by the science standards.

The fine arts curriculum can provide another model for inquiry learning. When presented with an artistic challenge, students are actively engaged in an arts-based creative process; they are involved in problem solving. Students may or may not be aware that they are asking and answering their own questions during the creative process. They are taking risks, experimenting, and learning through trial and error. They are tolerating uncertainty and must be internally motivated to persist when the results do not meet their expectations. As Eric Booth notes, "when given free range, arts education becomes exemplary inquiry-based learning" (2013, 26).

CURIOSITY, EXPERIMENTATION, AND CREATIVITY

"Curiosity starts out as an impulse, an urge, but it pops out into the world as something more active, more searching: a question" (Grazer and Fishman 2015, 10). When inquiry questions come from students, they will be more motivated to pursue a line of inquiry. They will be more invested and active in the process because it springs from an authentic question that is relevant to them. Students will have support from their peers and educators who will push their thinking. Throughout the process, they will access multiple resources, interpret the information they find, and determine how it adds to their understanding. Students will enthusiastically present and share their findings. Educators will guide them in self-reflection and self-assessment throughout the inquiry. When the inquiry comes to a close, students will have gained a process as well as practiced a multitude of skills and dispositions that they can transfer to other learning contexts.

In today's library **makerspace** movement, students are involved in hands-on opportunities to practice the creativity and critical thinking that can lead to innovation. Students' makerspace activities may be facilitated by a team of educators that includes the school librarian. Curriculum-integrated makerspaces may have a focus on **STEM, STEAM, or STREAM** learning experiences. Through a curricular focus on science, technology, engineering, and mathematics, STEM learning signals an understanding that creativity is necessary for innovation and design. In STEAM experiences, the arts help learners expand their creativity. Formal experience with the arts has been proven to foster "reasoning ability, intuition, perception, imagination, inventiveness, creativity, problem-solving skills and expression" (Ruppert 2006, 13).

Curriculum-integrated, team-facilitated makerspaces have the potential to spread curiosity, experimentation, and creativity throughout the learning community. Makerspaces can support inquiry learning. The hands-on nature of makerspaces can give students a sense of autonomy when educators create an environment that encourages divergent strategies for problem solving. School librarians who coplan and coimplement makerspace learning with colleagues can ensure that students have choice and self-guided activities when they work in that space. "If we truly want our students to apply their learning and create new knowledge and ideas, we need to ensure students have opportunities to practice this kind of learning throughout the day and across disciplines" (Couros 2015, 101).

Curriculum-integrated, team-facilitated makerspaces have the potential to spread curiosity, experimentation, and creativity.
#buildingconnections4learning

SKILLS AND DISPOSITIONS

The Partnership for 21st Century Learning (P21) is a "catalyst" organization that builds partnerships in order to effect educational change (http://p21.org). P21 promotes learning and innovation skills that prepare future ready students for the increasingly complex and competitive working and living environments they will encounter. P21's 4Cs are creativity and innovation, critical thinking and problem solving, communication, and collaboration (see figure 1.1). These are precisely the skills that students learn and practice while engaged in inquiry learning. And these are exactly the skills that educators employ and model as they cofacilitate an inquiry process.

Students practice the 4Cs during inquiry learning. Educators model and encourage students to exercise creativity in how they approach the task or problem. Students employ critical thinking and problem solving as they make decisions throughout the inquiry process. They also decide which questions to ask, which questions to pursue or abandon, and why. Students determine which resources and tools to use, how to organize their findings to make them useful, and they interpret information and draw conclusions. During inquiry, students practice effective communication and collaboration skills with classmates, educators, and experts in the field. They determine how to present their learning using various formats, devices, and tools. Empowered students have choice and voice.

As Ken Robinson and Lou Aronica (2015) noted, educators are responsible for creating environments in which students want to learn—where they develop the dispositions that will help them persist when learning is difficult. Throughout the inquiry process, students will come to understand that the ambiguity associated with searching to discover something new is part and parcel of the journey. Inquiry requires that students take ownership of the learning process and become more self-reliant in their motivation and decision-making. "Learning can be transformed into understanding only with intrinsic motivation" (Booth 2013, 25). Inquiry learning has the potential to result in deeper understanding for students who have invested their whole hearts, minds, and bodies in pursuing personally meaningful questions and in solving real-world, relevant problems.

Inquiry learning has the potential to spark students' intellectual curiosity because educators and students codesign learning experiences that connect the curriculum to students' interests. Curiosity motivates people; it helps them persevere when learning is not easy. Open-mindedness is associated with other dispositions such as flexibility and adaptability. These are precisely the dispositions that students learn and practice while engaged in inquiry learning. And these are precisely the dispositions that educators employ and model as they cofacilitate an inquiry process.

INQUIRY LEARNING PHASES

School librarians may be aware of or versed in a number of inquiry learning models. Figure 3.2 shows inquiry phases for three of the models used in schools today.

FIGURE 3.2

Learning Phases of Various Inquiry Models

Guided Inquiry Design (2012)	Stripling Model (2003)	WISE (2011)
Open	Connect	Wonder
Immerse	Wonder	
Explore		
Identify	Investigate	Investigate
Gather		
Create	Construct	Synthesize
Share	Express	Express
Evaluate/Reflect	Reflect	Reflect

All three of these models begin with a phase in which educators spark learners' curiosity and invite them to wonder about a topic, concept, problem, or dilemma. In the **Stripling Model** (Stripling 2003), this initial phase puts a particular emphasis on students' prior knowledge and experiences. The Guided Inquiry Design provides students and educators with two additional phases for motivating, connecting, and engaging learners before they hone in and use resources to help them identify their initial inquiry questions. Stripling and the **WISE** inquiry-based research model use the term "investigate" at this point in the process when students are interacting with various texts.

Again, the GID has an additional phase in which students continue to gather ideas and information. Students may revise their initial questions based on new information and interests. All three models have a "create" stage in which students synthesize their learning and construct a learning product or performance. Both Stripling and the WISE model call the next phase "express" in which students "share" their learning, the term used in the GID. The final phase of all three processes involves students in self-evaluating their inquiry process and final products. Reflecting on their learning is also an essential component of this phase and is integrated into all of the phases in the GID.

In inquiry-based classrooms and libraries, the GID involves students in pursuing curriculum-based topics while exploring questions of personal interest. Figure 3.3 shows the eight phases of the guided inquiry process: open, immerse, explore, identify, gather, create, share, and evaluate.

FIGURE 3.3

Guided Inquiry Design Process

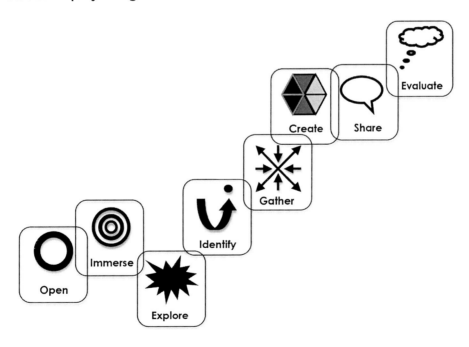

Republished with permission from ABC-CLIO, from *Guided Inquiry Design: A Framework for Inquiry in Your School* by Carol Collier Kuhlthau, Leslie K. Maniotes, and Ann K. Caspari, ©2012; permission conveyed through Copyright Clearance Center, Inc.

From the Open to the Evaluate phase, school librarians, classroom teachers, and specialists design the inquiry process to use highly motivating resources and tools that empower student engagement, choice, and voice. Coteachers provide interventions at the point of need and monitor student progress throughout the process. They further students' inquiry by asking probing questions, and offering content- and process-oriented prompts as needed. Coteachers design **scaffolds** and assessment tools to support students as they engage in the inquiry process.

LAUNCHING THE GID: OPEN, IMMERSE, AND EXPLORE

When educators launch the GID process, their initial goals are to spark students' passions and pique their curiosity as they frame the inquiry unit in terms of the required curriculum. The Open phase is intended to serve as an invitation to explore—an invitation that inspires and motivates learners to take a shared journey into the unknown and discover new knowledge. They present big ideas around which students (and/or educators) can build **essential questions**. "Big ideas go beyond discrete facts or skills to focus on larger concepts, principles, or processes" (Wiggins and McTighe 2005, 10). Educators help make curriculum-based inquiry relevant to students by connecting this Open phase to students' lives, inside or outside of school, or to real-world events. In the Open phase, educators create the conditions in which students are bursting with questions.

The Open phase relates directly to instructional design. Effective lessons and units of instruction begin by actively engaging students with the process and content of learning. Two (or more) educators with different areas of expertise or with divergent perspectives can codevelop more creative ways to launch an inquiry process. They might present a dilemma in the form of a discussion or debate between two (or more) opposing viewpoints. Educators could present a problem with a skit involving two (or more) actors. They may frame the inquiry using a broad essential question. By working together on inquiry design, educators may improve their ability to pique students' curiosity and spark their passions.

Educators can also maximize the impact of coplanning and coteaching in the Immerse and Explore phases of the GID. In the Immerse phase, educators guide students as they connect to their background knowledge. For a topic on which students lack background knowledge or may have misconceptions, educators use the Immerse phase to help learners build shared understandings. Educators can jointly identify resources to support this effort, including oral stories, books, field trips to museums or nature preserves, videos, podcasts, web- or social media-based information, current events, and more. While immersed in the overarching topic for the inquiry, educators encourage students to begin to think about how the connections they are making warrant further exploration.

In the Explore phase, educators provide a **text set**, (electronic) **pathfinder**, or other sources of information for students to browse and explore. Kuhlthau, Maniotes, and Caspari call this the "dip-in phase." During these skimming and scanning explorations, learners continue to build their background knowledge and further develop their thoughts about what is most compelling to them about the topic, problem, or dilemma. Students may also begin to jot down ideas and questions that spark their curiosity. In this phase, educators may help students form **inquiry circles** to provide each other with peer support throughout the process (see Kuhlthau, Maniotes, and Caspari 2015, 32–36).

THE "RESEARCH" PHASES OF THE GUIDED INQUIRY DESIGN

The Identify, Gather, and Create phases of the GID encompass what is thought of as traditional preK–12 "research." One critical difference is that in the Identify phase, students' own questions will develop organically because they are grounded in the background knowledge and motivation built during the first three phases of the GID. As a result, students' questions will be more personally meaningful, which in turn can help sustain their engagement and increase the likelihood that they will persevere throughout the process. Students' self-generated questions will be aligned with curriculum-based topics, and their questions will be authentic because they originate in the students' own interests and personal connections.

In the Identify phase, students develop their inquiry questions. They benefit from having two or more educators to support them as they hone their question(s). Through one-on-one or one-to-small-group inquiry question conferences, educators can help students clarify their question(s). They can ensure that students' questions are doable in terms of resources and time. In conferences, educators can also provide students with feedback related to their mastery of content, process learning, skills.

The Gather phase requires that students go beyond the resources provided by the educators in the first three phases. In this phase, students will access, evaluate, select, and use information to answer their question(s). With two or more educators facilitating the Gather phase, students receive more support as they locate and learn from "just-right" materials at their own levels of reading proficiency. This phase is often where school librarians and classroom teachers coteach information literacy skills, such as strategies for free-range web searching and using databases. Educators also teach or offer **mini-lessons** on the importance of critically evaluating sources in terms of their currency, relevance, authority, accuracy, purpose, and perspective or bias.

During the Gather phase, it is essential that students learn to make notes in their own words, record quotes and paraphrases, and keep a log of their references. **Notemaking** and annotating are essential lifelong learning skills. Students learn to use **text features**, such as subheadings, and to identify keywords that help them determine the main ideas in the information they read. As a result, students improve their ability to sift, sort, and prioritize information in order to meet their information needs.

When students determine that they have gathered the necessary information, they interpret and synthesize it in the Create phase. As Daniel Pink, who studies human motivation, proclaims: "If schools truly want to engage students, they need to downgrade control and compliance—and upgrade autonomy" (Azzam 2014, 12). If students are encouraged to pursue personally meaningful questions, it is logical that educators would provide students with a range of choices for demonstrating their learning. Students might employ **cloud-based tools**, or build a physical model. They could choreograph a dance, or write a script and perform their work. They might choose to give a speech, or write an editorial and submit it to a print or online newspaper or magazine. They could even choose to compose a traditional report. If students know limitless choices await them at the end of their inquiry journey, their motivation to persist throughout the process may be much stronger.

Creating digital learning products requires that students review information related to fair use and copyright guidelines. This is an area of expertise for school librarians who may take the lead in teaching the conventions of digital making. Capturing original media or locating and using **open education resources** (OER), including media with Creative Commons licenses, are essential aspects of students' learning during this phase. Educators may provide pathfinders that lead students to images, videos, music, and sounds that may be freely used or remixed and distributed on the Web. Setting the expectation for and teaching the ethical use of ideas, information, and media are essential if students are to learn and practice digital and **media literacy**.

SHARING, EVALUATING, AND REFLECTING

School librarians may take the role of advocates for students' diverse and creative expressions of learning.

#schoollibrarianleadership

Similar to the first three phases of the GID, the Sharing, Evaluating, and Reflecting phases may be new or expanded activities for students and classroom teachers who have had more experience with traditional research projects. During coplanning, school librarians and classroom teachers think about what "counts" in terms of inquiry outcomes. School librarians may take the role of advocates for students' diverse and creative expressions of learning. Future ready learning means students are empowered creators. When school librarians codevelop learning experiences and outcomes assessments, they can influence their colleagues and school learning communities in terms of assessing a diversity of learning products. Empowered students can exercise choice and voice while meeting educators' student learning objectives. Educators must make this clear from the outset.

Using various technology tools and social media, students can also reach audiences far beyond their classrooms, schools, and immediate communities. School librarians can help students tap into authentic audiences for their work and possibly receive feedback that can spur them on to even deeper learning. Learning products can go global or viral as students share their ideas with others, including near and far peers, experts, and decision-makers. Engaging in a personally meaningful inquiry and then sharing the results of that inquiry with a real-world audience is one way to define future ready work. Students gain experience in the development of the online "cultural competencies and social skills needed for full involvement" in **participatory culture** (Jenkins et al. 2009, xiii). Web-based tools and **social media** make this possible.

Inquiry learning requires that students engage in self-assessment and reflect on their learning journey throughout the process. Using educator- or student-created assessment tools, students learn to determine how and if they have reached the learning targets. Reflective writing helps learners see their thinking "on the page" and supports metacognition. Students can be encouraged to keep an inquiry journal where they jot down notes and record formal reflections (some based on educators' prompts) as they move through each phase of the inquiry process. Educators can also use students' inquiry journals in student conferences, and students and educators may use these journals as assessment tools as well.

MAKING THE CASE FOR INQUIRY LEARNING

In recent years, many state-level learning standards have been moving from a "research" to an "inquiry" focus. For example, the Texas Essential Knowledge and Skills in English language arts standards use strategies such as developing a research plan, formulating open-ended questions, clarifying and revising or broadening or narrowing initial research questions, and developing an argument that shows complexities and discrepancies in information (http://ritter.tea.state.tx.us/rules/tac/chapter110). Student learning objectives such as these are associated with inquiry learning rather than with traditional fact-finding, teacher-centered research projects. In other states, the Common Core State Standards focus on higher-order thinking and align with inquiry learning through their emphasis on citing evidence, drawing inferences, solving problems, connecting to real-world relevance, and demonstrating deeper learning. Although not all of these standards use the term "inquiry," students will not be able to meet these targets without moving beyond traditional preK–12 research practices.

Some educators may have an inaccurate conception of inquiry as an "anything goes" style of teaching and learning. In fact, while it includes the flexibility needed to respond to students' interests and questions, inquiry learning requires systematic planning on the part of educators. It requires mini-lessons to teach the various subskills noted in figure 3.4. It also requires educators to carefully observe and regularly monitor students' progress. In fact, educators' appropriately timed interventions are a key component of the GID (Kuhlthau, Maniotes, and Caspari 2015, 133–48).

Other educators may be reluctant to engage students in inquiry learning because of the challenges associated with assessing divergent lines of inquiry and a wide variety of final learning products. School librarians can share this added challenge by codesigning appropriate and flexible assessments that relate to the phases of the inquiry process, as well as to students' final products and presentations (see figure 7.2, "Sample Analytic Rubric"). When school librarians make the commitment to coassess student learning throughout all phases of the inquiry process, some classroom teachers may be more willing to take the risks inherent in providing students with increased opportunities for choice.

FIGURE 3.4

Guided Inquiry Subskills

GID Process Phase(s)	Description of Phase	Subskills (*tested on standardized tests)
Open, Immerse, Explore	**Educators** • Launching inquiry problem/concept/context **Students** • Immersing • Exploring	• Brainstorming – included in writing tests* • Webbing – included in writing tests* • Identifying main ideas (while recording brief notes)*
Identify	**Students** • Developing, revisiting, and refining questions at this phase and throughout the process **Educators** • Coaching for deeper, meaningful, doable questions	• Determining questions **Examples** • math word problems* • question/answer relationships*
Gather	**Students** • Collecting and responding to ideas and information to answer questions • Accessing, selecting, evaluating resources that meet their purposes • Making notes • Organizing information so it is useful **Educators** • Providing mini-lessons and interventions • Monitoring and supporting	• Using text features* • Identifying main ideas (while using notemaking graphic organizers that show relative importance)* • Making inferences* • Interpreting information* • Composing summary notes • Composing paragraphs (on writing tests)* • Keeping bibliographic records
Create	**Students** • Selecting tools • Fine-tuning audience(s) **Educators** • Providing mini-lessons and interventions • Monitoring and supporting	• Drafting (on writing tests)* • Storyboarding (on writing tests)* • Creating (on writing tests)* • Citing sources
Share	**Students** • Presenting **Educators** • Monitoring	• Presentation Skills including speaking and listening • Disseminating learning/findings
Evaluate	**Students** • Self-assessing • Peer reviewing **Educators** • Assessing	• Using exit slips, rubrics, and other self-assessment instruments to assess process and product • Peer and educator feedback
Reflect	**Students** • Reflecting **Educators** • Reflecting	• Practicing metacognition* • Oral or written reflections throughout the process for students and educators

Figure 3.4 shows the many subskills that students are learning and practicing throughout the GID process. (Figure 3.4 is also available as a downloadable Web Extra.) It is important for school librarians to help principals and classroom teachers understand how these subskills help students develop both content and process knowledge. School librarians can point out to administrators and colleagues that many of these skills are also utilized on standardized tests.

School librarians can be leaders on their campuses by building connections to spread inquiry learning to all classrooms, grade levels, and disciplines. They can help build a school-wide culture in which inquiry-based learning thrives. By engaging in instructional partnerships with classroom teachers and specialists, school librarians support these colleagues in taking the necessary risks associated with inquiry learning. School librarians will know if students have had prior inquiry learning experiences in other classrooms or content areas. They can codesign instruction that builds on what students already know and are able to do. School librarians can also connect colleagues with educators in other classrooms whose students may be embarking on similar inquiry journeys in order to provide support for students and educators alike.

INQUIRY AS A PROFESSIONAL DEVELOPMENT STANCE

As a lifelong skill, inquiry learning is not only for students. All educators and school communities can view their own evolution through an inquiry learning lens. Similar to students pursuing inquiry learning, educators involved in professional learning communities are also on a quest to discover strategies to improve student learning. In taking an inquiry stance, educators ask questions, test, and verify, modify, and retest various solutions. They share the findings of their learning and teaching questions. They reflect and generate more questions to explore.

When a school faculty takes an inquiry stance toward their own professional development, educators have a firsthand opportunity to learn and practice the inquiry process. This will help shore up their ability to guide students' inquiry learning. They will experience the various affective aspects of inquiry learning, such as uncertainty, optimism, confusion, or accomplishment. Educators will also have an authentic reason to further develop their own skills: creativity, communication, critical thinking, and collaboration. Their dispositions, like open-mindedness, perseverance, and flexibility, will be tested. Professional learning that takes an inquiry stance can strengthen the learning culture in the school (see Activity 3).

An entire school faculty could use the eight phases of the GID to frame an inquiry-based PD process. In this way, educators can become "learners of their own teaching." A principal might open the inquiry by posing a problem or dilemma the faculty is facing. Administrators could also challenge a group of teacher leaders to open the inquiry with an essential question that would engage the passions of their colleagues. With a commitment to being accountable to one another, faculty can be internally motivated to work together as a community to ask meaningful questions, explore educational research, and seek more information. They can develop, test, and retest possible solutions to the problem. Along the way, faculty will share their practices and student learning outcomes data more openly. They will coplan, coteach, and collectively reflect on practice. They will build deeper and more trusting relationships in a culture of continuous learning.

ADVOCATING FOR INQUIRY LEARNING

Inquiry learning is future ready learning.
#schoollibrarianleadership

Inquiry learning is future ready learning; it is a critical piece in an empowered learning culture. The school librarian serves as a connector for creating and sustaining a culture of learning in which inquiry can thrive. School librarians have a responsibility to serve as instructional partners alongside classroom teachers and specialists in order to ensure that students have opportunities to engage in inquiry learning. When the school librarian supports an inquiry-based learning model, the library provides a physical and virtual space for:

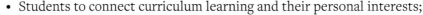

- Students to connect curriculum learning and their personal interests;
- Classroom teachers to connect disciplines to provide a richer **interdisciplinary approach** to learning;
- Teachers to connect to each other in order to provide the best learning experiences for students;
- Students and educators to connect to the wider world of information (Todd, Gordon, and Lu 2011, 27–28).

Today's youth will use information and conduct print and online research in their schooling and everyday lives, and they will participate as active citizens in local, national, and global communities. If they are given multiple opportunities to engage in inquiry learning, students will internalize this process and use it throughout their academic, professional, personal, and civic lives. The process, literacies, skills, and dispositions that students learn and practice during inquiry are transferrable to other contexts. In fact, students' ability to transfer what they have learned shows whether or not they deeply understand it. Empowered students are given more opportunities to seek and use information and tools to answer questions, solve problems, and present their discoveries. As a result, they may find greater relevance and purpose in their in-school learning.

School librarians who become experts in coplanning and coteaching inquiry can be leaders in advocating for these processes for students' learning as well as for educators' professional development. With a commitment to improving student learning today and to helping youth develop lifelong learning skills and strategies for tomorrow, school librarians are leaders who take action to utilize the most effective learning strategies for future ready students. They coteach traditional literacies that form a foundation of support for inquiry learning. School librarians can advocate for a school-wide culture of inquiry that serves as the spark that ignites a culture of learning throughout the school community.

BOOK STUDY GUIDE

I. Discussion Questions

QUESTION #1: How were you taught to conduct preK–12 "research"? How has that influenced your thinking and practices related to assigning research or inquiry projects in your classroom or library?

QUESTION #2: What experience have you had with the inquiry process as described in this chapter? If you have seen inquiry learning in action, describe it. What questions do you have about inquiry? What do you find most challenging about facilitating the inquiry process?

QUESTION #3: What experiences have you had in an adult learning/professional development situation where you used an inquiry process? How would staff development organized around an inquiry process differ from more traditional PD?

- *Individual Thinking*: Compose individual responses to the questions asked above.
- *Partner Sharing*: Share your individual responses to these questions with a colleague in your own school or another school.
- *Group Sharing*: As a small or whole group, discuss the feelings, ideas, hopes, and challenges that occurred to you as you responded to these questions or listened to your colleagues' responses.

II. Activities

Although these activities can be undertaken by individuals, they are designed for group work.

Activity 1

Research Reimagined as Inquiry, Part 1

Using the GID, work in partners or in grade-level or disciplinary teams to reimagine a regularly taught traditional research unit of instruction. Reports on animals or U.S. states could be elementary-level examples. At the secondary level, examples include social studies or English language arts research projects. (Depending on how it's structured, the senior project might or might not be a good example.)

Focus your attention on the first three phases (Open, Immerse, and Explore). Brainstorm surprising, curiosity-provoking ways to launch an inquiry. How would you connect the curriculum with students' lives outside of school? Consider the experiences in which you might immerse students, and the resources you could offer for them to explore. How would this be the same or different from previous launches of this research project?

Pairs or small groups can complete this activity for all three initial phases, or if time is an issue, they can divide the phases among the groups. Use electronic mind-mapping tools such as Cacoo.com, Padlet.com, or Popplet.com and share the results. Discuss the similarities and differences between the reimagined inquiry process and the original research project.

Activity 2

Research Reimagined as Inquiry, Part 2

Using the GID, work in partners or in grade-level or discipline teams to reimagine a regularly taught traditional research unit of instruction. (See the examples in Activity 1 above.)

Focus your attention on the last three phases of the GID process (Create, Share, and Evaluate/Reflect). Brainstorm the possible forms and formats that students' learning products could take. Match these formats with possible audiences and show how students might share their work with an authentic audience beyond the classroom or school. Could this inquiry motivate students to take action in some way? Finally, discuss how students and educators would assess the learning targets. How would this be the same or different from previous assessments used for this research project? What reflection prompts might educators pose throughout the process and at the conclusion of the project?

Pairs or small groups can complete this activity for all three phases, or if time is an issue, they can divide the phases among the groups. Use electronic mind-mapping tools and share the results. Discuss the similarities and differences between the reimagined inquiry process and the original research project.

Activity 3

Building Capacity for Inquiry Learning

Asset-based community development (ABCD) is a process used to identify strategies to help people and communities work together to achieve positive change. The assets that people use are their own knowledge, skills, and lived experience about the issues they encounter in their lives in the community.

With a grade-level, department, whole faculty, or school library cohort group, create a matrix that shows the SOAR (Strengths, Opportunities, Aspirations, Results) assets in your school learning community that support inquiry learning.

Assets	School	District	Community
Strengths			
Opportunities			
Aspirations			
Results			

After completing the matrix, use it as the "open" phase of an inquiry process. Taking a strengths-based approach, identify areas of strength that are unique to or strongest in your school, district, or community. Hone in on one strength that is the most salient at this point in time. Locate additional information and resources about this strength and codevelop inquiry questions to help you further capitalize on this strength. Pursue answers to your questions through the inquiry process described in this chapter. Take action to make the best use of this asset to build capacity in your school, district, and/or community.

III. Reflection Prompts

Choose from these possible reflection prompts or compose one of your own.

1. Reflect on your thoughts, feelings, and next steps as you read this chapter and/or as you engaged in the discussion questions or activities.
2. Reflect on your role in implementing inquiry-based learning. What do you already know and what are you already doing in your classroom or library that is related to inquiry learning? What do you need to learn?
3. Especially for school librarians: Reflect on the strengths you bring to inquiry learning. What roles do you currently play in supporting inquiry? What more do you need to learn in order to effectively institutionalize inquiry learning throughout your school or district?

CHAPTER FOUR

Traditional Literacy Learning

Guiding learners to become engaged and effective users of ideas and information and to appreciate literature requires that students develop as strategic readers who can comprehend, analyze, and evaluate text in both print and digital formats.

AMERICAN ASSOCIATION OF SCHOOL LIBRARIANS

◇◇◇◇

LITERACY IS A CULTURAL PRACTICE. IT IS THE WAY PEOPLE create meaning and communicate with others. Traditional literacies provide the foundation on which people build new understandings. Generalizable reading and writing skills are aspects of literacy in every discipline (McKenna and Robinson 1990). Listening and speaking are two additional literacy skills. During the early days of the World Wide Web, Jay Lemke wrote that "literacies are legion" (1998, 283). While multiple literacies are even more "legion" today, the traditional literacies of reading, writing, listening, and speaking remain at the heart of learning.

As students successfully pursue knowledge, they must be able to problem solve reading comprehension challenges when they interact with unfamiliar texts. "The degree to which students can read and understand text in all formats (e.g., picture, video, print) and all contexts is a key indicator of success in school and in life" (AASL 2007, 2). Whether students are reading print or digital materials, **reading comprehension strategies** are essential foundational skills for all readers. As Jacques Barzun, the cultural historian and former Columbia University dean, once said: "No subject of study is more important than reading . . . all other intellectual powers depend on it." Students must be able to make sense of **text** in order to be information-literate and to learn.

The same can be said for the ability to communicate one's ideas in writing. It is true that more and more products created by students to document their learning are **multimodal texts** that include print, audio, video, and hyperlinked components. Yet, students' ability to organize their ideas and demonstrate their learning still involves aspects of what is traditionally known as the **writing process.** Educators have the opportunity and responsibility to teach, model, and give

BEFORE READING

How are traditional literacies—reading, writing, listening, and speaking—taught and practiced in your school? Who is responsible for teaching students these foundational skills?

It may be most appropriate to conceive of literacy as a lifelong process—the process of *becoming* literate.

#schoollibrarianleadership

students daily opportunities to practice this foundational literacy. Applying reading and writing skills during inquiry learning is an authentic context for developing these essential skills.

With ubiquitous information and continually evolving texts and tools, it may be most appropriate to conceive of literacy as a lifelong process—the process of becoming literate. "Regardless of the content and whether ideas and information are communicated in print or multimodal texts, students begin and progress on their literacy journeys by learning and developing their ability to effectively read and write" (Moreillon 2017a, 87). Throughout their lifetimes, information seekers will be accessing and using information. They will seek to acquire medical, political, scientific, technical, and other information for which they have little or no background knowledge. They will need to apply strategies such as drawing inferences, questioning, and synthesizing in order to comprehend and use information. In this context, it is critical that preK–12 students develop strategies for making sense of difficult texts.

There has been a great deal of emphasis placed on efforts to ensure that all students are reading on grade level by third grade. While this is an essential first step in *becoming* literate, it may give students, educators, administrators, families, and communities a false sense that readers have learned all they need to know by the age of eight or nine. In fact, beginning in fourth grade, when curriculum-based reading involves more and more expository texts, students need additional tools in their strategy toolkits and more practice using these tools with diverse texts. At the middle and high school levels, "some 70 percent of older readers require some form of remediation. Very few of these struggling readers need help to read the words on the page; their most common problem is that they are not able to comprehend what they read" (Biancarosa and Snow 2006, 3).

In addition to reading, students will need to improve and perfect their ability to express themselves through the other three language arts: speaking, listening, and writing. As students' audiences for their ideas expand, they will also learn to speak, write, and represent ideas in various **genres** and **registers** in order to communicate effectively. They will use a variety of tools to voice their ideas and opinions. Students will learn and practice when and how to write in a style appropriate for social media and when and how to compose a formal essay for a college or a job application. Learning to write does not end with students' first tweets or with their first five-paragraph essays. They will produce written text throughout their preK–12 education and beyond.

The National Assessment of Education Progress reported that in 2015, an average of about one-third of fourth- and eighth-graders and 37 percent of high school seniors performed at or above the proficient achievement level in reading for their grade. Proficiency in the fourth grade ranged from 18 percent for African American students to 57 percent for Asian American students. At eighth grade, the percentages at or above the proficient level ranged from 16 percent for African American students to 54 percent for Asian American students. For high school seniors, 17 percent of African American students and 49 percent of Asian American students performed at or above the proficient level. Educators who believe that literacy gives people greater life choices cannot be satisfied with these low levels of reading proficiency.

School Librarians' Literacy Leadership Puzzle

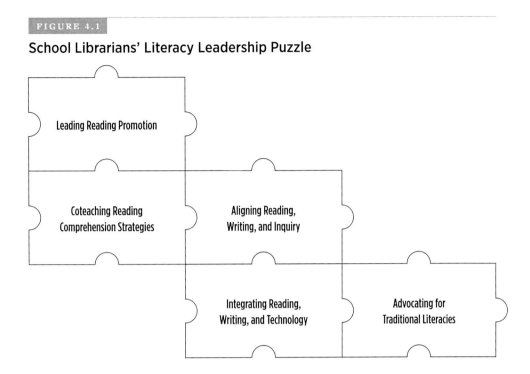

"From reading promotion to aligning reading and writing with inquiry learning, school librarians' ever-expanding roles as literacy leaders have grown alongside the explosion of information and the development of the technology tools used to access it" (Moreillon 2017a, 88). In order to serve as literacy leaders in their schools, school librarians build library-classroom connections through reading promotion; reading comprehension strategies; aligning reading and writing with inquiry; and integrating technology tools with reading and writing. School librarians also advocate for effective traditional literacy teaching and learning as a foundation for all literacies. Figure 4.1 shows these five interrelated activities that form school librarians' literacy leadership responsibilities. (This figure is also available as a downloadable Web Extra.)

School librarians can be coleaders with their principals and colleagues in establishing the school's or district's core beliefs about literacy. Shared beliefs can inform reading material purchases and choices, curriculum decisions, and instructional practices (Routman 2014). Educators can use common beliefs about literacy learning as a framework for coplanning and coteaching. Within this framework, school librarians can maximize the impact of the pieces of their literacy leadership puzzle and build a literacy culture in their schools.

Educators can use common beliefs about literacy learning as a framework for coplanning and coteaching. #schoollibrarianleadership

READING PROMOTION

Traditionally, school librarians have understood their reading responsibility as instilling a "love of reading" by promoting children's and young adult literature to students, classroom teachers, and families. Guided by the American Library

Association's "Library Bill of Rights" and "The Freedom to Read Statement," school librarians advocate for free choice and independent reading, which are core values in librarianship. "Intellectual freedom is every learner's right" is one of AASL's common beliefs (AASL 2018, 13). Educators respect and school librarians guard students' rights to privacy as well. Given intellectual freedom and the right to privacy, students develop the ability to think about their choices and explore within and beyond the school curriculum. These tenets provide a solid framework for the school librarian's promotion of reading, the library's literacy programs and events, and advocacy efforts related to reading.

Those school librarians whose literature promotions are most effective work in collaboration with students, classroom teachers, specialists, administrators, and families. This ensures that the entire school community is involved in establishing and sustaining a culture of reading. To this end, school librarians provide support for students and classroom teachers by developing book talks and online book trailers, and they coplan lessons that result in student-created versions of these activities. School librarians sponsor author/illustrator visits, family literacy nights, and poetry slams as ways to sharpen the learning community's focus on reading and writing. Promoting and participating in state, national, or international literacy initiatives can increase students' interest in literature and reading. These initiatives also provide focal points for collaborating with classroom teachers and specialists to align these literacy-building efforts with classroom curricula.

The American Association of School Librarians adopted a "Position Statement on the School Librarian's Role in Reading" (AASL 2009b). The following are some of the reasons why school librarians should be key contributors to achievement in reading in their schools:

1. Reading is a foundational skill for twenty-first-century learners.
2. Guiding learners to become engaged and effective users of ideas and information and to appreciate literature requires that students develop as strategic readers who can comprehend, analyze, and evaluate text in both print and digital formats.
3. The extent to which young people use information depends upon their ability to understand what they read, to integrate their understanding with what they already know, and to realize their unanswered questions.
4. Twenty-first-century learners must become adept at determining the authority and accuracy of information, and analyzing and evaluating that information in order to synthesize new knowledge from multiple resources.
5. The school librarian has a key role in supporting print and online reading comprehension strategy instruction in collaboration with classroom teachers and reading specialists.
6. School librarians codesign, coimplement, and coevaluate interdisciplinary lessons and units of instruction that result in increased student learning (AASL 2009a, 22–23).

As the position statement notes: "School librarians are in a critical and unique position to partner with other educators to elevate the reading development of our nation's youth" (AASL 2009a, 22).

Research studies have indicated that the presence of a state-certified school librarian is correlated with student achievement in reading. Recent time-series studies conducted by Keith Curry Lance and Linda Hofshire analyzed changes in library staffing and their possible correlations with students' reading scores on standardized tests (cited in Scholastic 2016). Their study of fourth-grade students' National Association of Education Progress scores suggests that students in schools which gained librarians between 2005 and 2009 had "significantly higher increases in fourth-grade NAEP reading scores than schools in states that lost librarians" (9). In their study of third- to tenth-grade students' reading scores on the Colorado Student Assessment Program tests, these researchers found that schools that gained or maintained state-certified librarians between 2005 and 2011 "tended to have more students scoring advanced in reading in 2011 and to have increased their performance more than schools that either lost their librarians or never had one" (Lance and Hofshire 2012, 3). The presence of a school librarian in every school is a first step toward providing students with an appropriate education. The quality of school librarians' contributions to student learning is a next step to address and study.

READING INSTRUCTION

School librarians cannot be satisfied with confining their impact on literacy learning to reading promotion only. They must take the next step of teaching and coteaching reading comprehension strategies at the point of need. School librarians can coteach these strategies in the context of inquiry learning across all grade levels and in all content areas. While proficient readers use these comprehension strategies automatically, striving and struggling readers need more opportunities to practice until they can access a range of strategies from their toolkits when needed in order to make sense of difficult text. All readers need a complete toolkit of reading comprehension strategies to help them make sense of unfamiliar text.

The study of reading comprehension online, as opposed to print, is a relatively new area of research. The following description of online reading strategies may sound a great deal like inquiry learning and information literacy skills to school librarians. Online reading comprehension "consists of a process of problem-based inquiry across many different online information sources, requiring several recursive reading practices: (a) reading online to identify important questions; (b) reading online to locate information; (c) reading online to critically evaluate information; (d) reading online to synthesize information; and (e) reading online to communicate information. During these events, new online and traditional offline reading comprehension skills are both required, often in complex and interrelated ways" (Leu et al. 2011, 5).

Whether reading on paper or online, students need to be able to apply reading comprehension strategies to make meaning; these are lifelong learning skills. Teaching these strategies is also important for educators and administrators who are being held accountable for student learning outcomes on standardized tests. "State reading assessments are increasingly dominated by skills such as the ability to infer; to identify an author's bias or persuasive techniques; to support interpretations of main ideas with evidence from the text; and to summarize, synthesize, analyze, and evaluate" (Schmoker 2006, 40). As students engage with increasingly complex texts, they will need opportunities to practice comprehension strategies throughout their preK–12 schooling.

"Strategies provide the tools to help students make sense of the content, and the content gives meaning and purpose to the strategies . . . The strategies might be content-general, applicable in a range of contexts, or they might be specific to the demands of the domain in which students are working" (Wilkinson and Son 2011, 367). In instruction on comprehension strategies, educators' goals are to increase students' engagement, their knowledge of content, and their understanding of the relevance of these processes to success in life. Educators are being held accountable for teaching literacy in their disciplines. And future ready school librarians are being held accountable through coteaching cultural, digital, information, and media literacies.

COTEACHING READING COMPREHENSION STRATEGIES DURING INQUIRY LEARNING

Educators model and coteach reading comprehension strategies when students encounter difficult texts during inquiry learning.

#buildingconnections4learning

Improvements in literacy instruction can spread throughout a learning community when educators collaborate. Educators model and coteach reading comprehension strategies when students encounter difficult texts during inquiry learning. Teaching comprehension strategies at the point of need helps students succeed with the task at hand. It also helps them understand that strategy lessons are not simply exercises, but have real-world applications. Along with literacy and reading coaches, school librarians are positioned to provide support for job-embedded PD. They can help ensure that classroom teachers are integrating reading comprehension strategy instruction throughout the school day at all grade levels and in all content areas.

Figure 4.2 shows how seven reading comprehension strategies align with inquiry learning and can be integrated into classroom-library lessons to support students' ongoing reading development.

Susan Zimmermann and Chryse Hutchins (2003) identified these seven core reading comprehension strategies. Readers use these strategies to help improve their text comprehension (Keene and Zimmermann 1997; Moreillon 2007, 2012a, 2013). Educators model these strategies with **think-alouds**, and students practice them with peer and educator support. When readers are proficient, these strategies become skills they can select from and apply at appropriate times to gain or regain comprehension and make meaning and use of texts.

FIGURE 4.2

Reading Comprehension Strategies Aligned with the Guided Inquiry Design Phases

Reading Comprehension Strategies	GID Phases
• Activating and Building Background Knowledge • Using Sensory Images • Questioning	Open, Immerse, Explore
• Questioning • Making Predictions	Identify
• Connecting to Background Knowledge (Text-to-Self, Text-to-Text, Text-to-World) • Using Sensory Images • Making Predictions • Drawing Inferences • Determining Main Ideas • Using Fix-up Options	Gather
• Drawing Inferences • Synthesizing	Create
• Synthesizing	Share
• Defining/Redefining the Purpose for Reading (A Fix-up Option)	Evaluate/Reflect

ACTIVATING OR BUILDING BACKGROUND KNOWLEDGE

During the Open phase of the Guided Inquiry Design, educators seek to awaken students' curiosity, tap into their passions, and connect with what students already know about a topic, problem, or dilemma. "How much a reader already knows about the subject is probably the best predictor of reading comprehension" (Fisher and Frey 2009, 2). In order to capitalize on students' background knowledge, educators guide students in thinking about the connections they can make in three ways: text-to-self, text-to-text, and text-to-world connections. Each of these can be made explicit through educator modeling with the think-aloud strategy, especially during the Open, Immerse, and Explore phases. Educators can conduct background knowledge mini-lessons with individual students, small groups, or the whole class as needed throughout the inquiry process.

Text-to-self connections are those for which students and educators have personal, firsthand experiences. For example, if the problem that educators present is related to how humans use natural resources, students will likely have had experience with recycling. Their prior knowledge about why and how they practice recycling in their homes, schools, or neighborhoods can activate their schema related to people's use of natural resources. Their prior knowledge provides a foundation on which the inquiry process can build.

Text-to-text connections involve students in noticing that the text presented is not the only example that spotlights this problem. In the Open phase, if educators share a provocative video of how people and industry are polluting oceans, students who are making text-to-text connections will note where else they have seen this problem presented. They might connect with other films, newspaper articles, blog posts, and books that address the impact of trash or industrial waste on the environment in general. Or they may cite examples of texts that spotlight the impact of pollution on the earth's oceans more specifically.

Text-to-world connections are those that extend to global issues. In the case of the ocean pollution problem, students may connect to the oceans as sources of food for people and as habitats and food sources for fishes and marine life around the world. They may note how damage to the ocean ecosystem affects the food chain. They may also connect with what they have heard about the world's growing population and the problems posed by food shortages. Text-to-world connections can lead students to think about how they could take action in their homes, schools, and communities. They may even seek to get involved with international programs such as the Jane Goodall Institute's Roots and Shoots project (http://rootsandshoots.org).

"Students must have opportunities to activate and build their background knowledge, or world knowledge, in order to form a firm foundation for comprehension. When reading expository texts, in particular, knowledge in the domain is the greatest indicator of readiness to read with understanding. Students' 'reading levels' vary based on prior knowledge, on their interest in the text topic, and on compelling reasons to comprehend" (Duke, Pearson, Strachan, and Billman 2011, 62). Educators who design learning opportunities that students perceive as authentic, real-world, and relevant to their lives outside of school create a context in which **deeper learning** can happen.

When educators launch an inquiry, they model their thinking in terms of the three ways of activating their background knowledge that have just been described. With two educators modeling with think-alouds, they demonstrate to students that not all people have the same prior knowledge. They model how to build background knowledge as a springboard for inquiry. They also show how people make different connections. With think-alouds, educators can demonstrate how people learn with and from each other's initial and subsequent understandings of a topic or problem.

During the Immerse and Explore phases of the GID, educators think aloud about the new information they encounter. They share how this new information aligns with or contradicts what they thought they already knew about the topic. Educators can support individual students or inquiry circle groups in sharing their own knowledge building. By asking probing questions, educators can help students make their own thinking visible to the students themselves and to their classmates. Through inquiry conversations and inquiry logs, students clarify and add to their understanding, identify gaps, and modify their prior knowledge related to the topic, problem, or dilemma. As educators continue to model this process, students continue to make these connections and develop **metacognition** throughout the inquiry.

USING SENSORY IMAGES

To ignite students' passions, educators can engage students' five senses in the Open phase of the inquiry process. Using experiences such as hands-on experiments, field trips, or multisensory media can capitalize on how people use their senses to understand their world. When educators launch an inquiry project, they can provide kinesthetic experiences that involve students' bodies as well as activating their brains. Sensory experiences are part of our background knowledge and part of the schema that people bring with them when they encounter new information.

When applied to reading comprehension, readers who enter fully into a text use all of their senses to make sense of it. Whether reading fiction or information texts, readers who achieve a "lived through" experience engage all of their senses. Buehl (2009) describes this as "breathing life" into abstract language. For example, when reading about a U.S. Civil War battle, a strategic reader can not only visualize the suffering and confusion on the battlefield, but also hear the sound of musket fire and smell the gunsmoke. Being able to enter into the text with all of their senses also activates readers' emotional responses. This helps them deeply connect with and comprehend a text.

Educators can offer students multisensory experiences throughout the inquiry process. Educators use think-alouds to show students how they are using their senses to deepen their understanding. They can share how mental images help students to retain and recall information. Educators can guide students in creating paper or digital mind maps to show thinking. Interacting with and creating **nonlinguistic representations** can also involve students in using art, drama, or music to experience information and ideas and express learning. Providing students with multimodal resources and encouraging students to present their learning with multimodal texts further emphasizes the importance of all five senses in meaning making (see figure 7.2).

QUESTIONING

Questioning is a central feature of inquiry learning. During the first three phases of the Guided Inquiry Design, educators encourage students to share their wonderings and pose their initial questions. These activities build curiosity and motivation and help students answer their superficial questions in order to go deeper. During the Identify phase, students develop relevant and meaningful self-generated questions. Students consider and reconsider the resource choices they make in terms of their questions, and they often return to their questions in order to reassess their inquiry progress.

As a reading comprehension strategy, students use questioning to monitor their understanding of texts. They can use this strategy in all phases of the process, but questioning the text may be most applicable in the Gather phase of the GID. The following are some possible questions a student might ask when first considering the usefulness or relevance of a text:

1. What is my *purpose* for reading this text?
2. How does this text relate to my *inquiry question(s)*?
3. Will the *genre* of this text help me access the information I want to find?
4. What *specific information* am I searching for?
5. What do I want to *learn* from this text?

After this initial questioning process, the student may ask additional questions related to analyzing the text for currency, accuracy, authority, or bias. School librarians consider these questions to be critical information literacy skills. These are also text comprehension questions. When educators model how to ask text analysis questions using think-alouds, they demonstrate to learners the importance of using credible sources. They sharpen students' focus on the quality of information rather than the quantity of it. Working in collaboration with content-area teachers, school librarians can also ask discipline-specific questions (see figure 5.1). The process of asking questions while engaging with information helps readers monitor their learning.

MAKING PREDICTIONS OR DRAWING INFERENCES

At any time during the inquiry process, students can benefit from making predictions based on their background knowledge and the clues found in texts. Similar to detectives following clues, whenever students are reading a text, they make predictions as to the next piece of information they will uncover, or the next plot twist. Strategic readers ask and answer prediction questions as a way to propel themselves through a text. They read on to find out if their predictions were correct. This is also a way that learners motivate and engage themselves throughout an inquiry process.

Drawing inferences, or reading between the lines, is similar to making predictions, since both rely on readers' prior knowledge combined with information found in the text. However, when students make predictions that can confirm or refute their predictions as they read further within the text, or within the course of the inquiry, the answers to predictions are knowable. On the other hand, inferences are not confirmed within the text. Inferences rely on readers making reasonable interpretations based on their background knowledge and the information at hand.

In the Gather phase of the inquiry process, inquirers will make predictions and draw inferences as they interact with information. More sophisticated readers will draw inferences as they synthesize and create learning products from the information in multiple texts. With think-alouds, educators show how different readers make different inferences. As long as each student can cite evidence in the text that leads to his or her conclusion, students will learn that there can be multiple inferences based on the same evidence in a text.

DETERMINING MAIN IDEAS

Whenever students are seeking information, they must sift and sort through content to uncover what information is important in helping them answer their inquiry question(s). It may be most appropriate for educators to coteach how to determine a text's main ideas during the Gather phase, when students are engaging with multiple resources. With a focus on their questions and their purpose for reading, students learn to determine the relative importance of the information they gather. During an inquiry process, students must be able to organize information so it is useful. Gathering a large quantity of disorganized and random facts will most likely not help them answer their inquiry question(s) or help them create an effective demonstration of their learning.

There is often an assumption that students know how to *make* notes when in fact they may only know how to *take* notes. The term "notemaking" can be used intentionally to distinguish it from "notetaking," in which students hand-copy or copy and paste information verbatim from a text. By contrast, the process of notemaking requires that students filter information through their prior knowledge, their purpose for reading, their inquiry question(s), and the relative importance of this piece of information compared with other information gathered. Notemaking requires critical thinking.

Educators must model the thought processes that are involved in notemaking. Using think-alouds, educators demonstrate how to read a chunk of text, identify key words and concepts, and question whether or not the information is useful in answering one's inquiry question(s). When information is useful, educators model the type of note that should be made: a single word, a phrase, a bulleted list, a reference to a page number, or a quote. They also model how to keep a running record of the resource from which the note came and how to link the resource and the note in some way. Determining main ideas and the relative importance of different pieces of information are essential strategies for inquirers.

USING FIX-UP OPTIONS

When students are engaged in inquiry learning they will regularly encounter difficult texts—texts that are beyond their level of reading proficiency. Zimmermann and Hutchins (2003) offer readers sixteen "fix-up options" that readers can use to regain comprehension. Figure 4.3 is a graphic organizer that can be used when educators model and students practice these strategies during "**close reading**" strategy lessons. (This figure is also available as a downloadable Web Extra.)

For close reading interventions, educators select a shorter text or a small chunk of text. Educators model and students read, reread, and apply strategies to gain or regain comprehension of this text. Readers use questioning and "fix-up options" to go beyond the surface level of the text to uncover the author's deeper meaning. This can involve the other six reading comprehension strategies described in this chapter, as well as looking at specific word choice, phrases, and sentence structure.

FIGURE 4.3

Fix-Up Options Self-Monitoring Sheet

Options	Option Used	Example(s)
1. Reread.		
2. Read ahead.		
3. Stop to think.		
4. Try to visualize.		
5. Ask new question.		
6. Make a prediction.		
7. Study the illustration or other text features.		
8. Ask someone for help.		
9. Figure out unknown words.		
10. Look at the sentence structure.		
11. Draw an inference.		
12. Connect to background knowledge.		
13. Read the author's or illustrator's note.		
14. Write about the confusing parts.		
15. Make an effort to think about the message.		
16. Define/redefine the purpose for reading this text.		

From *Coteaching Reading Comprehension Strategies in Elementary School Libraries: Maximizing Your Impact* (American Library Association 2013) and *Coteaching Reading Comprehension Strategies in Secondary School Libraries: Maximizing Your Impact* (American Library Association 2012)

The goal of close reading and using fix-up options is to give readers strategies for monitoring their own comprehension and interrogating texts to arrive at a deep understanding of them (see Activity 2).

Using a chunk of complex text, educators can model this intervention at any time during the inquiry process. Educators can encourage students to use the fix-up options graphic organizer independently when they encounter difficult text during the GID Gather phase. "Defining or redefining the purpose for reading" is one of the options that can help students self-monitor their selection of texts and their reading comprehension, and monitor their progress toward achieving their inquiry goals. Students may also refer to the fix-up options during reflection at any time during the inquiry process.

SYNTHESIZING

Students apply the synthesizing reading comprehension strategy during the Create phase of the GID. When they have gathered information from multiple sources, students must pull ideas together and draw inferences from them. They must note and resolve discrepancies, form interpretations, and draw conclusions. Synthesis is part and parcel of inquiry learning and helps students document new knowledge.

The process involved in synthesizing information is not simple. Most students require a great deal of practice before they can master synthesis. Educators use think-alouds to model synthesizing information from multiple sources. They show students how to organize their notes in such a way as to be able to compare similar information and identify discrepancies. Combining think-alouds with **shared writing** can be particularly effective. One of the fix-up options is to "write about the confusing parts" of the text (see figure 4.3). Educators model the process of noting conflicting information in the text and talking through or writing down their confusion. Hearing educators' think-alouds or seeing the confusion documented in print can help educators and students work together to sort out discrepancies.

Figure 4.4 shows a selection of lesson topics in which instruction in reading comprehension strategies can be applied during inquiry learning. These seven strategies and lessons are presented in detail in *Coteaching Reading Comprehension Strategies in Elementary School Libraries* and *Coteaching Reading Comprehension Strategies in Secondary School Libraries* (Moreillon 2013, 2012a). Each book contains twenty-one sample classroom-library lesson plans at three different levels of reading proficiency. All of the lessons are intended to be cotaught by a school librarian and a classroom teacher or specialist team who use think-alouds to model the strategies.

When strategic readers delve deeply into texts, they are exploring the writer's craft. They learn how writers evoke imagery, inform, and persuade. They learn how writers set a tone in their writing in order to elicit a particular mood in the reader. They learn about text features and **text structures**, such as compare and contrast or cause and effect. They understand the purpose and forms of various genres of text. Through deep comprehension, readers learn how authors use language

FIGURE 4.4

Reading Comprehension Strategy Lessons and Inquiry Learning Connections

Instructional Levels	Topics	Reading Comprehension Strategies	Inquiry Connections
Advancing 2nd – 3rd Grades	Spanish language	Making Predictions	Language use and culture
Advancing 2nd – 3rd Grades	Penguins	Determining Main Ideas	Arctic (or other biome) ecology
Advanced 4th – 5th Grades	Overcoming discrimination	Drawing Inferences	Civil rights—then and now
Advanced 4th – 5th Grades	Kids' inventions	Determining Main Ideas	Innovators and the innovation process
Challenging 5th – 6th Grades	Jazz music	Synthesizing	Influence of art and history on contemporary culture

From *Coteaching Reading Comprehension Strategies in Elementary School Libraries: Maximizing Your Impact* (American Library Association 2013)

Instructional Levels	Topics	Reading Comprehension Strategies	Inquiry Connections
Advancing 7th – 8th Grades	Slave trade	Using Sensory Images	Economics – contemporary global slave and other labor issues
Advancing 7th – 8th Grades	Health and wellness	Questioning	Nutrition, personal fitness, and lifestyles
Advanced 9th – 10th Grades	Ocean currents	Building Background Knowledge	Climate change
Advanced 9th – 10th Grades	Editorial cartoons	Questioning	Bias in reporting, journalism, and media
Challenging 11th – 12th Grades	Harlem Renaissance	Synthesizing	Influence of art and history on contemporary culture

From *Coteaching Reading Comprehension Strategies in Secondary School Libraries: Maximizing Your Impact* (American Library Association 2012) creatively in order to evoke a particular response from readers or convey information effectively. And when students improve their reading proficiency through deep comprehension, they have the opportunity to improve their writing skills as well.

Coteachers also integrate students' use of technology tools while reading and writing. School librarians may have more experience in applying specific digital resources and tools during inquiry learning. Working together, educators can take risks to field-test new resources and tools that can support student learning. Coteachers increase each other's knowledge of the most effective tools to support students in developing digital, information, and media literacies (see chapter 6, "Digital Learning").

ADVOCACY FOR TRADITIONAL LITERACIES

For school librarians who are integrating reading comprehension strategies and writing interventions into inquiry learning, the key phrase is "at the point of need." Rather than teaching reading comprehension strategies and the writing process in isolation from curriculum content, educators provide instruction when students need to use these strategies in order to make sense of text or to express their learning. Learners who are engaged in inquiry inevitably bump up against texts, whether in print or online, that are above their proficient reading comprehension level. Students who can reach into their reading toolkits and apply a strategy may be more likely to solve these comprehension challenges. "Comprehension instruction is most effective when students integrate and flexibly use reading and thinking strategies across a wide variety of texts and in the context of a challenging, engaging curriculum" (Harvey and Goudvis 2013, 434). Inquiry provides a golden opportunity for coteaching reading comprehension strategies.

Taking a problem-solving approach is one way to describe what strategic readers do in order to make meaning from a text. It is also what writers do when they compose texts to document their learning. When school librarians and classroom teachers coteach these strategies during an inquiry unit, they help students develop the necessary skills of lifelong readers and writers who will be challenged by reading difficult texts and by writing effectively throughout their lives.

Traditional literacies form a foundation for an empowered learning culture.
#buildingconnections4learning

Traditional literacies form a foundation for an empowered learning culture. Effective and efficient readers and writers have the strategies they need to be effective and efficient inquirers. Reading and writing strategies and inquiry processes support independent learning. Reading, writing, and inquiry are necessary for future ready students to achieve college, career, and community readiness and success. An interdisciplinary team-oriented approach that includes ongoing PD and involves content-area teachers as well as specialists has a greater chance of improving students' literacy levels (Biancarosa and Snow 2006).

When school librarians coteach reading and writing with classroom teachers, they use **formative assessments** and **summative assessments** to assess the impact of their teaching on what matters—student learning outcomes. While they focus on reading and writing processes, educators measure results. Documenting improvements in students' reading and writing proficiency will engender advocates for the school librarian's contributions to the school's academic program. The librarian's colleagues, administrators, students, and their families will recognize and advocate for her role in students' learning and achievement in reading and writing.

One of the common beliefs in school librarianship is that "reading is the core of personal and academic competency" (AASL 2018, 11). School librarians build connections by coteaching traditional literacies through classroom-library instructional partnerships. They promote job-embedded PD as they practice reciprocal mentorship with classroom teachers to improve students' traditional literacy learning. School librarians can advocate for and lead PD focused on literacy teaching in the context of inquiry learning. PD and coteaching can help ensure that principals' initiatives for literacy teaching are practiced and implemented in classrooms and in libraries. Through shared knowledge and instructional practices, educators ensure that students develop the necessary toolkit for deeper learning.

BOOK STUDY GUIDE

I. Discussion Questions:

QUESTION #1: How do you know when you have lost comprehension while reading, listening, or viewing? What strategies do you use to recover comprehension? How can you share your own comprehension challenges with students in order to reinforce the idea of *becoming* literate as a lifelong process?

QUESTION #2: How do you improve students' proficiency and development in reading comprehension strategies before, during, and after inquiry learning?

QUESTION #3: List aspects of the writing process that support students' inquiry learning and work products (regardless of the media used). What are your strategies for improving student writing?

- *Individual Thinking*: Compose individual responses to the questions asked above.
- *Partner Sharing*: Share your individual responses to these questions with a colleague in your own school or another school.
- *Group Sharing*: As a small or whole group, discuss the feelings, ideas, hopes, and challenges that occurred to you as you responded to these questions or listened to your colleagues' responses.

II. Activities

Although these activities can be undertaken by individuals, they are designed for group work.

Activity 1

Reading Difficult Text

When readers have no background knowledge on a particular topic, they have an immediate loss of comprehension when they begin to read about it. Find someone on the faculty who has expert knowledge on a topic that is not taught in the school. Ask that expert to "assign" a text. Research or scientific articles on unfamiliar topics are examples of difficult texts.

Distribute the article to faculty and **think-pair-share** with a partner how you would begin to build background knowledge in order to comprehend this text. Which of the fix-up options in figure 4.3 would you use to make sense of the text? What questions would you ask? What resources would you use? If the expert is on the faculty, he or she could comment on the strategies suggested by the faculty.

Reflect on this activity.

Activity 2

Close Reading

Conduct a close reading of a text. Two educators (preferably a classroom teacher and a school librarian) can take the roles of educators guiding a classroom of students through a close reading intervention. Using figure 4.3 in this book, these two educators use think-alouds to model applying comprehension strategies with the first chunk or two of text. They use the following four questions to guide their interactions with the text, and they write or project these on the whiteboard:

1. What is the author *telling* me at this point in the text?
2. What are the *important vocabulary words?* What are the *challenging words?*
3. How does the author use *language* to convey information and add meaning?
4. What does the author want me to *know and feel?* (adapted from Boyles 2012, 40).

Other educators will follow along, marking their graphic organizers during the modeling. Then, working as individuals, partners, or small groups, all educators will complete the reading, mark their graphic organizers, and compare their results.

Educators can use the 8-2 sample lesson plan in *Coteaching Reading Comprehension Strategies in Secondary School Libraries: Maximizing Your Impact* (Moreillon 2012a, 151–54). This lesson plan uses Emily Dickinson's poem "Part Four: Time and Eternity XXVII" from *The Complete Poems* (1924) as the mentor text: www.bartleby.com/113/4027.html.

Reflect on this activity.

Activity 3

Shared Writing

Conduct a shared writing activity. Use a curriculum-based topic and a genre of writing tested at a particular grade level. Build background knowledge and develop a prompt. Another option is to write about an event for the school's newsletter. One or two faculty members can take the role of educator and/or scribe. Employ all five steps of the writing process. Use think-alouds for each of the five writing process steps. If appropriate, use web-based tools. If the faculty composed an article for a newsletter, publish the article.

Reflect on the process.

III. Reflection Prompts

Choose from these possible reflection prompts or compose one of your own.

1. Reflect on your thoughts, feelings, and next steps as you read this chapter and/or engaged in the discussion questions or activities.
2. Reflect on the benefits to students and your roles in integrating reading comprehension strategies and the writing process across the curriculum and into inquiry learning, in particular.
3. Especially for school librarians: Reflect on what you need to learn in order to effectively integrate reading comprehension strategy and writing instruction into inquiry learning.

CHAPTER FIVE

Deeper Learning

Having students create questions is a shortcut to deeper learning. As students become more curious and engaged and take on a new ownership of their learning, they will leave school as sophisticated questioners who can use the skill of question formulation in higher education, the workplace, their lives, and our democracy.

DAN ROTHSTEIN, LUZ SANTANA, AND ANDREW P. MINIGAN

◇◇◇◇

N THE INNOVATION AGE, EDUCATORS MUST CREATE OPPORtunities for students to experience deeper learning. The Hewlett Foundation has identified six deeper learning competencies: "master core academic content, think critically and solve complex problems, communicate effectively, work collaboratively, learn how to learn, and develop an academic mindset" (Hewlett Foundation 2013). To achieve deeper learning, students cannot be merely passive recipients of ideas and information. Rote learning and collecting facts do not lead to rigor. Students must be actively engaged in order to master hands-on, minds-on literacies, skills, and dispositions.

School librarians can link deeper learning competencies to more rigorous, personalized, future ready learning. Some have confused rigor with providing more advanced coursework offerings, increased workloads, or increasing the total number or difficulty of texts. "Rigor is not defined by the text—it comes from what students do. It is not standard across a curriculum—it is individual to each student's needs. It is not quantified by how much gets crammed into a school day—it is measured in depth of understanding. Rigor is a result, not a cause" (Sztabnik 2015). Increased rigor can be one result of authentic inquiry learning that is sparked by students' curiosity. Unlike fact-finding "research," inquiry leads to deeper understandings. With authentic questions and "learning how to learn" as the centerpieces of inquiry, students can achieve a level of rigor that will lead them to success in achieving their life goals.

The 2017 Horizon Report cited deeper learning as a long-term trend driving technology adoption (New Media Consortium and Consortium for School Networking 2017). Deeper learning must not be reserved for one or two content areas in which "research" has traditionally been taught. "Subject matter silos prevent

BEFORE READING

What does the term "deeper learning" mean to you? Describe when you had an opportunity to deeply explore a topic, question, problem, or dilemma.

students from seeing the relevance of courses and concepts, leading them to justifiably pose their most frequently asked question: 'Why do I need to know this?'" (Chen 2012, 36). Students must develop the ability to respond to a problem, dilemma, or challenge; ask meaningful questions; and pursue, comprehend, and analyze relevant information in all disciplines. They need opportunities to create new knowledge in all subject areas. They must experience how these processes may be similar or different in various domains.

Deeper learning requires that students apply metacognitive strategies in order to self-regulate and guide their interactions with information and ideas. Students must actively engage with texts in order to transform information and ideas into knowledge. When educators design a curriculum that requires learners to marshal thinking strategies in the service of deep understanding, students develop the ability to self-regulate, reflect on, and assess the process as well as the content of their learning. In the process, students develop the literacies, skills, and dispositions they need to be independent, knowledgeable, and engaged members of their learning communities and society.

Many educators feel pressure to "get through the material" rather than allow students to investigate it thoroughly. A focus on "coverage" can make it difficult for educators to dedicate the kind of time necessary for students to engage in deeper learning. Covering the curriculum on a superficial level means that far too often learners don't have opportunities to actively apply knowledge, generate analogies, make logical deductions, create and use memory aids, practice resilience (the ability to recover from setbacks), and reflect on their learning (Resnick 1999, 38–39). But with time and effort, as Lauren Resnick notes, educators can help students learn strategies to harness their cognitive efforts to "create ability" rather than accept the limits of what has been called their "aptitude."

Critical thinking is part and parcel of deeper learning. It involves approaching issues with an open mind, considering multiple perspectives, and resolving conflicting information. The goal of critical thinking is for learners to analyze and evaluate an issue or topic and then be able to form a conclusion based on evidence. In *Setting the Standard for Project Based Learning: The Why, What, and How of Gold Standard PBL,* the Buck Institute for Education authors set out project design elements that help students meet deeper learning goals. These involve:

1. A challenging problem or question that stimulates an authentic need to know in students;
2. Sustained inquiry that requires active learning over time, multiple resources, and opportunities to revisit and change inquiry questions when students identify that need;
3. Authenticity in terms of real-world processes, tasks and tools, and performance standards that may have meaning for students' personal lives;
4. Student voice and choice that can motivate and increase students' investment in the project;
5. Reflection throughout the process;
6. Critique and revision-based formative assessment from educators and peers, and through self-assessment;

7. A public product, or artifact, that can be reviewed and discussed by an authentic audience, including students' families (Buck Institute et al. 2015).

These instructional design elements also guide deeper learning. Choice and voice in real-world learning lead to student agency. In the Guided Inquiry Design, students' own questions assert choice and voice. "Our students will enter a world where their ideas—their genius—will only matter if they have the agency to develop and share them. Helping students become their own biggest advocates is key" (Sheninger and Murray 2017, 77). Inquirers are empowered learners. Educators advocate for students' right to guide their own learning.

Inquirers are empowered learners.
#buildingconnections4learning

DEEPER LEARNING IN A CULTURE OF INNOVATION

The 2017 Horizon Report identified "advancing cultures of innovation" as another long-term trend. It involves applying entrepreneurship, collaboration, project-based learning, and creativity to transform school culture. To achieve a school culture of innovation, districts must prioritize "recruiting and retaining teachers and school leaders who are ready to pioneer new systems with expertise and an 'all-in' mindset" (New Media Consortium and Consortium for School Networking 2017, 12). As George Couros notes, "innovation is a way of thinking that creates something *new* and *better*" (2015, 19).

While there are many pathways to instructional innovation, providing an interdisciplinary curriculum is one that offers students a deeper and more expansive intellectual experience. In interdisciplinary studies, "concepts and modes of thinking from more than one discipline are brought together synergistically to illuminate issues that cannot be adequately tested through one discipline" (Wineburg and Grossman 2000, 18). Interdisciplinary studies require students to view human knowledge and activity through various lenses. More than a **multidisciplinary curriculum**, which uses multiple disciplines to support a single disciplinary focus (such as writing up science lab results), interdisciplinary studies can set educators and students firmly on the path to innovation.

Each of the four broad academic disciplines has a specific way of thinking and demonstrating knowledge: the arts and humanities, mathematics, science, and history. The arts and humanities use an aesthetic lens to respond to the world and apply various **sign or symbol systems** to communicate knowledge. Mathematical knowledge relies on the application of logic to solve problems. The structure of scientific knowledge depends on proposing logical hypotheses and theories backed up by empirical evidence. History is constructed by an authority (the historian) who assumes a cause-and-effect perspective with regard to the impact of history on past or current events (Woolman 2000). In an interdisciplinary curriculum, "each disciplinary perspective contributes specific concepts or findings as well as specific modes of thinking to shed light on a particular problem" (Wineburg and Grossman 2000, 27).

Figure 5.1 shows some discipline-specific and cross-discipline questions that may be used to guide interdisciplinary teaching and learning. (This figure is also available as a downloadable Web Extra.)

FIGURE 5.1

Cross-Discipline and Discipline-Specific Questioning Matrix

Discipline	Types of Questions
All Disciplines	• How does this information, or how do these ideas, relate to my purpose for reading? • How is this text organized; what is the text structure and what are the text features? • Is my prior knowledge reliable, or do I need to build more background knowledge in order to comprehend this text? • Which additional reading strategies can I use to deeply comprehend this text?
Arts and Language Arts	• Why did the author write this text? • What is my response to this text? • How does the genre of this text impact its meaning to me? • Whose voices are heard in this text; whose are left out? • How do cultural, historical, and political factors influence this text?
Mathematics	• How is the problem being presented? • What do the numbers, symbols, graphs, tables, and charts mean? • Can I define all of the vocabulary in terms of mathematical concepts? • What patterns do I detect in this information? • Why are these patterns important?
Science	• What is the hypothesis, and what information leads to this hypothesis? • When does this process occur and how does it work? • Can I define all of the vocabulary in terms of scientific concepts? • Can I explain how these data are supported by evidence? • How do I know this information is accurate, logical, reliable, replicable, and clear?
Social Studies	• From whose perspective is this text written and on what assumptions is it based? • How do I know that this information is factual, or how do I know it is an opinion? • How do I know this information is comprehensive, authoritative, well organized and supported by reliable references? • What do the illustrations, maps, realia, and language used in the primary source documents, time lines, and charts mean? • After this event, what changed and what remained the same? Who made it happen, who benefited, and who did not?
Technology	• Who made this tool, device, or information resource, and for whose benefit was it made? • Why is this tool, device, or resource important? • How does this tool, device, or resource impact communication and access to ideas and information? • Who has access to the data generated by this device, tool, or resource, and how can they use it? • What are the laws or rules governing the production, distribution, or use of this tool, device, or resource?

Combining questions usually reserved for specific disciplines helps educators and students go deeper. Using an interdisciplinary approach, students can examine phenomena through different perspectives and may arrive at different interpretations. For example, students who study World War II and the Holocaust from a historical perspective can simultaneously view the same events through a sociological lens. They can comprehend how post–World War I economic and political repercussions interacted with Germany's changing society, including scapegoating Jews and the patently false theory of the biological superiority of the Aryan race. They can understand the complexity of the context that made the destructive policies of the Third Reich palatable to a majority of the German population at that time in history.

An interdisciplinary curriculum can also support students in applying inquiry learning, reading comprehension strategies, and digital tools across the curriculum. Learning strategies to make meaning from texts must not be limited to the English language arts curriculum. Some "struggling readers may have learned [reading comprehension] strategies but have difficulty using them because they have only practiced using them with a limited range of texts and in a limited range of circumstances. Specifically, they may not be able to generalize their strategies to content-area literacy tasks and lack instruction in and knowledge of strategies specific to particular subject areas, such as math, science, or history" (Biancarosa and Snow 2006, 8–9). Students need to be taught comprehension strategies and given opportunities to intentionally apply the strategies in all content areas.

COLLABORATIVE LEARNING AND DEEPER LEARNING APPROACHES

Collaborative learning approaches were identified as midterm impact trends in both the 2015 and 2016 Horizon Reports. In future ready classrooms and libraries, educators organize instruction to include, if not center on, collaborative learning. As noted in chapter 1, collaboration is a theme running through many thought leaders' visions for education. Heterogeneous groupings in collaborative learning support students who struggle by putting them in a **zone of proximal development** where they can learn with and from more proficient peers (Vygotsky 1978). Collaborative learning not only boosts the learning of less proficient students, but it also helps more advanced students practice explaining their thinking and knowledge to others. Students learn through dialogue with their peers. In collaborative learning activities, students can learn to listen as well as speak, and follow as well as lead.

Collaborative learning challenges students and educators to rethink how to design learning activities and assess learning outcomes. The curriculum designer and author David Hunter notes: "The two most common missteps teachers make when executing group work are (1) not having a group-worthy task and (2) not requiring individual accountability" (quoted in McKibben 2016, 3). Inquiry learning can provide the open-ended, complex, meaningful tasks that are worth the team's time. The GID framework also supports educators in holding individual learners accountable.

The inquiry process and assessments must foster positive **interdependence** among group members. For example, educators may require and assess individual students' inquiry logs or journals; teams may also share their journals among members. Students' graphic organizers and other formative assessments, such as quizzes, can be assessed individually. Students' learning products or performance may be codesigned, codeveloped, and copresented. However, project assessment rubrics may have criteria for individuals, as well as collective criteria for the entire team's process and product. Reflections on an individual student's or the group's progress or final product may also be accomplished individually or by the team.

Figure 5.2 shows selected deeper learning competencies chosen from the "AASL Standards Framework for Learners" (2018, 34–39). Students learn and practice these competencies in both individual and group work. Developing these competencies over time, in all disciplines, and in various contexts helps students master these lifelong learning skills and strategies.

FIGURE 5.2

Selected AASL Deeper Learning Competencies

Shared Foundation	Domain	Competency
I. Inquire	B. Create	Learners engage with new knowledge by following a process that includes: 2. Devising and implementing a plan to fill knowledge gaps.
II. Include	A. Think	Learners adjust their awareness of the global learning community by: 2. Adopting a discerning stance toward points of view and opinions expressed in information resources and learning products.
III. Collaborate	D. Grow	Learners actively participate with others in learning situations by: 2. Recognizing learning as a social responsibility.
IV. Curate	C. Share	Learners exchange information resources within and beyond their learning community by: 3. Joining with others to compare and contrast information derived from collaboratively constructed information sites.
V. Explore	D. Grow	Learners develop through experience and reflection by: 1. Iteratively responding to challenges.
VI. Engage	C. Share	Learners responsibly, ethically, and legally share new information with a global community by: 1. Sharing information sources in accordance with modification, reuse, and remix policies.

Excerpted from *National School Library Standards for Learners, School Librarians, and School Libraries* by the American Association of School Librarians, a division of the American Library Association, copyright © 2018 American Library Association. Available for download at www.standards.aasl.org. Used with permission.

"Inquiry does not necessarily begin with a question, but with exploring and searching to find a question that's worth pursuing" (Short and Burke 1991, 56). For deeper learning to occur, students must be given ample time to discuss issues, problems, questions, and solutions with peers, mentors, and experts in the field. Time to practice oral and written communication may be especially important for youth who may have not yet learned to listen and empathize with their discussion mates and mentors (Turkle 2015). Educators can push students to take discussions even deeper by demonstrating effective listening skills, empathy, and how to take a critical stance with regard to the ideas and information that others share.

A QUESTIONING-FOCUSED LEARNING ENVIRONMENT

As Albert Einstein said, "The important thing is not to stop questioning." Anyone who has spent time with young children knows that "why" questions are one of the primary ways that preschool children seek information. Once they enter formal schooling, however, there seems to be an unwritten expectation that educators are responsible for asking questions, and students are responsible for providing answers. Inquiry learning offers a framework for disrupting these expectations and positions student-initiated questions at the heart of learning. It is important, then, for educators to create the conditions in which students learn, relearn, and practice asking meaningful questions. By rethinking how learning happens, educators can create opportunities for deeper learning.

By rethinking how learning happens, educators can create opportunities for deeper learning.
#schoollibrarianleadership

In their book *Make Just One Change: Teach Students to Ask Their Own Questions*, Dan Rothstein and Luz Santana (2015) suggest that student-led questioning is a way to ensure that students are learning and practicing thinking skills. The ability to question, whether applied to reading and responding to literature, identifying perspective or bias in a political cartoon, or analyzing the data in a scientific journal article, is an essential, lifelong learning skill. What are the questions that matter in a deeper learning environment? "Information gaps make good bait" (Leslie 2014, 43). During inquiry, students uncover gaps in their own background knowledge and gaps in the information they are reading. When students take the bait, these gaps offer invitations to inquire and explore more deeply. When educators guide students and listen carefully, they can help students identify and investigate the gaps in their own understanding.

When readers question the texts they encounter, they are engaged in active learning. This process has the potential to increase students' content knowledge as well as improve their overall reading proficiency. "Comprehension begins when we merge thinking with content. Here's where kids use thinking strategies so that understanding takes root—engaging in connecting, questioning, inferring, visualizing, determining importance, and synthesizing information" (Harvey and Goudvis 2013, 435).

Educators know that all questions are not created equal. The quality of the questions that educators and students ask matters. Every discipline has questions that frame inquiries conducted within that field of study. These can be called "essential questions." According to Jay McTighe and Grant Wiggins, there are seven defining characteristics of essential questions. (Italics are preserved from the original.) An essential question:

1. Is *open-ended*; that is, it typically will not have a single, final, and correct answer;
2. Is *thought-provoking* and *intellectually engaging*, often sparking discussion and debate;
3. Calls for *higher-order thinking*, such as analysis, inference, evaluation, prediction. It cannot be effectively answered by recall alone;
4. Points toward *important, transferable ideas* within (and sometimes across) disciplines;
5. Raises *additional questions* and sparks further inquiry;
6. Requires *support* and *justification*, not just an answer;
7. *Recurs* over time; that is, the question can and should be revisited again and again (McTighe and Wiggins 2013, 3).

Educators can use essential questions to frame a lesson, an instructional unit, inquiry learning, or an entire course. Students can also identify how their inquiry learning aligns with the essential questions of a particular field of study. Essential questions help educators teach and students learn like artists, published authors, mathematicians, scientists, historians, and more.

STRATEGIES FOR TEACHING QUESTIONING

Educators provide interventions throughout the inquiry process to prompt learners to think more clearly and deeply about the texts and information they encounter. Educators can use the various questioning strategies in figure 5.3 to help students deepen their inquiry. These strategies can help students get to a place of passionately needing to know and understand. Students uncover meaningful questions while they immerse themselves in a problem and explore ideas and information related to that problem. These will be the questions that are worth pursuing. "A beautiful question is an ambitious yet actionable question that can begin to shift the way we perceive or think about something—and that might serve as a catalyst to bring about change" (Berger 2014, 8). That change is learning.

Dan Rothstein, Luz Santana, and Andrew P. Minigan from the Right Question Institute suggest a brainstorming method to elicit students' questions as a way of frontloading a lesson or inquiry unit (see http://rightquestion.org). In the Question Formulation Technique's brainstorming, all contributions are accepted, weighted equally, and then prioritized. "Having students create questions is a shortcut to deeper learning. As students become more curious and engaged and take on a new ownership of their learning, they will leave school as sophisticated questioners who can use the skill of question formulation in higher education, the workplace, their lives, and our democracy" (Rothstein, Santana, and Minigan

FIGURE 5.3

Questioning Strategies for Deeper Learning

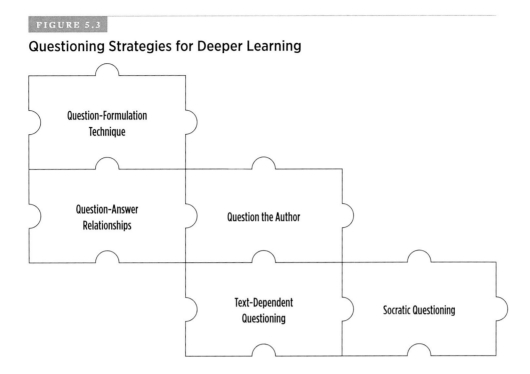

2015, 75). Empowered students use the Question Formulation Technique to take ownership of their learning.

The **question-answer relationship** (QAR) strategy is one way that students can explore the connections, predictions, inferences, and questions that occur to them as they read. Dan Ouzts (1998) notes that studying question-answer relationships can help students distinguish between "locate-type" questions and answers and "think-type" questions and answers. In this model, students are asked to classify questions by the source of their answers. If the question is literal, students will find the answer "on the line" or "right there" in the text. These types of questions are often the five W's: who, what, where, when, and sometimes why. Answers to these questions may be found on a specific page or screen in the text. If they are "think and search" questions, they may also require readers to synthesize information found at various points in the text or in multiple texts.

The answers to inferential questions are found "between the lines" when readers combine information found in the text with their own background knowledge. These can be called "author and me" questions because the answers are co-constructed between the author and the reader. "Why" questions, such as why the author wrote a particular piece, often require students to infer. Determining the theme of a poem, story, novel, or essay involves reading between the lines. Answers to questions related to point of view, bias, and persuasion may also be found between the lines.

Evaluative questions require students to make a judgment or state an opinion. If the question wasn't answered in the text, where can an answer be found? These questions can be called "on my own" questions. When students categorize questions, including their own questions, by type and by where the answers can be found, they can better understand the ways in which questioning supports comprehension. In many school districts, identifying QARs is an aspect of test preparation because students need to understand that many answers to test questions are not stated directly in the text.

The goal of the **question the author** (QtA) comprehension strategy is to increase readers' interaction and engagement with texts (Beck et al. 1996). QtA involves students in a dialogue with the author and the text. With QtA, readers learn to deconstruct the writer's craft and to share authority with the author through questioning and their interpretations. When readers ask why authors use a particular genre to convey ideas or information, they learn more about the choices that writers make when they compose a text. When readers question the way in which authors use language and media to inform or persuade, they learn about authority, perspective, and bias while they also determine the accuracy of information.

In narrative or persuasive texts, authors use word choice to create a particular tone. The tone is designed to evoke a particular mood in the reader. Authors can play a prediction game with the reader, dropping clues and leaving gaps in information as the plot unfolds. Readers find that filling in the gaps propels them through the text. Mysteries that leave readers asking "how and why" questions require that readers "read between the lines" to make inferences—to connect clues with their own background knowledge. With topical informational texts, authors might capitalize on text features, such as graphs, charts, and maps, to organize and convey information; they may also use the same features in a persuasive manner to evoke a particular response from the reader.

Similar to QtA, Douglas Fisher and Nancy Frey suggest a metacognitive **text-dependent questioning protocol** (TDP) as a path for readers to follow as they read and analyze literary and informational texts. Educators model this strategy with think-alouds. They use the following questions as probes to invite individual readers to think more deeply, and they post them for students' reference:

1. What does the text say?
2. How does the text work?
3. What does the text mean?
4. What does the text inspire you to do? (Fisher and Frey 2015, 82–83).

In TDP, the first text-dependent question is literal; what are the facts? The second question relates to how genre and text structures support comprehension; it is about the writer's craft. The third question is inferential; what does the text mean to the reader? Readers will need to use their background knowledge and cite evidence in the text to support their interpretations. The fourth question prompts readers to take action. The action could be asking a new question. Or it could be enacting a response in the world. TDP is intended to raise readers' awareness of the need for thinking deeply and critically about the text. As with other metacognitive strategies, the ultimate goal is for readers to ask these questions of themselves as they independently engage with texts.

Socratic questioning, attributed to the ancient Greek philosopher Socrates, includes six types of questions that prompt deeper thinking. Educators can model asking these questions, and students can learn to ask these questions of themselves and their peers. Figure 5.4 shows types of Socratic questions, the purpose for each, and sample questions that relate to each question type. (This figure is also available as a downloadable Web Extra.)

FIGURE 5.4

Socratic Questioning

Type of Question	Purpose: To help students	Sample Questions
Seeking Clarifications	Think more clearly about the concept	• Can you say more about that? • Can you give an example? • How does this relate to your background knowledge or experience, or how does this relate to our discussion?
Probing Assumptions	Think about the assumptions on which they are basing their opinions or arguments	• What are your assumptions that cause you to believe that? • How did you arrive at that assumption, and can you prove it is true? • Are there other plausible assumptions?
Probing Reasons and Evidence	Think about their reasoning and the evidence they are using to support their arguments	• How do you know this is true? • What is your evidence? • What evidence could be used to refute your argument?
Questioning Viewpoints and Perspectives	Think about equally valid alternative viewpoints and perspectives	• How could you look at this from another perspective? • What is the difference between your viewpoint and another perspective? • Why is your perspective more valid than another viewpoint?
Probing Implications and Consequences	Think about the logic and desirability of their perspectives	• How does this affect . . . ? • What are the intended consequences of that outcome? • What might be the unintended consequences?
Questioning the Question	Think about the effectiveness of the question itself	• Was this an effective question in terms of thinking about . . . ? Why or why not? • What question would have been more effective? • Why do we ask questions to support learning?

Socratic questioning, in particular, can help students see the complexity of issues in light of what students believe and think about those issues. Questioning supports "human curiosity, which depends on friction, on the struggle to close information gaps, on uncertainty, mystery, and the awareness of ignorance" (Leslie 2014, 56). Modeling questioning strategies in all areas of a curriculum is essential practice for educators. Practicing questioning strategies in all disciplines is essential for students.

METACOGNITION ACROSS THE CURRICULUM

Metacognition, or "thinking about thinking," is essential if students are to transfer their learning from one context to another. In their report *How People Learn: Brain, Mind, Experience, and School,* the National Research Council (2000) states that metacognition must be taught and nurtured. In order to teach metacognition, educators use think-aloud strategies. Research has shown that people learn better when they are more aware of their own thinking processes. Think-aloud strategies were once thought of as primarily useful in elementary school classrooms, but effective educators are now encouraged to apply these strategies to instruction across the K–12 spectrum (Wilhelm, Baker, and Dube 2001).

Using think-alouds, educators provide learners with an apprenticeship in text-based thinking. When educators model how to approach a text, they demonstrate how to wrestle with unknown vocabulary and challenging text structures and concepts. Educators can make think-aloud demonstrations interactive by inviting students to make comments and ask questions about their observations of educators' thinking processes. With these models, students can also demonstrate their thinking by practicing think-alouds with educators and peers. In the process, students will show their thinking about content-specific vocabulary and concepts, and demonstrate various reading comprehension strategies. The ultimate goal for think-alouds is for strategic readers and inquirers to internalize these processes, select the most useful strategies for solving a particular comprehension challenge, and apply them when reading independently.

Questioning helps students apply thinking skills to increase their content knowledge. Educators collaborate with each other and with students to practice thinking skills and make the curriculum content relevant to students' lives. Kuhlthau, Maniotes, and Caspari call this convergence the "**third space**" where the students' out-of-school experiences, the first space, and state-mandated curricula, the second space, overlap to make space for authentic learning. In this third space, "real questions are about something genuinely important to students and to which they do not already know the answer" (Kuhlthau, Maniotes, and Caspari 2015, 17). With a shared attitude of discovery, students and educators continuously negotiate the third space as they pursue deeper learning through inquiry.

Questioning
helps students
apply thinking
skills to increase
their content
knowledge.
#buildingconnections4learning

INQUIRY LEARNING AND NEW STANDARDS IN THE CONTENT AREAS

While questioning is surely important, Einstein also possessed an extraordinary ability to connect seemingly unrelated ideas and information. His endless curiosity in combination with his deep knowledge of physics and his mastery of reasoning skills are what made his many discoveries possible. Whenever new standards are introduced in any discipline, educators have an acute need to revisit the curriculum and to identify and align new resources with existing ones. They need to develop new methods to support student achievement, and develop new assessments to measure progress. Educators also need to engage in professional development to ensure effective implementation. School librarians can serve as leaders in coimplementing new standards, particularly those based in inquiry.

In 2013, the National Council for the Social Studies (NCSS) released the College, Career, and Civic Life (C3) Framework for Social Studies State Standards. That same year the National Research Council (NRC) published the Next Generation Science Standards (NGSS). These two inquiry-based initiatives share a goal of increasing rigor and are guided by overarching themes: change, innovation, and discovery. They also share the expectation, whether in history or in science, that students will be able to build arguments and support their claims with evidence. Both initiatives have the goals of developing learners who think like historians and scientists and who will take up the challenge to discover solutions to the world's pressing problems.

"The C3 Framework provides guidance to states on upgrading state social studies standards to include the application of knowledge within the disciplines of civics, economics, geography, and history as students develop questions and plan inquiries; apply disciplinary concepts and tools; evaluate and use evidence; and communicate conclusions and take informed action" (NCSS 2013, 6). The NGSS also create a timely opportunity for school librarians and classroom teachers to design deeper learning experiences for students. The NGSS home page states: "a high-quality science education means that students will develop an in-depth understanding of content and develop key skills—communication, collaboration, inquiry, problem solving, and flexibility—that will serve them throughout their educational and professional lives" (www.nextgenscience.org).

Both the NCSS 3Cs and the NGSS require students to engage in deeper learning. With these standards, students are not being asked to conduct superficial fact-finding research or conduct science labs following a lockstep protocol. Instead, students are required to think critically about real-world problems. They are expected to gather information and cite evidence, synthesize their learning, and draw conclusions. Together, educators and students assess the quality of the questions that students pursue. Educators guide students as they reflect on the content they have learned and the processes they used to learn it. These initiatives require students to engage in inquiry.

School librarians can serve as leaders in coimplementing new standards, particularly those based In Inquiry.
#schoollibrarianleadership

SCHOOL LIBRARIANS AS DEEPER LEARNING LEADERS

There are an infinite number of ways for school librarians to maximize their leadership role in implementing deeper learning. In coplanning, school librarians bring their knowledge of print and online resources and their commitment to identify and curate new resources to meet curriculum requirements. These new resources can include **open education resources** (OER) that are free or licensed for educational use. OER can include textbooks, streaming videos, software, full courses, course materials, tests, learning modules, and any other tools, materials, or techniques that are used to support access to knowledge (Hewlett Foundation 2014). School librarians practice curation with online pathfinders when they organize and add value by providing annotations for resources and additional information that create a learning context for students.

In addition to their knowledge of resources, future ready school librarians connect their expertise to the classroom curriculum through coplanning and coteaching. They coteach technology-supported learning and outcomes-based technology tool integration. Combined with their ability to guide inquiry learning and coteach reading comprehension strategies, school librarians bring considerable professional knowledge to the collaboration table. Taken together, these connected areas of expertise enable school librarians to maximize their impact on deeper learning. Colleagues and administrators will value their leadership.

In a collaborative school culture, principals "endorse a whole school, 21st-century learning environment where educators model collaboration for students as they collaborate; encourage a culture of innovation, risk taking, and high expectations, and acknowledge the actions school librarians take to shape a school culture of deep learning" (Todd, Gordon, and Lu 2012, xxii). With a school-wide approach, educators will develop a shared vocabulary that describes the various learning processes used within the community. Ideally, the school or district will select an inquiry model, such as the Guided Inquiry Design, that students will follow in all grade levels and content areas. Students will spiral through this process with increasing sophistication. With each encounter, students will refine the inquiry process until they internalize it. Students will be confident and successful because they will have the support of every educator in the school who shares their understanding of this process.

Deeper learning is authentic learning. It is a critical piece of future ready learning. Students must care about the topics, questions, problems, and dilemmas that frame their inquiries. As they develop content literacies through inquiry learning, students will have the necessary prior knowledge to ask deeper questions and to explore innovative solutions. "Knowledge begets comprehension begets knowledge is just the sort of virtuous cycle we would like students to experience" (Duke, Pearson, Strachan, and Billman 2011, 55).

School librarians can be leaders in collaboratively designing learning experiences that guide inquiry learning in compelling directions—in ways that ignite students' passions and spark their curiosity. School librarians can serve as advocates for student choice, voice, and relevance throughout the inquiry process. While designing and implementing inquiry, school librarians and classroom teachers will build connections. They will capitalize on school librarians' expertise in effectively integrating multimodal resources and digital tools into teaching and learning. The resulting deeper learning through cotaught interdisciplinary inquiry offers an ideal context for developing digital literacy, which is one important piece of the future ready learning puzzle.

BOOK STUDY GUIDE

I. Discussion Questions

QUESTION #1: What would have to change in your school's physical facilities and resources to make deeper learning more commonly experienced by students in all content areas?

QUESTION #2: What would have to change in your own instructional practices to ensure that students have deeper learning opportunities?

QUESTION #3: How would the learning culture in your school change if the facilities, resources, and instructional practices supported deeper learning?

- *Individual Thinking*: Compose individual responses to the questions asked above.
- *Partner Sharing*: Share your individual responses to these questions with a colleague in your own school or another school.
- *Group Sharing*: As a small or whole group, discuss the feelings, ideas, hopes, and challenges that occurred to you as you responded to these questions or listened to your colleagues' responses.

II. Activities

Although these activities can be undertaken by individuals, they are designed for group work.

Activity 1

Force Field Analysis

Conduct a force field analysis of the forces that support or constrain deeper learning in your school (see chapter 2, Activity 1). Brainstorm strategies for moving ahead with deeper learning and develop an action plan.

What strategy can you develop from the most promising driving force? What kind of action plan can the group develop to support that strategy? If there isn't a promising strategy, discuss the most obvious constraining force and develop an action plan to deal with that constraint.

Activity 2

Essential Questions

In this activity, faculty suggest and negotiate shared essential questions (questions that matter the most) in each of the content areas taught in your school.

In elementary schools where most teachers are responsible for all subjects, educators at each instructional level will divide up and take responsibility for one of the disciplines (English language arts and reading, math, science, social studies, various fine arts, and more). At the secondary level, they will form disciplinary groups. Specialists will work with these groups as appropriate.

If a cadre of school librarians is conducting this activity, they can divide into small groups focused on reading comprehension instruction, information-seeking processes, information ethics, digital literacy or citizenship, or any area of focus in their practice.

Each individual or small group will contribute to a collective cloud-based mapping tool or a Google Drive doc (which is created and organized into disciplines by the school librarian). Use the seven defining characteristics proposed by Jay McTighe and Grant Wiggins and cited in this chapter. Use the following prompts to develop essential questions for each domain:

1. If you had to distill your domain into *one* or *two* concepts that you expect students to master, what would it/they be?
2. Turn these must-learn concepts into essential questions for students.

Information-seeking example:

- *Concept*: Students must understand that all information is presented from the author's viewpoint.
- *Essential Question*: Why is it essential for readers/viewers to determine if the author's perspective is biased?

After groups contribute to the shared document, each group will report out. A facilitator will guide the group in looking for essential questions that transfer across disciplines and those that are unique to particular subject areas. Discuss how framing an instructional unit around one or more of these questions might strengthen or change what and how you and your colleagues teach this content. Note where there are opportunities for interdisciplinary teaching and learning.

Activity 3

Think-Alouds with Socratic Questioning

This activity is designed for educators to learn from each other's practice of think-alouds with follow-up Socratic questions (use figure 5.3 to support this activity). One educator at any instructional level, in any discipline, or the school librarian will be responsible for selecting a text for partner or small-group practice. Texts that work especially well include persuasive speeches and current events articles or editorials.

Create a graphic organizer with three columns like the one below. Fill in a selection of short passages from the text, one per row. Add rows as needed for additional passages. For maximum benefit, audio-record the activity so that group members can review the recording and share other possible think-aloud comments and Socratic questions.

Short Passage from the Text	Think-Aloud	Socratic Question

III. Reflection Prompts

Choose from these possible reflection prompts or compose one of your own.

1. Reflect on your thoughts, feelings, and next steps as you read this chapter and/or engaged in the discussion questions or activities.
2. Reflect on the benefits of interdisciplinary inquiry learning in which students use various disciplinary lenses to deeply explore a topic, concept, problem, or dilemma.
3. Especially for school librarians: Reflect on what you need to learn in order to cofacilitate deeper learning opportunities for students across grade levels and disciplines.

CHAPTER SIX

Digital Learning

Beyond providing basic access to training, schools will also have to tackle the deeper challenge of ensuring that educators receive the guidance and support needed to embed these tools fully and effectively into instruction and to align technology with students' needs and learning goals.

EDUCATION WEEK, "TECHNOLOGY COUNTS REPORT"

◇◇◇◇

ODAY'S EDUCATORS ARE RESPONSIBLE FOR TEACHING students to navigate the digital landscape that shapes their academic, civic, cultural, economic, and social lives. Educators must also advocate for equitable access to high-speed Internet, digital resources, and technology devices and tools. They must seek guidance for effective technology-supported pedagogy. "An effective school library plays a critical role in bridging digital and socioeconomic divides" (AASL 2018, 14). The ability to use **information and communication technology** (ICT) for teaching and learning is arguably the hottest topic in preK–12 education. ICTs present educators and students with a wide array of resources and tools to empower learning. Since all students deserve to be and should be "connected," they must develop digital literacy. Students must learn strategies for evaluating information in order to effectively use the richness of web-based information. They must learn to use digital devices and tools, use information ethically, and avoid plagiarism.

From the moment they begin to participate in the online environment, students must make informed decisions about how to manage and protect their online footprints and avoid potential dangers such as bullying, fraud, and identify theft. Parents and communities can join with educators to help all young people develop the necessary skills and strategies for learning and living in a digital world. Yet, the expectation is that schools will take on the primary responsibility for teaching digital literacy, facilitating **digital learning**, and for guiding youth in practicing **digital citizenship**.

The American Library Association's Digital Literacy Task Force defined digital literacy in this way: "Digital literacy is the ability to use information and communication technologies to find, understand, evaluate, create, and communicate

BEFORE READING

There is no universally agreed-upon definition for "personalized learning." What does this term mean to you, and how do you or how could you enact it in your classroom, library, or school?

digital information, an ability that requires both cognitive and technical skills" (ALA 2013). On the Digital Learning Day website, the Alliance for Excellent Education (AEE) defines digital learning in this way. "Digital learning is any instructional practice that effectively uses technology to strengthen a student's learning experience. It emphasizes high-quality instruction and provides access to challenging content, feedback through formative assessment, opportunities for learning anytime and anywhere, and individualized instruction to ensure all students reach their full potential to succeed in college and a career" (Alliance for Excellent Education 2016a). These definitions provide administrators and educators with targets for digital learning in preK–12 schools.

Just as they work with colleagues to help develop common beliefs about literacy learning, school librarians can also be coleaders in determining specific core beliefs about digital literacy. These beliefs guide educators as they collaborate. During coplanning, school librarians have the opportunity to suggest digital resources and ways to integrate digital tools that can transform learning. School librarians take or share responsibility for teaching and assessing students' work in inquiry process areas such as evaluating digital resources for their currency, relevance, authority, accuracy, and bias. They teach and assess students' ability to make notes from digital texts and locate and use electronic media for their projects. School librarians teach students to ethically use, organize, annotate, and curate electronic resources in order to make them useful and accessible to themselves and others. They also teach students to cite original media and media that have been accessed, remixed, and reused. While coteaching digital literacy, school librarians and classroom teachers develop a shared vocabulary, instructional practices, and expectations for students' digital learning.

School librarians and classroom teachers develop a shared vocabulary, instructional practices, and expectations for students' digital learning.

#buildingconnections4learning

DIGITAL CONVERSION, SHIFT, AND TRANSFORMATION

There are many U.S.-based and international organizations that offer a wide array of resources, research data, and reports related to digital learning. Figure 6.1 quotes the vision or mission statements of eight of the leading organizations. Educators who are leading digital transformation in their schools and districts will want to stay abreast of the resources, support, and publications that these organizations provide.

There are quite literally hundreds of digital learning leaders who present at conferences, provide workshops, write books, and publish on social media. There is one often-spoken or written sentence that may summarize a shared understanding among these leaders: "It's about the learning, not about the technology." In the face of the daily release of new online tools and applications and the annual rollout of new devices, it may be difficult for educators to keep a focus on this truism. Knowing tens or hundreds of websites or apps is not as important as finding, field-testing, and applying a few tools that meet the learning needs and objectives

FIGURE 6.1

Leading Digital Learning Organizations

Organization	Mission – Quotes from About, Home, or Mission Web Pages	URL
Alliance for Excellent Education	"The mission of the Alliance for Excellent Education is to promote high school transformation to make it possible for every child to graduate prepared for postsecondary learning and success in life."	all4ed.org
Digital Promise	"Digital Promise works at the intersection of education leaders, researchers, and learning technology developers to improve learning opportunity."	digitalpromise.org
Edutopia	"Our vision is of a new world of learning based on the compelling truth that improving education is the key to the survival of the human race.... It's a world where schools provide rigorous project-based learning, social-emotional learning, and access to new technology."	edutopia.org
Future Ready Schools	"Future Ready Schools helps district leaders plan and implement personalized, research-based digital learning strategies so all students can achieve their full potential."	futureready.org
International Society for Technology in Education	"As the creator and steward of the definitive education technology standards, our mission is to empower learners to flourish in a connected world by cultivating a passionate professional learning community, linking educators and partners, leveraging knowledge and expertise, advocating for strategic policies, and continually improving learning and teaching."	iste.org
New Media Consortium	"The NMC Horizon Project charts the landscape of emerging technologies for teaching, learning, and creative inquiry."	nmc.org
Partnership for 21st Century Learning	"P21's mission is to serve as a catalyst for 21st century learning to build collaborative partnerships among education, business, community and government leaders so that all learners acquire the knowledge and skills they need to thrive in a world where change is constant and learning never stops."	p21.org
Project Tomorrow	"The Speak Up data represents the largest collection of authentic, unfiltered stakeholder input on education, technology, 21st century skills, schools of the future and science instruction. Education, business and policy leaders report using the data regularly to inform federal, state and local education programs."	tomorrow.org

of the students and educators in one's own building. As George Couros wrote: "*Learners* are the driver; technology is the accelerator" (2015, 148).

There are different ways that schools and districts describe their evolution or revolution from an analog environment to a digital one: **digital conversion**, **digital shift**, and **digital transformation**. The term "digital conversion" suggests a change in tools that results in a technology-infused learning environment. This is often rolled out as a 1:1 initiative in which every student at a grade level or all students in the school get a laptop computer, tablet, or other device for their use on a 24/7 basis. In the Mooresville (North Carolina) Graded School District, Superintendent Mark Edwards noted that digital conversion in his district involved a "culture of caring and a relentless focus on data to improve student achievement" as well as on hardware and software considerations (Edwards 2014, x–xi).

The term "digital shift" suggests a modification in instructional practices—a shift from print or paper to digital or electronic resources and tools. The goal of such a shift is to leverage digital tools in order to improve teaching and learning. Appropriating digital tools can break down the barriers between the technologies used inside school and those used outside of the school. Technology-enabled connections among students, classrooms, and local, national, and worldwide communities can increase the relevance of in-school learning. In the most technologically evolved schools and districts, instructional decisions are based on the best tools or resources for the purpose of achieving specific student learning outcomes. Although analog and print options may be selected, a school culture that is undergoing a digital shift has begun to privilege digital tools and resources.

The ultimate goal of both digital conversion and digital shift is digital transformation. "Educational leaders need to think about digital transformation from a whole-systems perspective and build a culture that encourages ubiquitous leadership and fosters innovation" (Steve Webb cited in Sheninger and Murray 2017, 197). In order for digital transformation to occur, students and educators must participate in learning experiences that could not have been as easily accomplished or even have been possible in a purely analog world. Digital transformation requires that educators, students, and families take risks together. Educators and students must act with a shared understanding that, since the global community is shaped more and more by technology, new digital tools must be leveraged to enable school-based learning.

DIGITAL LEARNING STANDARDS AND DISPOSITIONS

In 2016, the International Society for Technology in Education (ISTE) released the organization's latest standards for students. These standards "are designed to empower student voice and ensure that learning is a student-driven process of exploration, creativity and discovery no matter where they or their teachers are in the thoughtful integration of ed tech" (ISTE 2016a). Indicators are listed under each of seven standards:

1. Empowered Learner
2. Digital Citizen
3. Knowledge Constructor
4. Innovative Designer
5. Computational Thinker
6. Creative Communicator
7. Global Collaborator (ISTE 2016a).

Simultaneously with these revised standards, ISTE published "Redefining Learning in a Technology-Driven World: A Report to Support Adoption of the ISTE Standards for Students" (2016b). In this report, ISTE used an evidence-based model and cited relevant literature and research studies to support each of the seven standards—standards which are focused on pedagogy rather than on the tools themselves.

Student agency is one of the recurring themes in the ISTE report and is a cornerstone of the standards. With the goals of students expressing their own voices and making choices in terms of their learning, the ISTE standards seek to support students as empowered agents as they prepare for their futures. According to the report, agency can help motivate students as they develop positive dispositions, such as perseverance and the ability to tolerate ambiguity. Agency also supports students as they personalize, self-regulate, and own their learning, including negotiating unequal access to tools and resources.

As noted in the report, "What has not been fully realized [in schools] is the potential for technology to mend gaps in equity, engage students as unique individuals, and prepare them for an uncertain future" (ISTE 2016b, 2). With their global view of the learning community, school librarians have an essential role to play as technology stewards who help address gaps in technology access. "Information technologies must be appropriately integrated and equitably available" (AASL 2018, 11). Ensuring equitable access to information and technology is a central mission of school librarianship.

Along the path to improving digital literacy for all, school librarians are developing and helping others develop the dispositions they need to become effective digital learners: flexibility, open-mindedness, perseverance, risk-taking, and more. "The key aspect of these dispositions, even though they are manifest in the exhibition of specific skills and actions, is that they cannot be directly taught or directly tested . . . These qualities, these dispositions, have to be developed over time. They must be nurtured across a variety of circumstances so that they become ingrained and are likely to emerge when the situation calls for them. Dispositions must be encultured—that is, learned through immersion in a culture" (Ritchhart 2015, 20).

Collaborating school librarians play a key role in helping students develop these dispositions in authentic contexts. When educators coteach, they model dispositions associated with teamwork—flexibility and open-mindedness. When they coteach technology-supported learning experiences, educators model perseverance and risk-taking. When educators guide students in real-world online learning, they model curiosity and grit. A digital learning environment is an ideal context for enculturating students in future ready dispositions.

BLENDED AND PERSONALIZED LEARNING

Blended learning, or hybrid learning, involves students and educators interacting with content in both the face-to-face classroom and the online environment. Blended learning can be used to deepen students' engagement with ideas and information. As more and more postsecondary education is conducted with hybrid or 100 percent online instruction, this trend in K–12 schools helps prepare students for continuing their education after high school graduation. In the online environment, students have control of and responsibility for the "time, place, path, and pace of instruction" (Staker and Horn 2012, 3). With a focus on hands-on learning in the face-to-face classroom, blended learning can also be used to increase the individualized support that students receive in the classroom from educators and peers. In addition, blended learning can support community-embedded projects such as fieldwork and internships.

The **flipped classroom** is a blended learning approach in which educators provide students with tasks to perform or texts to view and respond to *as homework* before they come to class. "Instead of a lecture in class and hands-on work at home, instructors assign material to be reviewed ahead of time, allowing for problem-solving activities during class time" (Fawley 2014, 19). This approach supports students as responsible agents in their own learning. When students come to class prepared to discuss or take some sort of action as a result of their homework, the classroom can become more student-centered. Students can use class time for responding to and discussing what they did and did not understand about the homework. They can share what they question, believe, or feel about the topic. Educators can use class time to challenge students with additional prompts, and they can monitor students' conversations and provide individual or small-group support.

With a plethora of digital tools from which to choose, **personalized learning** can give students more control over when and how they learn. With 24/7 access to information and web-based tool choices, students who get up early and those who stay up late can make more decisions about their learning process. Educators, who create flexible learning environments in school and online, can vary the organization of instruction to include one-on-one tutoring, peer-to-peer mentoring, and small-group collaboration as well as whole-class instruction. Learning management systems, software, and cloud-based tools abound that can facilitate students' opportunities to choose divergent learning paths as well as collaborate on shared projects. Like blended learning, personalized learning can also extend outside traditional schooling to include students participating in internships or apprenticeships with experts, businesses, or organizations in the community.

A focus on personalized learning can help educators differentiate digital resources and technology-supported instruction to meet the needs of individuals

Digital learning environment is an ideal context for enculturating students in future ready dispositions.

#buildingconnections4learning

and small groups of learners. Offering choice in terms of resource format can increase students' motivation to engage in the learning process. Using digital tools to differentiate learning tasks can support student success. Educators who have more experience and greater comfort with a traditional print-based teacher-centered model for education will need professional development in order to rise to this challenge. School librarians are prepared and positioned to offer colleagues differentiated digital learning professional development. They can advocate for students' digital learning opportunities, resources, and tools through coplanning and coteaching blended and personalized learning activities.

DIGITAL CITIZENSHIP

When engaged in digital learning, students are acquiring the skills and strategies of digital citizenship that they will use in the personal, professional, and civic arenas throughout their lives. In *Digital Citizenship in Schools: Nine Elements All Students Should Know*, Mike Ribble (2015) suggests and describes nine digital citizenship elements: digital access, commerce, communication, literacy, etiquette, law, rights and responsibilities, health and wellness, and security. As this list of elements suggests, digital citizenship is complex. In order to be future ready, students must learn and practice digital citizenship. Many educators agree that teaching these elements should be part of the curriculum taught in any school.

School librarians are prepared and positioned to offer colleagues differentiated digital learning professional development.

#schoollibrarianleadership

Digital citizenship is a foundational set of skills and behaviors that can be taught, practiced, and applied in blended, 100 percent online, and personalized learning situations. Common Sense Education provides a free K–12 curriculum to support educators, including classroom teachers, school librarians, and technology specialists, in teaching digital citizenship (https://www.commonsensemedia.org/educators). Their cross-curricular scope and sequence offers eighty lessons that address student learning in eight categories: Internet safety, privacy and security, relationships and communication, cyberbullying and digital drama, digital footprints and reputation, self-image and identity, information literacy, and creative credit and copyright. The units are organized into four grade-level ranges: K–2, 3–5, 6–8, and 9–12. The lessons are aligned with the Common Core State Standards and the 2016 ISTE Standards for Students. Other organizations, such as ConnectSafely .org, DigitalCitizenship.net, and OnGuardOnline.gov, offer resources that address creating and maintaining a secure online identity, considering issues of privacy, and learning about how online data is collected and used.

The goal of teaching digital citizenship is to ensure that students are active, ethical, legal, responsible, and safe online learners. In many schools and districts, school librarians have taken a leadership role in implementing or coteaching digital citizenship lessons. In these lessons, students engage in critical thinking about the digital information they consume and the information they download, create, upload, and share on the Web. A whole-school or whole-district approach to integrating digital citizenship learning into the taught curriculum is an ideal strategy. Involving families in this effort further strengthens students' success.

EVALUATING THE QUALITY OF DIGITAL LEARNING

The Arizona Technology Integration Matrix (TIM) is an interactive tool that educators can use to evaluate the effectiveness of their digital lessons (www .azk12.org/tim/). The goal of the TIM and other technology integration initiatives is to improve educators' technological literacy and proficiency so that students will have opportunities to utilize digital devices, tools, and resources in school-based learning. The TIM offers descriptions and examples of five levels of technology integration (entry, adoption, adaptation, infusion, and transformation) that are categorized by five characteristics of learning environments: active, constructive, goal-directed (reflective), authentic, and collaborative. The TIM provides videos and K–4, 5–8, and 9–12 sample lessons at each level and in each category. Educators can use these lessons as models and can use this matrix to guide and assess their technology-supported lesson plans as well as their own digital literacy.

The Organisation of Economic Cooperation and Development (OECD) is an international governmental group. One of the OECD's objectives is to "ensure that people of all ages can develop the skills to work productively and satisfyingly in the jobs of tomorrow." The OECD's "Students, Computers, and Learning: Making the Connection" report stresses the importance of strengthening students' ability to navigate digital texts. The report also includes an analysis of the relationships between computer access in schools, computer use in classrooms, and students' performance on the 2012 Programme for International Student Assessment (PISA). One of the findings that may surprise many is that "even where computers are used in the classroom, their impact on student performance is mixed at best. Students who use computers moderately at school tend to have somewhat better learning outcomes than students who use computers rarely. But students who use computers very frequently at school do a lot worse in most learning outcomes, even after accounting for social background and student demographics" (OECD 2015, 3). It could be that when it comes to information and communications technologies in schools, "less is more."

It is equally likely that, as the OECD postulates, educators have not yet developed the most effective pedagogies to capitalize on the potential benefits that ICTs can provide. Utilizing technology tools in the context of the curriculum and addressing required standards can help keep educators' focus on pedagogy rather than on the glitz of the latest gadgets and applications. "When infusing technology, there needs to be a 'Return on Instruction' (ROI) that results in evidence of improved student learning outcomes" (Sheninger and Murray 2017, 25). School librarians can help colleagues maintain a student learning-centered approach. They can take a leadership role as educators critically evaluate the potential of a particular technology tool to help students meet specific learning outcomes.

Educators can collaboratively assess the usefulness or appropriateness of technology tools in terms of cognitive goals. For example, citation generators that automate footnotes and bibliographies and electronic notemaking tools save students time. But do they deepen students' understanding of intellectual property rights, fair use and copyright law, and practices to avoid plagiarism? If educators' goals are to help students develop perseverance and self-reliance, two dispositions identified by Jean Donham (2014), do particular tools shortcut students' thinking or shortchange their opportunities to develop future ready dispositions? The same tool may be perfectly appropriate to achieve some learning objectives and inappropriate in achieving others.

When educators question how much a tool does *for* the student and how much the student can do *with* the tool, educators can keep a focus on the goal of helping students become independent learners. In a culture of collaboration, school educators engage in critical conversations about pedagogy. They can raise and discuss dilemmas that arise at the intersection of pedagogy and technology. School librarians can share research related to digital technologies as a way to maximize their instructional leadership. Digital Promise is one excellent source for the latest digital learning research (http://digitalpromise.org).

FUTURE READY SCHOOLS

The Alliance for Excellent Education (AEE) and the U.S. Department of Education are taking a leading role in the effort to "maximize digital learning opportunities and help school districts move quickly toward preparing students for success in college, a career, and citizenship" (http://all4ed.org/issues/future-ready). AEE is a Washington, D.C.–based policy and advocacy organization dedicated to ensuring that all students, particularly those who are traditionally underserved, graduate from high school ready for success. In 2015, AEE created a separate project called Future Ready Schools (FRS) to help school districts develop comprehensive plans to achieve successful student learning outcomes by (1) transforming instructional pedagogy and practice while (2) simultaneously leveraging technology to personalize learning in the classroom.

FRS offers a framework of seven "gears" to guide implementation plans. The foundational attributes of the FRS are the increased use of digital content and providing learners with a range of high-quality media that are accessible 24/7. In this context, students will have more opportunities for personalized learning, and more time to engage frequently in a deeper understanding of complex topics, think critically, and reflect on their own work.

The "seven gears" of the Future Ready Framework are:

1. Curriculum, Instruction, and Assessment
2. Use of Space and Time
3. Robust Infrastructure
4. Data and Privacy
5. Community Partnerships
6. Personalized Professional Learning
7. Budget and Resources (Alliance for Excellent Education 2016c).

Each of the gears is fleshed out in the Future Ready District Assessment, which includes rating scales for each criterion related to each of the gears. In step one of the action plan, AEE suggests that superintendents form a planning team consisting of a range of stakeholders from district-level departments and school sites; AEE's recommended team includes a school librarian. Together, the team will spend time applying AEE's digital learning assessment to gauge their district's FRS progress.

On the FRS website, AEE lays out a framework for this initiative, offers an interactive planning dashboard as a tool to help school districts assess their readiness for implementing digital learning, a five-step action plan, a research base for future ready leadership, resources for professional development, and the Future Ready District Pledge. "The effort provides districts with resources and support to ensure that local technology and digital learning plans align with instructional best practices, are implemented by highly trained teachers, and lead to personalized learning experiences for all students, particularly those from traditionally under-served communities" (Alliance for Excellent Education 2016c).

FUTURE READY (SCHOOL) LIBRARIANS

The Future Ready Librarians (FRL) initiative, which developed out of Follett's Project Connect, was launched by AEE in 2016. The initiative describes how the work of school librarians can support future ready school goals, as well as how school librarians can best develop their own knowledge and skills in order to be more "future ready." Figure 6.2 shows the ten FRL "gears" that school librarians can use to guide their practice and their own professional learning.

School librarians who develop this knowledge and practice these skills and behaviors can maximize the impact of their contributions toward transforming teaching and learning. When they position their work at the center of their schools' and districts' transition to digital learning, they can serve as leaders on their campuses.

School librarians are perfectly positioned to bridge the two worlds of analog and digital learning. There are many options for school librarians to develop hybrid print and digital literacy instruction or events. They may also facilitate 100 percent digital learning or digitally focused events. Today's school library collections include e-books and audiobooks, as well as hardcover and paperback print titles. By integrating multiple genres and formats into text sets, educators can differentiate instruction and motivate more students through their preferred reading platforms. In collaboration with classroom teachers and specialists, school librarians also help students become more proficient at reading electronic books for pleasure and for information and can learn to more effectively use bookmarking, notemaking, and other affordances of digital devices and apps.

Literacy programming can capitalize on some students' preferences for digital learning. Fan fiction, literature map challenges, virtual field trips, and gaming can supplement or supplant traditional print literacy programs. Gamification in the library may involve following an online narrative and earning a number of points. The rewards for participation or completion may be printed books. Badging is another form of competition that may motivate and engage students. School librarians can collaborate with colleagues to set proficiency levels for "micro-credentials"

FIGURE 6.2

Future Ready Librarians Framework

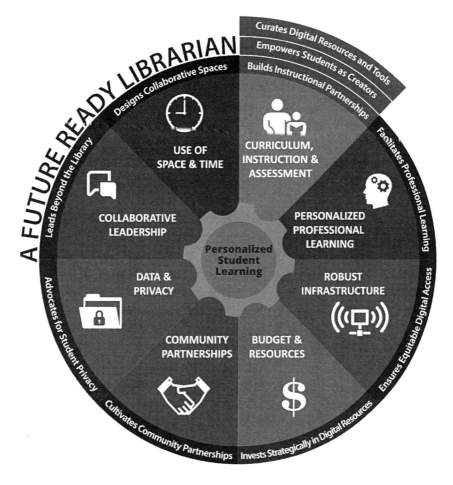

Image copyright: Alliance for Excellent Education 2016. Used with permission.

and integrating badging into the curriculum. This can include various aspects of experimentation or innovation that students explore in a classroom, library, makerspace, computer lab, or other school learning zone.

Hour of Code (HoC) is a global movement to introduce students to computer science (CS). It began as a one-hour event held in December during Computer Science Education Week. The HoC website offers tutorials and ways to earn certificates of participation. As noted on the site: "The success [of HoC] is reflected in broad participation across gender and ethnic and socioeconomic groups, and the resulting increase in enrollment and participation we see in CS courses at all grade levels" (https://hourofcode.com/us). Setting various achievement levels for computer **coding** is one possible way to motivate students to further develop their problem-solving skills, logic, and creativity. Now, in many locations around the globe, HoC has expanded into involving students in coding clubs and includes "unplugged" activities that challenge them to deepen their understanding and further their enjoyment of coding principles.

School librarians can also support students' and classroom teachers' participation in Digital Learning Day (www.digitallearningday.org). This annual event, begun in 2012 and sponsored by AEE, gives schools across the country a way to spotlight how students are participating in technology-supported learning that improves learning outcomes. This event also showcases the exemplary work of educators who are designing learning experiences and facilitating students' effective application of digital tools in knowledge creation. School librarians can maximize their leadership by sharing their cotaught digital learning work on Digital Learning Day at the site, district, state, and national levels.

PROFESSIONAL DEVELOPMENT FOR DIGITAL TRANSFORMATION

In many current educational publications, personalized learning is discussed exclusively in terms of student access to this learning model. However, classroom teachers' access to personalized learning is a key to providing students with more opportunities for effective personalized, technology-supported learning. If this model is to be diffused into classrooms throughout a school or district, administrators and teacher leaders will need to develop strategies to support classroom teachers' personalized learning. One-on-one or one-to-small-group mentoring is one way to achieve this. Research studies focused on preservice classroom teachers, K–12 educators, and university faculty have shown that mentoring can help many educators overcome barriers to technology integration (Bullock 2004; Moreillon 2003; Polselli 2002; Swan and Dixon 2006).

A culture of collaboration and individualized support is the foundation on which a school learning community can build an effective technology integration model. Theodore Kopcha (2010) described how peer mentoring helps educators overcome perceived barriers, such as limited time and narrow beliefs about technology integration. "Using a systems-based approach to technology integration creates a teacher-centered process for integrating technology. The mentor provides just-in-time support, modeling, and apprenticeship that is situated in the context of teachers' classrooms" (Kopcha 2010, 186). Ultimately, peer mentoring results in an educator-led community of practice that can be effective and sustained. It is job-embedded and utilizes available tools and resources, addresses the required curriculum, and meets the needs of classroom teachers and their students. Mentoring may be especially important for first-year and late career educators.

Through reciprocal mentoring during coplanning and coteaching, educators gain support for effectively integrating technology tools into teaching and learning. Learning from and working with more proficient peers give educators the skills they need and the necessary comfort and confidence to take risks. When coteachers are available to experiment alongside their colleagues, more educators will be willing to stretch themselves and take those risks. School librarians who are sensitive to the needs and characteristics of adult learners can be particularly effective coteachers. School librarians serving in an instructional partner role

FIGURE 6.3

Selected Criteria and Possible Evidence for Future Ready Librarians

Selected Criteria	Possible Evidence Suggested by Judi Moreillon
From Future Ready Librarians*	The school librarian:
Designs Collaborative Spaces	Facilitates and promotes inquiry, creativity, collaboration, and community connections through a learning commons model.
Builds Instructional Partnerships	Codesigns collaborative lessons and units of instruction that involve deeper learning and innovative uses of technology tools.
	Coplans and coimplements instruction to help students practice critical thinking, digital, information, and media literacy, digital citizenship, and the active use of technology tools in the content areas.
	Ensures evidence-based practice through collaborative lessons that include formative and summative assessments to document student growth.
Empowers Students as Creators	Codesigns authentic learning experiences that challenge students to become self-directed learners who engage in real-world problem solving.
	Codesigns learning experiences that result in visual, digital, textual, and technological student products.
	Supports students in sharing their learning projects with authentic local, regional, national, and global audiences.
Curates Digital Resources and Tools	Shows leadership in selecting, integrating, and curating digital resources in order to transform teaching and learning.
	Mentors colleagues and students in digital curation practices.
Facilitates Professional Learning	Leads formal and informal professional development that focuses on digital-age skills, tools, and curricula.
	Engages in job-embedded professional development through coplanning and coteaching digital learning, literacy, and citizenship experiences.

*Future Ready Librarian criteria from: Alliance for Excellent Education: Future Ready Schools: Preparing Students for Success. "Future Ready Librarians - Future Ready Schools." http://futureready.org/about-the-effort/librarians

support the effective integration of technology tools into a shared curriculum. It is through coplanning and coteaching that school librarians can serve as change agents who help diffuse technology and other innovations and transform teaching and learning.

School librarians know that "education is incomplete without information AND technology skills" (Gordon 2016, 1). School librarians who have a strong background in information literacy, instructional design, **research-based instructional strategies**, and best practices in teaching and learning can be leaders in a digital learning environment. With this knowledge, they can support classroom teachers' learning objectives for their students and critically assess the appropriateness of digital devices, tools, and resources in helping students to achieve results. As

Lucy Santos Green notes, "No matter how much technology training and how many resources [school librarians] provide, without a corresponding emphasis on pedagogy, the training and resources have little to no impact on teachers' technology practice and on the interactions with technology their students experience" (Green 2014, 42).

Future ready school librarians document student learning outcomes in order to achieve evidence-based practice. Figure 6.3 aligns the first five Future Ready Librarian gears with suggested examples of the knowledge, skills, and behaviors that could provide evidence of meeting the goals of each of these gears. While all ten gears are important, these five (plus equitable access) relate directly to the school librarian's participation in instructional partnerships to achieve a deeper learning digital environment. (This figure is also available as a downloadable Web Extra.)

SCHOOL LIBRARIANS AS TECHNOLOGY STEWARDS

Stewardship is an activity that requires one to practice responsible planning and management of the resources one is given, or over which one has authority. In many schools, the library has been and remains the first room in the building where new digital tools and resources are provided and utilized for technology-supported learning and teaching. This fact positions the school librarian as a technology steward who ensures that these tools and resources are effectively integrated into the classroom curriculum. The goals of a school librarian acting in the role of a technology steward are to guide, teach, and lead others as educators codevelop learning experiences that are motivating, engaging, and relevant for students.

In AASL's "Definition for Effective School Library Program" Position Statement, the national association charges state-certified school librarians serving as instructional leaders and teachers with supporting the "development of digital learning, participatory learning, inquiry learning, technology literacies, and information literacy" (AASL 2016a). School librarians' roles as information specialists, instructional partners, and leaders situate them at the center of their schools' digital transformation initiatives. As technology stewards, school librarians are called upon to be knowledgeable guides who support students, classroom teachers, and specialists in accessing texts in multiple formats and genres and using the latest and most effective digital tools for reading, inquiry, and knowledge creation.

School librarians who support educators' professional development in the area of digital tools can help meet the challenge cited in *Education Week*'s "Classroom Technology: Where Schools Stand" report. "Beyond providing basic access to training, schools will also have to tackle the deeper challenge of ensuring that educators receive the guidance and support needed to embed these tools fully and effectively into instruction and to align technology with students' needs and learning goals" (*Education Week* 2017, 2). Future ready school librarians can be leaders in guiding and supporting their colleagues in achieving standards-based digital learning.

SCHOOL LIBRARIANS AS LEADERS IN DIGITAL LEARNING

There may be agreement in the educational community that future ready students "must achieve a high level of literacy and should excel at information problem solving, but it is not widely accepted that classroom-library collaboration is among the most effective strategies for teaching literacy and information literacy standards" (Moreillon 2008, 23). This could be the result of a lack of understanding of the potential for classroom-library collaboration to improve student learning. It could also be that many states and districts lack mandates for state-certified school librarians. Therefore, too many schools don't have professional librarians to support classroom teachers' instruction and students' learning. It could also be that school librarians who are providing exemplary instructional partnerships have not yet reached critical mass.

Through instructional partnerships, a future ready school librarian serves as a technology mentor. The one-on-one (or one-to-a-team) reciprocal mentorship of classroom-library collaboration for instruction is a model for job-embedded professional development. "Adult learning (and leading) in schools is best implemented at the point of practice" (Moreillon and Ballard 2013, vi). Through classroom-library coplanning and coteaching and by providing formal PD opportunities, school librarians can help principals diffuse innovations in teaching and learning throughout the school. When school librarians coteach with classroom teachers and specialists, they support their principals' initiatives for change, and they support their colleagues' and their own professional growth.

Through instructional partnerships, a future ready school librarian serves as a technology mentor.

#schoollibrarianleadership

The ultimate goal of schooling is to increase students' knowledge and develop lifelong learning literacies, skills, and dispositions. For school librarians, the best way to reach every student in their schools is to collaborate with the educators who spend the most time with students—classroom teachers and some specialists. Coplanning and coteaching in the context of digital learning may be the most effective way to advocate for the essential role of future ready librarians in future ready schools. In order to be one of today's change-makers, school librarians must also be lifelong digital learners. They must continuously upgrade their knowledge, assessment, and application of digital resources, tools, and devices.

To be future ready means that educators must share with students a passion for discovery and risk-taking. For school librarianship to thrive and for others to advocate for the school librarian's role in future ready education, school librarians must practice continuous learning and leadership in digital learning, literacy, and citizenship. Because they serve as centralized instructional partners who coteach with colleagues, school librarians are positioned to lead PD and implement future ready learning throughout the school. Facilitating and assessing all aspects of teaching and learning, including digital literacy, are critical pieces of an empowered learning culture. Assessing the effectiveness of their instruction and leadership is an essential activity for school librarians.

BOOK STUDY GUIDE

I. Discussion Questions:

QUESTION #1: How do you, your teaching team, school, district, or school librarian cadre define personalized learning? Discuss your definition(s) and how personalized learning is reflected in your curriculum and instructional practices.

QUESTION #2: What is your school or district's definition for digital literacy, learning, or citizenship? How are students engaged in these strategies, skills, and behaviors in your classroom, library, school, or community?

QUESTION #3: How do you currently collect data related to the use and effectiveness of digital tools and resources in helping students learn? How and with whom do you share these student-learning outcomes?

- *Individual Thinking*: Compose individual responses to the questions asked above.
- *Partner Sharing*: Share your individual responses to these questions with a colleague in your own school or another school.
- *Group Sharing*: As a small or whole group, discuss the feelings, ideas, hopes, and challenges that occurred to you as you responded to these questions or listened to your colleagues' responses.

II. Activities

Although these activities can be undertaken by individuals, they are designed for group work.

Activity 1

Levels of Technology Integration

Ask one or more educators to share a technology-supported lesson with a small group of peers who teach in the same or a different discipline or grade level. Use the Arizona Technology Integration Matrix (TIM) to plot the characteristics of the lesson (www.azk12.org/tim/). Determine the level of technology integration into the curriculum in terms of these characteristics: active, collaborative, constructive, authentic, and goal-directed. (Alternatively, use an "anonymous," freely available, technology-supported lesson plan for this activity.)

For each characteristic, work as a group to suggest ways to nudge, push, expand, or transform the lesson in order to achieve the next level of technology integration. Members of the group can use the TIM interactive matrix to view examples of K–12 lessons that are linked within the matrix itself. Follow up this activity with a discussion and reflection on technology-supported learning.

Activity 2

Digital Citizenship

Using the Common Sense Education (CSE) Digital Citizenship Curriculum, choose one of eight categories in the scope and sequence on which to focus a review (http://commonsense.org). Using CSE goals of empowering students to "think critically, behave safely, and participate responsibly in our digital world," analyze one or more lesson plans, and discuss them.

Activity 3

Guiding Question about Digital Learning

This activity can be conducted by any group of educators: a grade-level group, professional learning community, entire faculty, or school librarian cadre. Design a brainstorming focus such as "digital literacy, learning, or citizenship is essential for students' current and future success." Use the Question Formulation Technique (QFT) developed by the Right Question Institute and follow the QFT process (http://rightquestion.org) to formulate and prioritize an inquiry question to address:

1. Produce questions related to the topic through brainstorming.
2. Work with closed-ended and open-ended questions.
3. Prioritize questions.
4. Plan next steps.
5. Reflect (http://rightquestion.org).

Working with the top-priority question, launch an inquiry into how your group can begin to address this question.

III. Reflection Prompts

Choose from these possible reflection prompts or compose one of your own.

1. Reflect on your thoughts, feelings, and next steps as you read this chapter and/or engaged in the discussion questions or activities.
2. Reflect on the benefits of digital learning in terms of college, career, and community readiness.
3. Especially for school librarians: Reflect on what you need to know and be able to do in order to facilitate and coteach digital learning with colleagues in all grade levels, content areas, and across grade levels and disciplines.

CHAPTER SEVEN

Assessment

Our opportunity—and our obligation to youth—is to reimagine our schools, and give all kids an education that will help them thrive in a world that values them for what they can do, not for the facts that they know.

TONY WAGNER AND TED DINTERSMITH

◇◇◇◇

A SSESSMENT IS AN ESSENTIAL PIECE OF AN EMPOW-ered school culture. It should always be conducted in the service of learning. To achieve this goal, assessment must serve students by giving them feedback and opportunities for self-reflection in order to help them become independent, self-regulating learners. Assessment should serve educators and help them improve their practice of teaching and self-reflection. Likewise, school leaders are charged with assessing the impact of professional development on educators' practice as well as on its ultimate goal—improved student learning. Rick Stiggins (2011) would call this framework assessment *for* learning rather than assessment *of* learning.

Educators know that what gets measured gets done, but "what" should get measured and "how" it should be measured are questions that loom large. With their book *Understanding by Design*, Grant Wiggins and Jay McTighe (2005) provided a straightforward response to the "what" assessment question: What do we want students to know and be able to do as a result of learning? The thought leaders and organizations cited in this book might agree that "learning how to learn" is what students need to be able to do. Yet, the question of what specific knowledge students need to gain during their preK–12 schooling remains open to debate. As suggested in chapter 3, educators may take the stance that knowledge, literacies, skills, and dispositions can be all be taught, practiced, and ultimately mastered through inquiry learning. Still, educators must also determine "how" outcomes data in all four of these areas can best be collected, analyzed, and used to improve schooling for future ready students.

Assessment is a complex process. While holding students accountable for growth, school faculty must also hold themselves accountable for continuously

BEFORE READING

As you read this chapter, think about how you currently assess students' literacies, skills, and dispositions. In addition, think about how educators and programs are assessed in your school and the relationship between those assessments and professional learning.

developing more empowered learning environments. The "what" and "how" questions must apply to assessing and evaluating instructional practices and the professional learning of individuals, teams of educators, and the entire faculty. These questions must also be applied to programs, such as school library programs, and whole-school or district-wide transformation efforts as well. Today's assessments, whether applied to students, educators, or programs, must align with the components of future ready learning.

In education, formative and summative assessment and evaluation are used to determine the quality of outcomes. A formative assessment focuses on the learning in progress. It is a diagnostic tool to help educators and students understand the effectiveness of teaching and learning. The goal of a formative assessment is to measure outcomes for the purpose of improving them. Summative assessments, on the other hand, are associated with final products and overall performance. They measure achievement at the end of a learning process. Evaluation often compares students' or educators' achievement in relationship to their peers. Summative assessments and evaluation can be expressed in course grades, scores on standardized tests, educator and student-developed summative assessments, portfolio entries, or educator evaluations.

PreK–12 students are in a constant state of development. Individual educators, school library programs, and school transformation efforts are also works in progress. The entire school community, students and faculty alike, can best grow in a culture that thrives on continuous learning. In this safe yet demanding culture, the risks inherent in learning are seen as opportunities for further development. With an emphasis on meeting the needs for each individual to grow, schools can achieve the kind of personalized learning called for by ESSA and the thought leaders and organizations cited throughout this book. Viewing learning as a never-ending journey that students and educators undertake together keeps the focus on development (assessments) rather than on a final destination (evaluation).

ASSESSING STUDENT LEARNING OUTCOMES

Measuring students' knowledge, literacies, skills, and dispositions has never been a simple task. However, with the rapid-fire changes in society driven by technological innovations, assessment questions keep a growing number of educators up late at night. What facts and concepts can be relegated to spontaneous web-searching, and what content knowledge do students need to store in their **long-term memory** in order to use that knowledge to create and innovate? What learning experiences engage students in developing literacies and skills while also requiring them to apply content knowledge? How can educators assess future ready students' development of the dispositions they need in a rapidly changing world?

Emphasizing content knowledge over acquiring learning-how-to-learn skills is controversial today. "The role of education is no longer to teach content, but to help our children learn—in a world that rewards innovation and punishes the formulaic" (Wagner and Dintersmith 2015, 197). Traditionally, standardized,

FIGURE 7.1

Assessment Tools

surveys **checklists** journals exit slips
graphic organizers
Assessment Tools anticipation guides
multiple choice tests
gaming formats fill-in-the-blanks tests
portfolios **essays** skeleton outlines admit slips
reflections **polling**
rubrics

multiple choice, and fill-in-the-blanks tests have been used to assess students' content knowledge. By contrast, during inquiry, project-based, and problem-based learning, content knowledge is more often assessed through students' application of knowledge. These **performance-based assessments** measure how students apply content literacies, skills, and dispositions as they participate in real-world tasks.

Authentic tasks have multiple components and require students to apply both discipline-specific and interdisciplinary knowledge. Students must marshal multiple literacies, including information literacy, and skills, such as the 4Cs, when accomplishing these tasks. They also practice a number of dispositions as they move through a learning process. "Our opportunity—and our obligation to youth—is to reimagine our schools, and give all kids an education that will help them thrive in a world that values them for what they can do, not for the facts that they know" (Wagner and Dintersmith 2015, 222). Students and educators use various tools to measure performance-based objectives, including checklists, rubrics, portfolios, reflective essays, and more.

Figure 7.1 shows a plethora of assessment tools that students and educators can use before, during, and after learning activities.

Coteachers design and use these assessment tools in various combinations throughout a learning unit in order to capture students' development of literacies, skills, and dispositions. There are digital tools as well as traditional print tools for collecting these data.

Empowered students have a voice in codeveloping authentic tasks and the assessments that guide their learning. They must have experiences using assessments, and they must also self-assess their own progress and final products. With those experiences in their toolkits, educators invite individual, small-group, or whole-class collaboration in setting specific criteria for assessments. Some educators may have a portion of an assessment that applies to all students. Then students and educators can personalize the assessment tool using additional criteria for individual students or groups of students.

When students have a voice in the way their learning is assessed, there is a disruption in the traditional power structure in the classroom and library. Such

Educators who share the power of assessment with learners help students exercise agency.

#buildingconnections4learning

a disruption may be a way to create positive change in schooling and better prepare self-regulating learners. Educators who share the power of assessment with learners help students exercise agency. Agency helps students act on their own behalf. Honoring student agency shows trust between educators and students. Self-assessment encourages students to reflect on their own processes and products and to own their achievement.

FORMATIVE ASSESSMENTS

Educators, including school librarians, must gather data on student learning outcomes that reflect the effectiveness of their teaching and coteaching. Rather than the one-time snapshot that standardized tests provide, formative assessments can be used by educators, students, and families to chart student progress and guide further instructional interventions. The entire purpose of formative assessments is to monitor student growth. These assessments should provide students and educators with timely feedback and inform educators' subsequent instructional decisions.

Formative assessments provide students with **benchmarks**—mid-task feedback and assessments that allow for course corrections. Benchmark feedback provides students with opportunities to improve their work before they reach the end of a project. Benchmarks also provide educators with information to help them improve instructional interventions that can lead students to successful outcomes. "The integration of authentic learning tasks with diagnostic assessment and project monitoring is a powerful education instrument for [instructional] change and student achievement" (Moreillon, Luhtala, and Russo 2011, 20).

Formative assessments during instruction can be informal ones that are based on educators' observations; these can be particularly effective with two or more educators sharing their observations. These observations improve student-educator conferencing. Coteaching educators can also be especially effective in monitoring individual, small-group, or whole-class comprehension through checks for understanding. Various technology tools provide real-time feedback to students and educators. Polling, game formats, or other snapshot tools can be used routinely.

Educators collect formative assessments from various types of graphic organizers, composition drafts, or quizzes. Students can record evidence and reflect on their learning on exit tickets. They can compose brief journal entries immediately, for homework, or on the next day of class. During guided inquiry, students' journals can be particularly useful for conferences when students and educators discuss learning goals, benchmarks and timelines, progress, and next steps. Students may also use their journals for self-assessment and self-reflection. Collaboratively evaluating the effectiveness of their instruction through formative assessments offers educators a path to exemplary practice. All of these strategies provide students and educators with information that can be used to improve learning and teaching.

RUBRICS AS SUMMATIVE ASSESSMENTS

Rubrics are often used as performance-based assessments. Effective rubrics are guides that students (and educators) can consult as they journey through a longer-term learning experience. Rubrics establish the criteria for success and levels of proficiency. Educators must "teach" the rubric—even if students have codeveloped it. Ideally, educators also provide examples that show levels of achievement. These can be educator-created or based on the performances of students who previously completed a similar project.

FIGURE 7.2

Sample Analytic Rubric

STUDENTS' NAMES:

URL FOR PLANNING:

URL FOR STORYBOARD:

URL FOR MULTIMEDIA PRESENTATION:

Self-Assessment: Highlight or put your initials in the cell that best represents your work.

Criteria	RUBRIC POINTS			
	10	5	3	0
Planning	Students engage in **oral conversation and written electronic communication** to plan their group product. They **document** their negotiations on a wiki or by another means. **All team members actively participate.**	Students engage in **oral conversation and written (nonelectronic) communication** to plan their group product. They **document** the negotiations they made during the planning process. **All team members participate.**	Students **engage exclusively in oral conversation** to plan their group product. They document the negotiations they made during the planning process in some fashion. **One or two members dominate** the planning process.	Students **do not document** their planning negotiations.
Storyboard	Students use a Web 2.0 **storyboarding tool** to storyboard their presentation. They provide the URL and **all group members actively participate**.	Students use a Web 2.0 **storyboarding tool** to storyboard their presentation. They provide the URL and **all members participate.**	Students use a Web 2.0 **storyboarding tool** to storyboard their presentation. They provide the URL and **all but one** group member participates.	Students **do not use** a storyboarding tool to plan their project.

(continues on next page)

FIGURE 7.2

Sample Analytic Rubric (continued)

STUDENTS' NAMES: _____

URL FOR PLANNING: _____

URL FOR STORYBOARD: _____

URL FOR MULTIMEDIA PRESENTATION: _____

Self-Assessment: Highlight or put your initials in the cell that best represents your work.

Criteria	20	15	10	0
Narration	The digital story is narrated with fluency and **dramatic expression** that aligns with the topic.	The digital story is narrated with fluency and **appropriate expression** that aligns with the topic.	The expression in the narration may **not align** with topic or reading is **not fluent**.	The story is read **without** expression and fluency.
Creativity	The text and presentation align and show a **great deal** of creativity.	The text and presentation align and show **significant creativity**.	The text and presentation align and show **some** creativity.	The text and presentation **do not show** creativity.
Using Multimedia	Students **ONLY use original media components** that appeal to more than one sense.	Students **incorporate some original media components** that appeal to one or more senses.	Students **use only previously published media components** that appeal to one or more senses.	Students' product **does not communicate** sensory images.
Works Cited	Students **use only original media and cite ALL of it**.	Students **use and cite all original and previously published media**.	Students **use and cite previously published media only**.	Students **do not cite ALL of the media** they use in their product.

Total Score (100 Possible Points): _____

Note: Page 2 of the rubric is for comments by students, peers, and educators.

From J. Moreillon, *Coteaching Reading Comprehension Strategies in Secondary School Libraries* (Chicago: American Library Association, 2012). Licensed under the Creative Commons Attribution–Noncommercial–Share Alike 2.5 License: http://creativecommons.org/licenses/by-nc-sa/2.5/.

The effectiveness of rubrics is determined by how well students can use them to guide their learning process and self-assess their progress as well as their final product or performance. Analytic rubrics are organized by criteria (on the y-axis) and levels of proficiency for each criterion (on the x-axis). These rubrics include the necessary specificity to ensure actionable feedback to improve student performance. With specific evidence for each criterion, analytic rubrics provide a more objective assessment for students and educators.

Rubrics can become too complex if all of the criteria for an inquiry unit are represented on one assessment. Educators may provide checklists for some aspects of a unit. They may also develop rubrics with subsections to clarify varied criteria, or they may design multiple rubrics to assess a single inquiry-learning experience. Figure 7.2 is an example of a rubric that assesses students' planning and presentation, but not the actual content of their presentation. Educators and students would use an additional assessment tool or tools to measure student learning in other aspects of the inquiry unit.

Coteachers who develop and assess rubrics as a collaborative activity help one another increase the effectiveness of their assessment tools. Through coplanning and codeveloping rubrics, they can ensure that the lesson or unit objectives, learning tasks, and assessment(s) are aligned. They can check one another to make sure the language used in the rubric is clear, is at the students' comprehension level, and is comprehensible to students' families. Through collaboration and field-testing, educators provide rubrics that have achieved inter-scorer reliability. This level of accuracy and professionalism simply cannot be achieved by one educator working alone. School librarians can maximize their instructional leadership by codeveloping assessment tools and coassessing student learning outcomes.

PORTFOLIOS AS SUMMATIVE ASSESSMENTS

Many educators assert that **portfolios** serve as the most meaningful summative assessments. "Learning portfolios" are designed for students to not only showcase their best work, but to also show their learning process, including first attempts, missteps, and revisions (Couros 2015, 208–9). Rather than a snapshot from an objective test, learning portfolios show students' progress, and provide a more accurate picture of their growth and achievement over time. When students select the content of their learning portfolios, they demonstrate their ability to self-assess their work. They can also show how their most personally meaningful accomplishments were developed, revised, and achieved over time. Learning portfolios provide a more accurate and **authentic assessment** of where students started, how they progressed, and where they might want to go next in their learning.

Because they contain student-selected work, learning portfolios are ideal prompts for self-assessment and reflective conversations with peers, educators, families, and potential employers. Students can explain orally or in writing with their portfolio products how each example demonstrates their learning, what they accomplished, how they accomplished it, why they selected a particular work, and what that work means to them. Educators can require students to share storyboards and other planning documents, notes, first and final drafts, and other documents that show their learning as a process. By showing and reflecting on their progress, students are encouraged to self-regulate their learning.

With today's digital tools, electronic portfolios are more accessible, can be more professionally presented, and can be more effectively shared with various audiences. In some school districts, all students use a particular tool to archive and share their work. In other schools and districts, students use a variety of web-based tools as portfolio containers. Tools that support students in customizing their portfolios with design elements that reflect their personalities may be the most compelling ones, particularly when students share their work with peers. Blogs, wikis, websites, and other tools that allow students to link and embed learning objects and publicly share their work are ideal. Designing and maintaining a learning portfolio also help students develop their abilities as knowledge creators and curators.

ASSESSING SKILLS AND DISPOSITIONS

It is true that educators "cannot teach critical thinking without engaging students in rich and challenging academic content. The goal must be to choose the academic content selectively so as to create the required foundation for lifelong learning, without letting the quest for content coverage overwhelm the development of core competencies (skills)" (Wagner and Dintersmith 2015, 224). Creativity (and innovation), critical thinking (and problem solving), communication, and collaboration, the 4Cs, are widely considered to be essential skills for future ready students. Families, educators, education organizations, and employers increasingly point to these skills as indispensable.

In his article "Rigor Redefined," Tony Wagner (2008) described seven "survival skills" that are necessary for preparing students to be lifelong learners, workers, and citizens. He developed this list based on interviews with several hundred business, nonprofit, philanthropic, and education leaders and on classroom observations in some "highly regarded suburban schools." The "survival skills" he identified build on the 4Cs and include several dispositions cited by other education thought leaders:

1. Critical thinking and problem solving;
2. Collaboration and leadership;
3. Agility and adaptability;
4. Initiative and entrepreneurialism;
5. Effective oral and written communication;
6. Accessing and analyzing information;
7. Curiosity and imagination (Wagner 2008, 21–13).

One could argue that inquiry and problem-based learning, when conducted effectively, provide students with multiple opportunities to practice these skills.

Assessing dispositions is an essential piece of future ready learning (see figure 1.1). Some educators use the term "social and emotional learning" (SEL) to describe the attitudes and behaviors that are essential for success in school and in life. They specify SEL behaviors and character traits such as zest, self-control, gratitude, curiosity, optimism, grit, and social intelligence. They note that these are self-awareness and self-management characteristics (Elias, Perrito, and Moceri 2016). (See also the Collaborative for Academic, Social, and Emotional Learning's core competencies: www.casel.org/core-competencies.)

Students' development of successful dispositions must be noted by students themselves, by peers, and by trusted educators who have knowledge of students' past and current performance. Traditionally, educators have made notes on report cards related to students' behavior, character traits, preparation, motivation, and the like. Educators can best formalize this type of feedback when a school or district agrees upon and defines target dispositions and develops a shared means for students and educators to talk about growth in these areas. The resulting strategies for assessing dispositions are then tailored to individual schools and are owned by the school community.

Students develop self-efficacy by being keen observers of their own learning processes. When educators use terms associated with dispositions in their communications with students and families, students may be more likely to understand how their emotional and social intelligence affects their academic learning. Educators also model dispositions and share anecdotes related to how their own grit, curiosity, or sense of social responsibility made a difference in their lives. Within a culture of collaboration, all school stakeholders will enculturate students in these traits through immersion. Ultimately, school learning communities will strive for students who have internalized positive dispositions and can call upon them when needed for cognitive tasks.

Assessing dispositions is an essential piece of future ready learning.
#buildingconnections4learning

STUDENT SELF-REFLECTION

Reflecting on their learning experiences helps students **crystallize** new schema. Schema theory postulates that reflection is the way that all learners integrate new learning into prior knowledge or replace prior conceptions with new information. As noted in chapter 3, inquiry learning involves students in reflecting throughout the Guided Inquiry Design process. Seeing their thinking on paper or on the screen helps students practice metacognition. When students better understand themselves as learners, they can more effectively increase their ability to achieve their present and future learning goals.

In their book *Make Just One Change: Teach Students to Ask Their Own Questions*, Dan Rothstein and Luz Santana write about the importance for educators to design reflective activities that help students "name for themselves what they are learning, and when they do that, they own the skills more strongly and deepen their understanding of how they can use what they learned in other situations" (2015, 120). They offer a reflection process that includes designing the reflection activity, including whether students will engage in the reflection individually, in small groups, or in the larger group. They recommend that educators create and students use a regular classroom process or structure for participating in reflection activities.

Educators can support students with reflection prompts. Using the three areas of future ready learning (see figure 1.1), educators focus their prompts on the knowledge, skills, and behaviors associated with literacies, the 4Cs, and dispositions. Open-ended questions such as "What did you learn?" and "Why is this knowledge important to the discipline, the society, and important to you?" can help students reflect on their changes in cognition. The questions "How did you learn it?" and "How did you improve upon your past performance of these skills?" help students reflect on the 4Cs. Students' dispositions are often evidenced in how they feel about their learning process as well as their learning products. Questions such as "What character traits did you use to accomplish this task?" and "How did these traits help you achieve your goals?" connect students with the affective aspects of their learning.

As they reflect, students may notice the role that motivation and the effort they applied played in their learning. Motivation, perseverance, good study habits, and time management skills are some of the indicators that suggest how well students will do in college (Tough 2012, 153). Some call these **executive functions**. Educators can help students reflect on how these behaviors and dispositions influence their learning outcomes. Educators and students can discuss "grit," defined here as "self-discipline wedded to dedicated pursuit of a goal" (Angela Duckworth qtd. in Tough 2012, 136). Specifying executive functions increases students' awareness of them and their ability to marshal them for learning.

Students' self-reflections are also important data points for educators. "Seeing" students' learning from the students' own perspectives is essential in helping educators personalize learning. It shows respect for students' minds and acknowledges the complexity and uniqueness of each individual's learning process. Students' reflections, when combined with coteachers' individual and shared reflections, provide three data points that can lead educators to a holistic and more accurate assessment of student learning outcomes and instructional effectiveness.

SCHOOL LIBRARIANS AND STUDENT ASSESSMENT

It goes without saying that school librarians must participate in assessing student learning outcomes. However, there are classroom teachers, administrators, and yes, even school librarians who don't see the need or the value of school librarians performing this essential teaching task. Unless they participate in assessment, school librarians will be unable to collect evidence of the effectiveness of their teaching. They will lack the data they need to adjust their instruction in order to improve student learning outcomes. School librarians who want to be considered equals with classroom teacher colleagues will assess students' learning and use the resulting data to inform their teaching.

Some school librarians rely on library program management data to prove their effectiveness. They collect library circulation statistics, the number of individual student and class visits, the number of classroom-library collaborative lessons or units of instruction, or the number of professional development activities they have offered. They might collect analytics from the library's website, Facebook page, or Twitter handle. While these numerical data may indicate library use and resource access, they are not direct measures of student learning.

School librarians can use many different sources to collect data on student outcomes. Some librarians use tools that have been developed specifically for the library field, such as the Trails9 information literacy skills assessments (www .trails-9.org). The results from this assessment tool can provide pre- and post-data that identify various strengths and weaknesses in students' information-seeking skills. Other school librarians use locally developed pre- and post-tests to measure student learning outcomes. Whether teaching solo or coteaching with colleagues, school librarians must apply formative and summative assessment strategies.

Evidence-based practice places "a higher premium on direct measures of student learning" (Todd 2007, 71). During collaborative planning, school librarians and classroom teachers determine the assessment tools they will use to measure student learning. During the coplanning process is an optimal time for educators to discuss whether they will take individual or joint responsibility for assessing various components of a unit of instruction. If school librarians are to collect direct measures, "they must be proactive in creating the conditions in which they can collect, analyze, and use evidence of their impact on student learning" (Moreillon 2016, 30). In short, in order to maximize their leadership, school librarians must seek out instructional partnerships, and they must coplan, coteach, and coassess student learning outcomes.

The *National School Library Standards for Learners, School Librarians, and School Libraries* includes a "School Library Evaluation Checklist" (AASL 2018, 174–80). This tool is organized by the six shared foundations (inquire, include, collaborate, curate, explore, and engage) and includes criteria at the building and district levels. This is an example under "inquire" at the building level: "The school librarian collaborates with teachers to design and teach engaging inquiry-based learning experiences as well as assessments that incorporate multiple literacies and foster critical thinking" (174). The indicators at the district level focus on the work of school librarian supervisors or directors, as well as building-level librarians.

EDUCATOR EVALUATION AND SELF-ASSESSMENT

Every school district has an educator evaluation instrument. Depending on district policies and an educator's number of years of service, administrators perform observations and complete these evaluations at various intervals during the school year, or over the course of several years. In most districts, evaluations are developmental and show growth in teaching competence and other aspects of an educator's job. In some districts, evaluations result in merit pay or recommendations of plans for improvement or termination.

The Charlotte Danielson Framework, which has been used and adapted in many districts, includes four domains of teaching responsibility: planning and preparation, classroom environment, instruction, and professional responsibilities (https://www.danielsongroup.org/framework/). In many schools, school librarians are evaluated using the same instrument that is used to evaluate classroom teachers. Since some aspects of the job descriptions of classroom teachers and school librarians are not the same, this is likely an incomplete way to evaluate a school librarian or the school library program. That said, for the school librarian's instructional role, the teaching portion of such an evaluation instrument is appropriate if it includes coteaching.

School librarian evaluation is ideally conducted during coplanning, coteaching, and the coassessment of student learning outcomes. Principals and district-level library supervisors can discuss librarians' coteaching effectiveness in pre-observation and in follow-up conferences. This may be a substantial paradigm shift in many schools and districts. However, administrators who are building a collaborative culture of learning may be willing to experiment with or adopt this model for at least one of a school librarian's and an educator's evaluations. For school librarians who don't have a separate "library" curriculum, it is essential that they are observed and evaluated when teaching or coteaching the classroom curriculum.

In some states, such as New York and Texas, the state departments of education and school librarian organizations have collaborated to develop standards and evaluation instruments for school library programs or school librarians. In states that have yet to develop such specialized guidelines, some proactive school librarians have identified criteria on which others can evaluate their performance. For example, in Georgia a collaborative group of school librarians created a state-level School Librarian Effectiveness Instrument (Snipes 2017). Other instruments for evaluating school librarians have been created at the district level.

Figure 7.3 shows possible categories for creating an analytic school librarian self-assessment rubric. School librarians can collaborate with job-alike peers to develop levels of proficiency in each category and suggested evidence for each criterion, or they can use the criteria or indicators offered by each of these organizations. (This figure is also available as a downloadable Web Extra.)

School librarians can also use figure 1.4, "Responsibilities of School Librarians"; figure 2.2, "Levels of Library Services and Instructional Partnerships," and figure 2.4, "Coplanning and Coteaching Assessment" as guides for self-assessment.

Suggesting questions or prompts for self-assessment can help educators, including school librarians, focus in on their areas of strength and the areas they pinpoint for growth. For example, school librarians in Wisconsin developed a series of reflection questions related to each of the wedges on the Future Ready Librarians Framework (see figure 6.2). Using "how do you" as a sentence stem requires educators to provide evidence. School librarians can engage in conversations with colleagues, school librarian supervisors, administrators, or other decision-makers on the school librarian's current and future role(s) and responsibilities in the school.

School librarian evaluation is ideally conducted during coplanning, coteaching, and the coassessment of student learning outcomes.

#schoollibrarianleadership

FIGURE 7.3

School Librarian Self-Assessment Criteria

American Association of School Librarians (6 Shared Foundations)	Follett Project Connect (9 Challenges Framework)	Future Ready Librarians (8 Gears)	International Society for Technology in Education: Educators (7 Standards)
Inquire	Professional Development	Curriculum, Instruction, and Assessment	Learner
Include	Instructional Partnership	Personalized Professional Learning	Leader
Collaborate	Digital Citizenship	Robust Infrastructure	Citizen
Curate	Curriculum and Technology Integration	Budget and Resources	Collaborator
Engage	Information Literacy	Community Partnerships	Designer
Explore	Content Access and Curation	Data and Privacy	Facilitator
	Reading and Literacy Advocate	Collaborative Leadership	Analyst
	Learning Space Design/Making and Building (4Cs)	Use of Space and Time	
	Equity		

EDUCATOR PORTFOLIOS

Educators can use the categories of evaluation and assessment instruments as subheadings for their digital portfolios. Just as students' learning portfolios can show development, so can these performance-based assessments for educators. In a culture of collaborative learning, educators may welcome this opportunity to be transparent in demonstrating their growth as effective educators. Coteaching educators using digital portfolios can also link to their collaborating colleagues' work to show their collective achievements. Principals and school librarians can demonstrate leadership by being the first on their faculty to publish digital portfolios.

Educators' professional inquiry or **action research** can also be an informative component of their portfolios. Action research is an inquiry to improve the quality of practice. It involves determining an area of focus and an inquiry question (or two) followed by testing and monitoring various actions that may improve practice. The goals of action research are to gain insight and develop reflective practice, improve student outcomes, and effect positive changes in the school environment

(Mills 2010). While conducting action research, educators study various school community stakeholders—students, other educators, administrators, families, and community members. Study participants may provide data via various sources, including student learning artifacts, video capture, surveys, face-to-face or online interviews, focus groups, personal reflection or observational notes, and more.

Just as students' inquiry questions can be deepened by consulting with educators or peers, so can educators hone each other's inquiry questions. Educators may improve the results of an action research project by conducting it with a peer, a cohort of job-alike colleagues, or a university-based researcher. They can support one another in developing theoretical frameworks based on published research. They can also support one another by aligning the research methodology with the inquiry question(s). Collaborative inquiry can also increase the validity of the data analysis and the efficacy of the actions that educators take based on the conclusions the co-investigators draw from the study. Educators engaged in this level of professionalism should be acknowledged for their application of evidence-based practices. A digital portfolio is an ideal way to show the methodology, data, findings, and recommended improvements.

EDUCATOR SELF-REFLECTION

Reflection is a metacognitive practice that supports educators' professional growth. Many preservice classroom teachers, school librarians, and administrators are required or encouraged to keep a reflection journal during their student teaching, practicum, or internship experiences. Some continue this practice when they officially enter the field. Journaling can be a rich source of insight. Blogging is another way to curate professional learning reflections. Reviewing journal or blog post entries over a period of time helps educators see their own growth.

Reflecting with colleagues throughout an action research inquiry or a unit of instruction strengthens both the individual's and the partnership's ability to self-assess learning. "The notions of practitioner research and communities of practice are fundamental to collaborative inquiry. Both concepts assume that certain aspects of the human experience can only be richly understood when two or more people engage in spiraling cycles that alternate between having experiences and reflecting together on these experiences" (Harada 2005, 51). Reflecting with others requires that educators be open, listen to one another, seriously consider feedback, and make adjustments to improve their practice.

Self-reflection is an essential activity for educators. Research shows that "the ability of individual faculty members to engage in direct and rigorous self-analysis" related to student learning had even more impact than feedback from other faculty members and administrators (Guskey 2000, 27). Educators and cohorts of school librarians can collaborate to develop individual as well as shared self-reflection prompts. In addition to supporting self-reflection, collating data from multiple sources or school sites can be a powerful advocacy tool for instructional initiatives and school library programs.

Reflection is a metacognitive practice that supports educators' professional growth.
#buildingconnections4learning

ASSESSING EDUCATOR PROFESSIONAL LEARNING

It is important that leaders collect, analyze, share, and use data in order to further their professional development activities. While professional learning facilitated at the district level is still the norm in many schools, principals are increasingly taking responsibility for site-based faculty professional development. In the most progressive schools, principals are involving educators themselves in taking greater ownership by determining and coleading site-based PD. School librarians are among the educators taking the lead. Supporting educators in leading PD is both a distributed and strengths-based leadership approach.

In some schools, leadership teams or committees guide professional learning. Before launching PD, principals and teacher leaders survey the faculty for their professional learning needs. Principals, school librarians, and other teacher leaders can work together to design such surveys and review these data together. When new initiatives, such as 1:1 technology devices, are rolled out, it may be that the entire faculty will engage in PD together. Other PD strategies involve center rotations to facilitate educators in meeting individual learning needs. Technology camps are one example where educators teach each other how to use and apply educational technology to meet student learning objectives. Badging for PD related to specific literacies and skills is another strategy.

Thomas Guskey suggests five critical levels of PD evaluation:

1. Participants' reactions;
2. Participants' learning;
3. Organization support and change;
4. Participants' use of new knowledge and skills;
5. Student learning outcomes (Guskey 2000, 82–86).

In his book *Evaluating Professional Development*, Guskey (2000) offers a chart with a description of each data source, possible assessment questions, data collection methods, and how these data can be used. Participants themselves can provide feedback on levels 1 and 2. Blogging is one way to curate professional learning reflections. Administrators may be the most knowledgeable source for data related to the third level. School librarians in their instructional partnership roles will be able to collect data at levels 4 and 5 through coteaching with classroom teachers and specialists.

These connections between professional development and practice are essential for diffusing new strategies, methods, and innovations in teaching. Shared PD experiences can be a time for faculty to further build a collaborative culture of learning. Educators will want to push and help one another to become better educators and collaborative partners. Figure 7.4 is an example of a game-format challenge of what George Couros calls "competitive collaboration" (2015, 73). (This figure is also available as a downloadable Web Extra.)

In figure 7.4, "L" represents preK–12 learners, "E" represents educators, "A" is for administrators, "P" is for parents and families, and "S" extends from the school to the entire community. Educators can collaboratively develop challenges that

L.E.A.P.S. Challenge for Building a Positive School Climate and a Culture of Collaboration

Learners	Educators	Administrators	Parents	School
L	E	A	P	S
Invite student applications for the library learning commons advisory board. (@CactusWoman)	After each cotaught lesson, present coteachers with a collaboration certificate that includes standards addressed and student learning outcomes achieved. Share with administrator(s). (@thebookinator)	Invite an administrator to a classroom-library coplanning and/or coteaching session. (@CactusWoman)	Offer storytime for pre-K siblings, including book checkout for family members. (@auburnangie)	Host a Summer Reading Night for families. Collaborate with classroom teachers as well as public librarians to educate families on summer reading slide and how to avoid it. (@KelseyLCohen)
Host guest speaker events. Engage students in inviting the speaker, promoting the event/books, and planning the day. (@KelseyLCohen)	Host a snack time in the library. Use the arrival of a new book order as a curriculum conversation-starter and an invitation to coplan lessons/units. (@CactusWoman)	Invite an administrator to coplan and coteach a lesson with you. (@auburnangie)	Collaborate with the school's community outreach person, school counselor, or other colleague to offer a series of literacy workshops for parents or caregivers. (@CactusWoman)	For your school's version of Open House, invite school board members, business community members, elected officials, and others to visit the library during the event. (@thebookinator)
Host student clubs in the library and involve them in putting on literacy events held in the library. (@CactusWoman)	Start a Teacher Book Club. Read titles students are reading, professional texts, or newly published books. Use the opportunity to share other resources in the library collection that relate to the selected book(s). (@KelseyLCohen)	Free Space	Invite parents/caregivers to be expert sources of information/feedback for student inquiry learning (e.g., interviews or audience for final presentations/products). (@KelseyLCohen)	Coauthor a literacy-focused grant that will involve the entire school and greater learning community in building a culture of literacy. (@CactusWoman)
Create a school book award. Have students create categories, organize voting, design a logo for the award, and plan an awards ceremony for their peers. (@KelseyLCohen)	Coauthor and submit articles for school librarian and classroom teacher publications, or copresent at conferences. (@thebookinator)	Invite an administrator to a follow-up conference with a classroom teacher to review student learning outcomes from a cotaught lesson. (@CactusWoman)	Invite parents/caregivers to participate in a cotaught class activity (i.e., facilitate a learning center). (@CactusWoman)	Organize a student-parent (or other family member) book club. Publish an opinion piece in the local newspaper about the positive response to the club. (@auburnangie)
Invite a small group of students to coplan and coteach a lesson for younger students. Record and make the lesson available to teachers at the younger grade level. (@auburnangie)	Celebrate successful classroom-library coteaching and collaboration on the library website, in the library newsletter or e-mail blast, and on social media. (@CactusWoman)	Invite an administrator to a professional conference. Present and/or participate together. Share your learning with faculty afterward. (@KelseyLCohen)	Coplan and coteach a lesson in two (or more) languages. Inviting parents or other experts fluent in another language to participate. (@auburnangie)	Inspire students to take on a social action project that impacts the entire school or neighborhood. (@CactusWoman)

Note: The L.E.A.P.S. Challenge was crowdsourced with contributions from school librarians who have extensive experience in coteaching. Their Twitter handles are included to show one way to indicate educators' contributions on such a matrix relate to a specific PD focus. Challenges like this allow individuals to participate at various levels. Some will complete one row of this challenge bingo-style; others will want to challenge themselves to cover the entire "card." With a high level of trust, educators will share their "competitive collaboration" openly and will take these opportunities to further strengthen their collegial relationships.

ASSESSMENT AND ADVOCACY

Assessing progress toward future ready learning supported by coteaching can be a school-wide activity. To this point in this book, the focus has necessarily been on how principals and educators, especially school librarians, and students can build and strengthen a culture of learning in their schools. To be truly effective, however, families and community members, who also have a vested interest in students' success, must be invited into the conversation (see figure 7.4 above). They will also be part of the learning story that the community collaboratively creates and tells. Connecting future ready learning to college, career, and community readiness is a way for school librarians to maximize their impact on their schools' instructional program.

Leadership requires collecting the data needed for advocacy. All school stakeholders must have firsthand experience of the results of collaborative teaching in terms of student learning outcomes. They must be familiar with the roles that each constituent group plays in ensuring a culture of learning through collaboration. Advocacy is one way that leaders and stakeholders communicate with each other and with the greater community with regard to the results of the school's innovative and effective teaching and learning practices. Assessment and advocacy are critical pieces of an empowered learning culture.

BOOK STUDY GUIDE

I. Discussion Questions:

QUESTION #1: Conduct a shared investigation into the various ways that educators are assessing students' literacies. Working in grade-level teams, disciplinary teams, or in professional learning communities, make a chart with the types of assessments being used. How many of these are performance-based assessments? How are these assessments reported as grades in educators' gradebooks, and how do they determine grades on students' report cards? After a discussion, consider conducting an inquiry or action research project related to assessments in your school.

QUESTION #2: Do my/our current assessments align with what I/we value in terms of preparing future ready students? How can I/we best communicate my/our values to students, families, and community members through students' learning tasks and assessments?

QUESTION #3: How could a performance-based assessment system help prepare future ready students for college, career, and community readiness? If your school, school district, or state decided to adopt such an assessment system, what would have to change? What would have to change in terms of educator and school-level accountability?

- *Individual Thinking*: Compose individual responses to the questions asked above.
- *Partner Sharing*: Share your individual responses to these questions with a colleague in your own school or another school.
- *Group Sharing*: As a small or whole group, discuss the feelings, ideas, hopes, and challenges that occurred to you as you responded to these questions or listened to your colleagues' responses.

II. Activities

Although these activities can be undertaken by individuals, they are designed for group work.

Activity 1

Developing Rubrics for the 4Cs or Dispositions

Review the 4Cs skills and the various suggestions for dispositions discussed in this chapter. Working in grade-level teams, disciplinary teams, or PLCs, develop grade-level range (such as K–2) analytic rubrics with levels of proficiency for the 4Cs or for selected dispositions. Before field-testing these assessment tools with students, educators should self-assess their own proficiency in these areas. Conduct an open discussion about ways to improve educators' proficiencies and ways to model these skills and dispositions for students.

Activity 2

Library Services and Instructional Partnerships Self-Assessment

Using the matrix below, individual educators and school librarians, grade-level or disciplinary teams, and administrators can assess the level of library services and classroom-library instructional partnership activities in the school. Be specific about the evidence cited to show the level of library program integration. Use this formative assessment data to reflect and discuss how to maximize the school librarian's leadership and the library program's impact on student learning and classroom teachers' instruction.

Strategies	Activities	Evidence
Coplanning and Coteaching	Team Teaching	
	Parallel Teaching	
	Station/Center Teaching	
	Alternative Teaching	
Coplanning and Coordination	Coordinated Instruction	
Brief Conversation and Coordination	Coordinated Instruction	
Cooperation	Resources Provided or Other Library Services	

Activity 3

L.E.A.P.S. Challenge

Using figure 7.4 as a model, determine a specific school-wide goal and crowd-source indicators to include on a similar chart. Be sure to credit contributors with their names or social media handles. Each educator can set an individual goal. Some will choose a traditional bingo row, while others may challenge themselves to cover the entire "card." Share the outcomes and effectiveness of this challenge in prompting goal-oriented behaviors.

III. Reflection Prompts

Choose from these possible reflection prompts or compose one of your own.

1. Reflect on your thoughts, feelings, and next steps as you read this chapter and/or engaged in the discussion questions or activities.
2. Reflect on the benefits to students of authentic learning tasks and authentic assessments.
3. Especially for school librarians: Reflect on how you collaborate with colleagues to codesign assessments that help guide students' learning experiences, or how you assess the effectiveness and impact of the formal or informal professional learning you provide.

CHAPTER EIGHT

Leadership and Advocacy

Good leaders get people to work for them.
Great leaders get people to work for a cause that is greater than any of them—
and then for one another in service of that cause.

TERRY PEARCE

◇◇◇◇

L EADERSHIP AND ADVOCACY GO HAND IN HAND. THEY are two central activities for administrators and educators who are building a collaborative culture for future ready learning in their schools. One primary activity of leaders is to inspire and influence the thinking and behaviors of others. Today's education leaders want to move their faculty colleagues or organizations forward to embrace the instructional strategies and the tools of our times. In this age of innovation, maintaining the status quo is not an option. Principals and school librarians can maximize this leadership opportunity by advocating for continuous improvement in teaching and learning in order to better serve the needs of future ready students.

"Leadership is about social influence, enlisting the engagement and support of others in achieving a common task" (Haycock 2017, 11). With a goal to create empowered leaders among their faculty, school administrators who practice strengths-based leadership use advocacy as a tool to enlist active participation in the change process. They engender trust and a culture of collaboration as they build a future ready faculty. Leaders use effective strategies to ensure educators' professional learning and the diffusion of innovations throughout their schools. Influencing others to take up these efforts can occur at the level of an individual educator, within a grade-level or disciplinary team, or throughout the school faculty and staff. It can also extend beyond the school walls into the local community, or at the state, national, or international levels as well.

Leaders are mindful of the needs of their followers. In *Strengths-Based Leadership: Great Leaders, Teams, and Why People Follow* (2008), Tom Rath notes that based on the results of Gallup polls, followers have four basic needs: trust, compassion, stability, and hope (82). Trusting relationships lead to respect, integrity, and

BEFORE READING

Think about the last time you advocated on behalf of a particular student, instructional practice, or an educational, social, environmental, or political cause. What was your motivation—your "why"? How did you turn your passion into action and inspire others to take up the cause?

honesty. "Relationship flat-out trumps competence in building trust" (Rath 2008, 85). Genuine caring and showing compassion for followers is an important aspect of trust. "A good leader knows that integrity creates organizational certainty and collegial confidence" (Martin 2013, 60). Especially when participating in a change effort, followers need to know that the foundation on which the change is based is solid. Trust provides that foundation.

In the context of this book, a positive school climate and a supportive culture of collaboration offer the needed assurance of stability in the midst of change. According to Gallup, "the single most powerful question we asked employees was whether their company's leadership made them 'feel enthusiastic about the future'" (Rath 2008, 89). Leaders must communicate optimism to their followers. Optimistic leaders support people in taking the first and then the next steps in a change process. School librarians can be coleaders who positively affect school climate and culture through successful classroom-library instructional partnerships.

"We follow those who lead not for them but for ourselves" (Sinek 2009, np). Leaders must show followers their values and beliefs. They must display their values through action. This helps followers believe that what leaders provide is in the followers' own best interests. Advocates might say the same about the people who have enlisted them to take up their cause. When leading an appeal, leaders must make sure that stakeholders identify with the values of the appeal. Stakeholders must feel that they are joining the advocacy effort in order to achieve their own priorities; they must join "for themselves."

As Dale Carnegie is credited with saying, "People do things for 'their' reasons, not 'ours.' So, find their reasons." Before educators and school stakeholders will advocate for the transformation of teaching and learning discussed in this book, they must see how educational innovations align with their priorities. Whether those interests are personal, economic, political, or otherwise, it is important to know potential advocates' "reasons." In addition, knowing the needs of advocates helps leaders use language that resonates with their supporters.

When enlisting support, change agents and aides share verifiable data and authentic stories with various stakeholder groups. By aligning locally collected evidence and testimonials with the priorities of each group, leaders show respect for the needs of other people—their motivations, agendas, and time. While striving for the success of their advocacy appeal, leaders will demonstrate integrity as they reach out to build partnerships and alliances. Trust is a central feature of effective advocacy efforts. As respected colleagues, school librarians serve their schools as trusted instructional partners. They build connections that support advocacy for a future ready library program, including initiatives to transform teaching and learning.

BUILDING PARTNERSHIPS AND FORMING ALLIANCES

Advocacy requires building partnerships and forming alliances. The main goal of advocacy is to influence decisions. Educators who are working together to implement future ready learning will have shared understandings of the decisions that will help them achieve that goal. They will want to advocate for and enlist others to advocate for developing students' literacies, skills, and dispositions. They will advocate for deeper and digital learning through student-led inquiry, facilitated by a collaborative team of educators who are accountable for all students' success. They will make their case, argument, or claim supported by testimonials, data, artifacts, and other evidence.

Building a collaborative culture and the teaching and learning practices described in this book will present advocacy opportunities in school communities. The future ready practices within classrooms, libraries, and schools recommended in this book will affect all students, educators, and administrators. These innovations will also be felt in students' homes and in the community outside of the school. These changes may bump up against some long-held beliefs about schooling. The resulting friction creates an advocacy opportunity which will involve educating stakeholders about these changes and enlisting their activism in support of future ready teaching and learning.

Educators who value future ready learning have a robust set of beliefs—a strong *why*. They will need to clarify their "why" for the audiences they seek to influence. They will activate their values in "how" they educate students and they will gather evidence to show "what" their teaching accomplishes. "A WHY is just a belief; HOWs are the actions we take to realize that belief; and WHATs are the results of those actions. When all three are in balance, trust is built and value is perceived" (Sinek 2009, 85). School librarians can build trust and shared values through the connections they build. They will guide others to discover "solutions" to the challenges of educating today's students. Through their actions, school librarians will help others see future ready learning from this point of view.

The first seven chapters of this book focus on guiding the actions of the administrators and educators whose primary responsibility is to create a collaborative culture of learning in their schools. Before administrators and educators can advocate for future ready learning, they must effectively "walk their talk." They must practice and document the outcomes from a future ready academic program. Along the way, they nurture relationships with families, educational decision-makers and policy-makers at the district and state levels, members of the business community, and voters who are also stakeholders in preK–12 education. All of these stakeholders can be involved as advocates who can ensure the success of a future ready school or district. Their voices can be heard by decision-makers who provide the necessary support for transforming education.

THE ADVOCACY TEAM AND PRINCIPLES OF INFLUENCE

After building trusting relationships with one another, administrators and educators must use effective communication and hands-on involvement to enlist additional school stakeholders to join their advocacy team. This team has a leadership role to play in the school's success. The team will include parents and family members, business owners, elected officials, and other influential people in the community. One can think of an advocacy team as an extension of the school's ongoing leadership team or the school library's advisory committee. An advocacy team, however, is called upon at the point of need when people want to influence a particular decision that affects the school learning community and is about to be made. This team will be prepared with the necessary background knowledge that helps them launch an immediate and effective response to a specific need.

An effective advocacy team will be familiar with techniques of persuasion. The social psychologist Robert Cialdini suggests six "universal principles of influence." Those who seek to influence the behaviors of others can use these principles singly and in various combinations in order to achieve their goals:

1. Reciprocity—People tend to return a favor.
2. Consistency—If people commit to an idea or goal, they are more likely to follow through.
3. Consensus—People will do what other people are doing.
4. Liking—People are easily persuaded by other people whom they like.
5. Authority—People will tend to obey authority figures and experts.
6. Scarcity—Perceived scarcity fuels demand (Cialdini 2008).

In his book *Influence: Science and Practice,* Cialdini mostly describes these principles in terms of sales and fund-raising, but they have an equal application in nurturing advocates to support future ready learning. School leaders can apply these principles to enlist advocates within and beyond the library or school. Advocates can apply these principles as they speak up and speak out for future ready library program or school initiatives.

When educators involve stakeholders in the life of the school or library program, both groups experience mutual benefits. Most people naturally respond with reciprocity and expect their interactions with others to be characterized by give-and-take. Cialdini writes that helping people make commitments based on their values leads them to be consistent in their behaviors. Aligning educators' and advocates' values makes that commitment possible. People also align their behaviors with those of the people around them. This gives them the "social proof" they need, and helps them feel they are on the right track.

Various stakeholders will have advocacy roles to play. In a school with a positive climate, faculty and staff will strive to be good-natured and likeable. People will engage in conversations and activities with one another on a regular basis and become more familiar with one another due to the frequency and depth with which they interact in a collaborative culture of learning. There will be people within the school and in the advocate community on whom others rely because they carry the mantle of authority. Similar to Everett Rogers's opinion leaders, these people have a positive reputation and an extensive network in the community. When they speak on behalf of the school, they will share insider knowledge and opinions backed up by data. Their authority lends credibility to any advocacy effort. Advocating for future ready learning may be a way to spotlight positive directions in education when many hold negative opinions about preK–12 schooling.

School librarians can lead successful advocacy appeals for transforming teaching and learning and the library program. The remainder of this chapter is written specifically for school librarians. The information that follows is designed to help them launch effective advocacy campaigns. These campaigns could be to increase library staffing or the materials budget, raise funds for redesigning the library's learning spaces or purchasing technology tools and devices, or any programmatic development that is focused on improving student learning outcomes. All of this information can be applied more broadly to transforming a school's academic program in order to make it future ready.

School librarians can lead successful advocacy appeals for transforming teaching and learning and the library program.

#schoollibrarianleadership

PUBLIC RELATIONS AND ADVOCACY TOOLS

As coleaders in building connections for learning, school librarians must be in the right place at the right time in order to influence outcomes. "The best advocacy is, of course, being 'at the table,' not only when solutions are proposed but when problems are identified" (Haycock 2011). School librarians will be recognized as knowledgeable faculty members who have a global perspective on the learning community. With their connections in the building and beyond, school librarians will be able to identify strengths as well as challenges. They will be able to propose and field-test possible solutions.

But school librarians cannot speak alone. "Leaders understand the strategic nature of public relations and create an organized structure to communicate positive information to the community" (Martin 2013, 103). School librarians need an advocacy network, especially when challenges or possible solutions undermine the potential of the school librarian and library program to serve the literacy learning and resource needs of students, classroom teachers, and families. While collaborating with administrators and colleagues to build an effective school library program, school librarians will develop **public relations** promotional materials that spotlight the library's services, resources, instructional partnership activities,

---

FIGURE 8.1

Public Relations and Advocacy Tools

and impact on student learning. These materials tell readers and viewers who the school librarian "is" and what the school librarian and library program can "do" for and with them. (See figure 8.1.)

School librarians use many different types of printed materials as well as websites, blogs, social media, and other digital communication venues. These materials will be important when there is a specific advocacy appeal. School librarians use promotional materials to help educate stakeholders about the issue or decision under consideration.

All promotional materials should be imprinted with a recognizable brand. Many school librarians have used the American Library Association's advocacy campaigns to frame their brands. "Libraries Transform" is the current campaign. As an example, "School Libraries Transform Learning" could be a stand-alone brand, or it could be presented with an image or graphic. **Memes** or slogans are "self-replicating units of cultural information that spread virally from person to person and generation to generation, with a life of their own" (Reinsborough and Canning 2010, 32). A meme captures the theme of the story that advocates seek to tell. For example, #schoollibrarianleadership and #buildingconnections4learning are the Twitter memes for this book. All public relations tools can be used to support an advocacy effort.

Marketing is another critical component that comes before a successful advocacy appeal can be made. School librarians first seek to align library program services with stakeholders' values. They use surveys, focus groups, suggestion boxes, and informal conversations to ask stakeholders what they need from the library program. They also extend their data collection to those who rarely or never use the library. This helps librarians know what resources, services, and instructional supports users and nonusers are seeking, and the librarians can then take steps to meet their needs. Marketing also helps school librarians learn what areas others may need more information about, such as resources, library services, and instructional partnerships. After analyzing marketing data, school librarians revise the library's promotional materials to fill in the gaps in stakeholders' understanding of what the school librarian and library program have to offer.

"If your WHYs and their WHY correspond, then they will see your product and services as tangible ways to prove what they believe. When WHY, HOW, and WHAT are in balance, authenticity is achieved and the buyer [stakeholder] feels fulfilled" (Sinek 2009, 74). When school library programs are aligned with the needs of stakeholders, advocacy efforts have the potential for success. Through the strong relationships they develop and the values and information they share, school librarians can present the decision to be made and propose possible solutions to their advocates. Then, school librarians' voices will not be the only ones speaking up for their cause. Advocates from outside the library can be the most persuasive spokespeople. They can speak out with conviction and help influence the outcome of decisions that will affect students, educators, and the library program.

ADVOCACY FOR THE SCHOOL LIBRARY PROGRAM

Advocacy is an "ongoing process of building partnerships so that others will act for and with you, turning passive support into educated action for the library program" (AASL Advocacy Committee). Advocacy begins when library programs are aligned with the vision, mission, and strategic plan for their schools and districts. School librarians match library programs with the agenda and priorities of library stakeholders. Working from that shared vision, mission, and plan, school librarians codevelop a vital, integrated, and results-oriented school library program.

Advocacy is also a story. In schools, advocacy is the way the beneficiaries of an outstanding educational program express their gratitude and affirm their right to continue to reap the rewards of such a program. Advocacy must be based on the true story of values in action. Policies and programs and a school's climate and culture must be working for the benefit of all stakeholders. The positive stories that school librarians need to share about their work and their role in student learning and instructional improvement are not part of many people's existing schema for school librarianship. Far too many library stakeholders are not aware of the high level of involvement in the school's academic program that future ready school librarians enact.

It is essential that school librarians who have codeveloped a future ready school library program begin the conversation. They must speak up for themselves and their work on behalf of the students, classroom teachers, specialists, administrators, and families they serve. School librarians educate their stakeholders by spotlighting the various contributions their work, the activities of the library program, and the library's resources make to improve student learning outcomes. They are intentional in their efforts to engage in reciprocal mentorship with classroom teachers and specialists in order to maximize their influence on the school's academic program.

For today's future ready school librarians, building a coalition of support grows directly from the leadership role they take in their schools. "Advocacy involves a leadership effort, which goes beyond the school librarian as the sole voice for the program; it must be an effort to get others to speak for and about the school library" (Levitov 2017, 33). Coleading alongside their administrators, school librarians have the privilege of contributing to the welfare and growth of the entire system. School librarians, who serve as "centralized" instructional partners, work with all school library stakeholders. This is the most effective way to advocate for the program and build a cadre of advocates among library stakeholders.

As David Lankes noted, "the difference between good and great comes down to this: a library [librarian] that seeks to serve the community is good, and a library [librarian] that seeks to inspire your community to be better every day is great. You can love a good library [librarian], but you need a great library [librarian]" (Lankes 2012, 111). By virtue of their daily interactions with library stakeholders, effective school librarians aspire to lead "great libraries" that positively influence the decisions made in their learning communities. Through building connections,

FIGURE 8.2

School Librarians' Public Relations, Marketing, and Advocacy Checklist

	Assessment Question	Possible Evidence
☐	Have I done my school library program promotion homework and have clearly branded all communication tools?	• Ubiquitous brand • Meme/slogan • Website • Blog and other social media • Newsletters and reports • E-mail blasts • Brochures • Flyers • Business cards
☐	Have I listened to stakeholders, including library nonusers, by conducting and responding to marketing efforts?	Follow-ups from: • Surveys • Focus groups • Suggestion box • Informal conversations • Feedback after events
☐	Have I directly involved stakeholders, including students and families, in guiding library program policies and practices?	• Library Advisory Committee • Website Committee • Advocacy Committee
☐	Have I involved stakeholders directly in learning about the library program through hands-on experiences?	• Classroom-library collaboration • Library student aides • Stakeholder volunteers supporting instruction and literacy events
☐	Have I involved stakeholders in collection development and resource curation?	• Resource requests • Collaborative curation efforts • Pathfinders and other instructional tools • Book fair or other fundraising expenditure priorities • Publishing student work products
☐	Have I served on or taken leadership roles on school, district-level, and other professional or community-based committees?	• Site-based committees • District-level committees • Professional organization committees • Community organization boards
☐	Have I collaborated with people who serve in other literacy-focused organizations or agencies in the community?	• Public library children's/teen librarians • Early childhood educators and providers • Community recreation centers • Universities and community colleges
☐	Have I been interviewed or have I published in school librarian and non-school librarian news and information sources?	• Articles or quotes in articles • Letters to the editor • Opinion editorials • Social media, e.g., Twitter chats
☐	Have I made presentations to school, district, local, state, or national organizations or entities regarding the role of the school librarian and library in future ready learning?	• PTA presentations • School board presentations • Civic clubs or chambers of commerce • State or national legislative day participation • Other meetings with decision-makers

"great school librarians" educate stakeholders about the value added by their teaching and leadership. Effective school librarian leaders create advocates as an organic part of their work.

Effective school librarian leaders create advocates as an organic part of their work.
#buildingconnections4learning

PROMOTION, MARKETING, AND ADVOCACY

"While a crisis may foster a sense of urgency, building an effective library advocacy network requires a sustained effort. There must be ongoing recruitment, clear structure and regular communication to keep library advocates informed and involved" (ALA 2008, 4). By building a culture of collaboration with administrators and faculty, school librarians can reach their leadership potential within the school, and library programs can serve as hubs for their schools' academic programs. However, school librarians must also reach out to families, school board members, union representatives, business owners, elected officials, media outlets, community opinion leaders, and more. Figure 8.2 provides a checklist self-assessment for school librarians who seek to shore up the advocates within their buildings as well as those beyond school walls. (This figure is also available as a downloadable Web Extra.)

In many schools and communities, library stakeholders hold onto outdated stereotypes. Many administrators and classroom teachers have mental models of teaching as a solo activity, and they will need to experience successful classroom-library coteaching directly in order to acquire a different perception. Students, families, and the general public may only know school librarians as "shushers" who work in quiet book warehouses. These stakeholder groups must be educated regarding the essential role of school librarians and library programs in educating future ready students. School librarians can start by showing stakeholders the integrated, future ready way that librarianship is practiced today. They need to use all of the public relations, marketing, and advocacy tools in their toolboxes to update stakeholders' perceptions. (The American Association of School Librarians offers resources for the "School Librarians as Learning Leaders" initiative at www .ala.org/aasl/advocacy/tools/leaders.)

Effective school librarians use promotional tools to help educate stakeholders about the benefits that result from the daily learning activities that happen in the library. School librarians document how the school library program is making an impact on students' learning and classroom teachers' teaching. In schools where families are connected and regularly access information digitally, school librarians are particularly mindful of how they promote the library via online tools. Future ready librarians maintain and constantly refresh school library websites, blogs, and social media venues with announcements related to student learning opportunities. These include classroom-library coteaching, exciting print and electronic resources, literacy learning events, and more. School library newsletters and reports can be linked to the library website or blog and distributed in hard copy if that best meets the needs of the community.

Strategic school librarians approach their work as a long-term, ongoing advocacy effort.

#buildingconnections4learning

Strategic school librarians approach their work as a long-term, ongoing advocacy effort. In fact, while school librarians are building connections in a collaborative learning environment, they are also building a culture for advocacy. When there is a decision to be made that directly affects the library program, school librarians will have built positive reciprocal relationships. These librarians will have done their marketing homework and will have responded to stakeholders' needs. They will have created advocates along the way because they have been meeting the needs of stakeholders all along.

Stakeholders will understand and value the work of the school librarian and the influence of the school library program. Librarians and programs will clearly be perceived as assets for students, classroom teachers, and families. When stakeholders are included, they will have ownership and take pride in the library program. They will share the school librarian's conviction that the library program is worth fighting for because they understand how it is meeting stakeholders' needs. These advocates will have the essential connections, information, and firsthand experiences that prompt them to take up the library's cause.

REACHING OUT

The library program's reach extends beyond the school and out into the surrounding community. Through school librarians' public relations efforts, legislators, the media, business leaders, and the general public will know the roles that librarians and library programs play in schools. Through their marketing efforts, school librarians connect library values with priorities in the community, as well as the values of the individuals they are trying to influence. If there is a decision to be made, it is especially important that these potential advocates develop a sense of urgency about the issue and are clear about the consequences if decisions are not made in favor of school librarians and library programs. They must also be willing to commit the time and energy it will take to advocate for the issue.

When influencing those who have not had direct experience with the library program, it may be even more important to craft a compelling story. Stories personalize communication. They touch the heart as well as the mind. In *Whoever Tells the Best Story Wins: How to Use Your Own Stories to Communicate with Power and Impact*, Annette Simmons describes six different types of stories:

1. Who I am? Who are we?
2. Why I am here? Why are we here?
3. Teaching stories
4. Vision-building stories
5. Values in action
6. "I know what you're thinking" stories (Simmons 2007).

These story types may be useful to school librarians and advocates as they think about narratives that will build understanding and empathy for their cause. Some types of stories may be more powerful for various stakeholders and more or less appropriate in various contexts. Stories put "knowledge into a framework that is more lifelike, more true to our day-to-day existence. More like a flight simulator. Being the audience for a story isn't so passive, after all. Inside, we're getting into the act" (Heath and Heath 2007, 214). For some audiences, it will be especially important to strategically integrate data into the larger story—data that furthers the emotional appeal of the story. Librarians should frame the message in terms of values and benefits to the community, and they should clearly communicate the alignment between the library's values and those of the people they are trying to persuade (Lakoff 2014).

Ideally, people who hold similar positions in relation to the library will be the most effective in influencing their peers. Principals respect and listen to the opinions and experiences of other principals. Parents who know one another will be more receptive to acting on evidence shared by other parents. Superintendents, school boards, and legislators respond to appeals from families and other community members. When elected officials themselves become staunch advocates, they are well positioned to change the hearts and minds of their colleagues and of the general public as well.

A SAMPLE ADVOCACY SCENARIO

To begin an advocacy plan, school librarians must think about how the decision that is under consideration meets the needs of stakeholders in their learning community. They must be able to cite evidence of these benefits. School librarians then enlist stakeholders who can speak up for an advocacy effort. The most authentic and strongest voices help ensure that the decision will be made in favor of supporting the library program's initiative. The following provides the context and an outline for a sample advocacy plan.

Classroom teachers and school librarians have shared values for improving student learning outcomes. They know that open access to the school library and its resources before, during, and after school requires support staff. Educators also know that school librarians have greater opportunities to coplan and coteach with classroom teachers and specialists if they are not simultaneously managing the physical space of the library. Paraprofessionals are capable of managing the daily operations of a library. Classroom teachers and specialists whose students have benefited from classroom-library collaboration are the target stakeholders who can speak up for the need for library support staff. These stakeholders can most effectively advocate for this initiative with principals and district-level decision-makers.

In this scenario, all of the school librarians in the district have close relationships with coteaching classroom teachers and specialists. School librarians have done their marketing homework and have asked their colleagues what they need to be successful. Classroom teachers have identified time to meet with their librarians for coplanning during the school day as essential to effective collaboration. They have also identified the ability of the school librarian to coteach with them, not only in the library, but in the classroom, lab, on the athletic field, or on field trips into the community. In addition, classroom teachers express the need to involve future ready students in longer-term inquiry projects, and they realize that coteaching with school librarians supports student success. School librarians have aligned library programs to meet the specified needs of these educators, and they need library support staff to sustain those efforts.

In this appeal, school librarians intend to influence classroom teachers and specialists and ask them to advocate for paraprofessional library staff. They make it clear that they understand classroom teachers' needs for coplanning during the school day, coteaching with them in various locations in and around the school, and involving students in inquiry learning. Classroom teachers realize that in order to meet their needs, school librarians need a paraprofessional partner in the library who can manage the library space and give school librarians the flexibility to coplan and coteach as needed.

A SAMPLE ADVOCACY PLAN

Figure 8.3 shows the sample advocacy plan of a cadre of school librarians that is based on an appeal to hire full-time paraprofessionals for all school libraries. (School librarians' actual advocacy plans will be unique and tailored to the local community and will be more detailed in terms of dates and responsibilities.)

Planning for this advocacy appeal would have been started the previous spring. School librarian colleagues would have conducted market research followed by self-assessment to ensure that library programs were aligned with classroom teachers' and specialists' values and priorities. For this effort to be successful throughout the district, the cadre of school librarians will have been coplanning, coteaching, and collecting student learning outcomes data from the moment the bell rang for the new school year.

The next order of business for the cadre would be to reach a consensus on "why" this advocacy effort is needed. The management theorist Simon Sinek notes that great leaders are able to inspire others to act because they have and give others a strong sense of purpose (2009, 6). In the figure 8.3 example, these school librarians have expressed their "why" in terms of the benefits to students and classroom teachers as well as to district leaders. They have aligned their purpose with the purpose of the decision-makers they intend to influence.

Then, the cadre would plan with the end in mind. They would collaborate to develop a SMARTER goal for their advocacy effort. A SMART goal is one that is Specific, Measurable, Achievable, Relevant, and Timed. (This acronym is commonly attributed to Peter Drucker's "Management by Objectives" concept.) They would have added "E" for "evaluated" and "R" for "results" to the SMART goal as shown in this example. Once the cadre reached consensus on the goal, they would share it with and seek feedback from a select group of potential advocates. When they get the go-ahead, the cadre would begin negotiating a shared value, brand, meme, and sound bite in September or October. In late fall, they would have begun gathering

FIGURE 8.3

Sample Advocacy Plan

Why: Learning leaders need all faculty members serving at full capacity in order to prepare future ready students for college, career, and community.

Meme: Together! 4 #FutureReadyStudents
Advocates: Collaborating Classroom Teachers, Specialists, Principals, and Families
Target Stakeholders: Superintendent and School Board

SMARTER Goal: The superintendent will recommend that all school principals hire at least one full-time library paraprofessional who will begin training in the summer before the next school year and will be prepared and on the job by the time the new school year begins. At the end of the school year, principals, in collaboration with faculty, will evaluate the results of this staffing decision and submit data and their review to the superintendent for further guidance.

Sound Bite: When library programs have the support of library paraprofessionals, classroom teachers and school librarians can effectively coplan and coteach to ensure that administrators meet learning goals for future ready students.

Draft and Final Deadline: February (draft); March (Final)

Component	Notes
Library Value	Coteaching professionals improve student learning outcomes
Stakeholder(s) Value	Improved future ready student learning through effective instruction
SMARTER Goal	See above.
Sound Bite	See above.
Brand	Together! 4 #FutureReadyStudents (or #FutureReadySs)
Meme	Classroom-library coteachers prepare #FutureReadySs for college, career, and community. (Reproduced on an image or graphic of coteachers working with students)
Story Type (See Simmons 2007)	"Values in Action"
Emotional Appeal	All students deserve the support of coteaching educators in order to experience deeper future ready learning through inquiry.
Endorsements/Testimonials	Opinion leader principal(s) Change agent school board member(s) Collaborating classroom teachers and specialists PTA opinion leaders
Data	Inquiry learning outcomes data, including student learning products and reflections; faculty surveys, reflections, and other data related to classroom-library instructional partnerships; published research on coteaching benefits
Feedback on Draft from Stakeholders	Share and respond to feedback from several opinion leader principals and/or change agent school board member advocates (early February)
Revision and Fine-Tuning	February
Face-to-Face Appeal Dates	February/March – PTA Meetings March – Elementary and Secondary Principals' Meetings March/April – School Board Meeting
Print Media Promotion Plan	One-page fast facts for distribution at in-person meetings; available on library circulation desks, in school offices (with principals' permission), and linked to school and school library websites Opinion piece(s) for local newspaper Request interviews with local media outlets
Digital Storytelling Tools	Video, which includes testimonials (final March)
Online and Social Outreach Plan	Advocacy video, one-page fast facts. and sample cotaught lessons with student learning outcomes data (for each school): linked to school library websites, social media posts, school library e-newsletters, and supportive principals' e-newsletters/email distributions
Follow-Up Communications	Thank-you and next steps handwritten notes Follow-up phone calls to selected decision-makers Face-to-face meetings with superintendent, individual principals, and most influential district-level decision makers
Reflection and Self-Assessment	May

student outcomes data, identifying advocates and possible coalition partners, and collecting endorsements and testimonials.

For many change initiatives, it may be important for school librarians to seek out coalition partners. If there is another effort under way that aligns with or can enfold the library initiative, then joining a coalition may be the best strategy for success. However, if the library initiative runs the risk of being lost in another effort, then school librarians will want to focus their energies on identifying advocates who will provide endorsements rather than joining another effort. Ideally, advocates whose voices most effectively appeal to decision-makers will be at the ready to provide endorsements. Endorsement signatures are good, and face-to-face or digital testimonials are even better.

In this advocacy example, the school librarian cadre might form various subcommittees. One committee might be responsible for developing the printed and digital promotional materials. Another might plan and create a video. They may work with a site-based or district-level technology department to produce a professional **crowdsourced** video. The committee would be responsible for the video script and would line up video shoots for collecting the endorsements and testimonials if individual school librarians are unable to provide high-quality capture. The committee would also make sure that the entire cadre and selected members of the target audience had the opportunity to view and provide feedback on a video draft. They would weigh all feedback and make edits and revisions as needed. Members of another committee might be responsible for incorporating the promotional materials and video into a polished presentation.

For additional advocacy plan support, the American Library Association's *Library Advocate's Handbook* includes a "Developing Your Action Plan Worksheet" (2008, 14). The handbook also includes guidelines for telling the library's story, successful speaking tips (including a speaker's checklist), and tips for talking with the media and dealing with tough questions. This resource also provides information that can help school librarians guide and coplan advocacy efforts in their communities.

TAKING AN ADVOCACY STANCE

The ever-changing nature of future ready education and school librarianship requires a commitment to lifelong learning. Through coteaching and providing faculty development, school librarians engage in hands-on adult learning experiences that honor the knowledge and needs of their colleagues. Serving in a collaborative culture of learning, they support other educators in stretching their individual instructional expertise. In the process, school librarians build their own capacity to make connections and lead. With a global view of the school learning community informed by effective partnerships with principals, classroom teachers, and specialists, school librarians serve as on-site learning leaders who ensure that principals' and district-level initiatives succeed. Whether this leadership role is recognized formally or informally, school librarians are perfectly positioned to lead from the hub of the academic program—the school library.

School librarians also benefit from advocacy at the national level. The American Association of School Librarians and initiatives such as Future Ready Librarians and the Lilead Fellows Project offer guidelines for exemplary programs and provide support for advocacy appeals. School librarians in districts with school library supervisors, in particular, may benefit when their district-level administrators' work is influenced by the activities of their job-alike Lilead fellows. These library leaders are developing "a strong national voice that articulates how effective school library programs can make a difference in the lives of all members in their communities" (Weeks 2016, 15). Their work creates a network of excellence, and their advocacy benefits everyone in the school library profession.

"Good leaders get people to work for them. Great leaders get people to work for a cause that is greater than any of them—and then for one another in service of that cause" (Pearce 2013, 40). When educators determine the "why" that motivates them and inspires others, they can join forces and collaboratively create the future ready learning opportunities that students need. Finding your element "is a two-way journey: an inward one to explore what lies within you and an outward journey to explore opportunities in the world around you" (Robinson 2013, 5). To become leaders who inspire commitment to a shared cause, school librarians must find their passion—not only for serving the needs of youth, but also for serving the needs of their colleagues, administrators, and other library stakeholders as well.

Educators must also find their courage. As Martin Luther King Jr. said, "Our lives begin to end the day we become silent about things that matter." As advocates for future ready learning, educators cannot afford to be silent about what youth need to succeed. The stakes are high for today's students. They must compete in a global economy. They are growing up in an economically stratified society, and many have not had the advantages of some of their peers. To maximize their impact, education stakeholders must join forces and collectively commit to giving all students the chance in life they deserve. Leadership and advocacy are necessary for achieving future ready learning. School librarians have a unique role in sustaining connections in an empowered collaborative culture of learning.

As advocates for future ready learning, educators cannot afford to be silent about what youth need to succeed.

#schoollibrarianleadership

BOOK STUDY GUIDE

I. Discussion Questions:

QUESTION #1: What is your school's "why" or purpose? How is "why" reflected in your school's vision or mission statement? (Some organizations would call a vision or mission statement their "why.") How does your school's "why" reflect the values of your learning community?

QUESTION #2: What evidence can you cite that shows your learning team is doing its "homework" in terms of public relations and marketing efforts in order to enlist advocates for your school or library program's transformation efforts?

QUESTION #3: What is the current level of involvement and interaction between your school and families, district-level administrators, local business leaders, elected officials, and other school stakeholders? How are these stakeholders empowered to participate in your learning community and become advocates for your school or library program?

- *Individual Thinking*: Compose individual responses to the questions asked above.
- *Partner Sharing*: Share your individual responses to these questions with a colleague in your own school or another school.
- *Group Sharing*: As a small or whole group, discuss the feelings, ideas, hopes, and challenges that occurred to you as you responded to these questions or listened to your colleagues' responses.

II. Activities

Although these activities can be undertaken by individuals, they are designed for group work.

Activity 1

Develop Promotional Materials

As a group, determine an aspect of your school's academic program that your faculty or team would like to spotlight for families, district-level administrators, local business leaders, elected officials, or other school stakeholders. Coming to a consensus about the value this activity adds to your program and how this value aligns with the values of the target audience for these materials. Negotiate a brand, meme, and sound bite that represent this value.

Determine the most effective types of promotional materials that will reach and speak to your target stakeholders. Work in partners or small groups to develop, seek feedback on, and revise these materials. Distribute the materials to your target audience and collect data to determine their effectiveness.

Activity 2

Conduct a Market Survey

As a group, determine a target audience with which to conduct a market survey. Brainstorm possible questions about your academic program, school climate, school library program, or an issue that will be of interest to this group of stakeholders. Prioritize the questions. Invite a focus group to respond to the most pressing questions, and contribute additional questions for a market survey on this topic.

Determine the best method and distribute a survey to the target stakeholders. Discuss the survey results and your team's current level of effectiveness in meeting this stakeholder group's perceived needs. Do you provide additional services about which this stakeholder group is unaware? Realign your program to meet stakeholder needs, and/or educate stakeholders with new information. Revise your promotional materials to spotlight this realignment and to educate stakeholders about additional benefits which they may be currently unaware of.

Activity 3

Develop an Advocacy Plan

As an individual, group, whole faculty, or school librarian cadre, determine an issue about which a decision will be made soon. Begin by coming to a consensus regarding the "why" of your advocacy appeal. Make sure your "why" aligns with that of your advocates. Collaboratively develop a SMARTER goal. Using the example in figure 8.3, develop an outline for how to launch and implement an advocacy appeal.

Execute the plan, self-assess, and reflect on the process and results. Share your process, evaluation, and results with others who may have similar advocacy needs.

III. Reflection Prompts

Choose from these possible reflection prompts or compose one of your own.

1. Reflect on your thoughts, feelings, and next steps as you read this chapter and/or engaged in the discussion questions or activities.
2. Reflect on the benefits of and processes involved in inviting families, district-level decision-makers, business and civic organization leaders, elected officials, and other community members to be advocates for your school and library program transformation process.
3. Especially for school librarians: Reflect on the library's current collection of promotional materials that are used to educate stakeholders about the value of the library program. Do they meet the guidelines set out in this chapter? When did you last conduct market research? If they were needed tomorrow, are you prepared to enlist the support of an advocacy team? If not, what do you need to do in order to be prepared?

CHAPTER NINE

Sustaining Connections in a Collaborative Culture

A team is not a group of people who work together. A team is a group of people who trust each other.

SIMON SINEK, DAVID MEAD, AND PETER DOCKER

◇◇◇

N THIS AGE OF INNOVATION, EMPOWERED ADMINISTRATORS and educators have the potential to transform school learning environments and the quality of students' learning experiences. Together, they must also transform educators' instructional practices. They can facilitate learning opportunities that are authentic, relevant, and meaningful to empowered students. Transformation means to "make a thorough or dramatic change in the form, appearance, or character of" (https://en.oxforddictionaries.com). Creating an empowered learning culture from a systems thinking perspective involves an understanding of the long-term implications of actions taken in the present time. School librarians who are building connections to support a learning culture help create the foundation for transforming teaching and learning. Maintaining those connections is critical for sustaining change and achieving a shared purpose.

Transformation involves all school stakeholders in a change process. John Kotter is considered an authority on leadership and change. In his book *Leading Change,* he explains eight steps for creating major change:

1. Establishing a sense of urgency;
2. Creating a guiding coalition;
3. Developing a vision and strategy;
4. Communicating the change vision;
5. Empowering broad-based action;
6. Generating short-term wins;
7. Consolidating gains and producing more change;
8. Anchoring new approaches in the culture (Kotter 2012, 22).

BEFORE READING

Reflect on a positive change you have made in your life that you have also had difficulties sustaining. What support did you need, and what strategies did you use to stay on or get back on track?

Kotter suggests that leaders follow these steps in this sequence. He unpacks each step and also notes the errors that leaders can make at each step that can ultimately lead to failure. School leaders may apply these eight steps to transform their schools for future ready learning.

There is an ever-increasing sense of urgency for transforming teaching and learning. The pace of change and the need for solutions to the world's pressing problems add a sense of urgency. Ubiquitous information of varying reliability and the evolving role of technology in society are additional drivers. Researchers studying the brain are learning more every day about how people learn. Their findings must be applied by educators as they reimagine curricula and refine instructional practices that engage empowered students. Education decision-makers at the local, state, and federal levels, along with business leaders and families, add to the urgency with high expectations for schools to prepare all students for college, career, and community.

Maximizing School Librarian Leadership: Building Connections for Learning and Teaching is about forming a powerful team of administrators, educators, and advocates who believe that it takes a village to enact future ready learning. They share the American Association of School Librarians' common belief: "Learners should be prepared for college, career, and life" (2018, 11). In classrooms and libraries, educators practice reciprocal mentorship in order to improve student learning outcomes. They take risks together to coteach, and they believe that their instructional practices can develop at a much greater rate with more assured improvements when they collaborate. Within and beyond the school walls, a future ready school conveys a team spirit that allows them to build successful partnerships and form alliances in the community. The school includes students, families, and community members in decision-making regarding the environment, content, and processes of teaching and learning. This future ready school has a collective growth mindset. All school stakeholders are committed to continuous learning and an ongoing assessment of their change process.

All school stakeholders are committed to continuous learning and an ongoing assessment of their change process.

#schoollibrarianleadership

One way to measure a school or library program's evolution toward a transformed learning culture is in the pronouns that leaders and members use as they talk about their schools and libraries. "The leaders who work most effectively, it seems to me [Peter Drucker], never say 'I.' And that's not because they have trained themselves not to say 'I.' They don't think 'I.' They think 'we;' they think 'team.' They understand their job is to make the team function. They accept responsibility and don't sidestep it, but 'we' gets the credit. That is what creates trust, what enables [leaders] to get the task done" (Drucker 2006, 19).

A clear vision is essential for a change effort to succeed. A vision may begin as the "why" of a learning leader principal or other administrator and a guiding coalition of like-minded educators. The components of future ready learning—literacies, skills, and dispositions—may be reflected in a future ready school's vision or it may be part of the strategy to achieve that vision. A school's vision must be consistently communicated in words, actions, and deeds. This involves:

1. Clarifying why a vision is necessary;
2. Developing the vision;

3. Analyzing the vision;

4. Clarifying the role of the team developing the vision (Cohen 2005, 65).

As noted in chapter 1, a shared vision takes time to develop and still more time to be embraced and enacted in daily practice.

The vision must be communicated. Change agent principals and change aide school librarians and other members of the change team are charged with consistently modeling the expected behaviors. They believe in the wisdom of the change, and they walk the talk. This team can work together and with the entire faculty and staff to remove obstacles that stand in the way of actualizing change. The change could consist, for example, in how classes are scheduled, when and how educators engage in coplanning and coteaching, or how professional development is carried out.

The team can be responsible for making sure that "short-term wins" are achieved and celebrated in the learning community. The school librarian's efforts in building a collaborative culture through coplanning, coteaching, and cofacilitating PD can result in these exemplars of practice. When one third-grade teacher or one social studies teacher successfully coteaches with the school librarian, they can join the change team in advocating for instructional partnerships. Then members of their teaching teams—other third-grade or social studies teachers—will think it is safe and advantageous to take a risk and will want to experience similar successes for their students and themselves.

With leadership, a successful change process breeds more change. "People at all levels need to be consistent in holding people accountable, evaluating their performance, and rewarding them. Short-term gains demonstrate that change is gaining momentum and is here to stay" (Cohen 2005, 88). Once a learning community has taken the first steps toward coming together to create a collaborative culture of learning, the most challenging work begins. For all stakeholders to work together over time, a learning culture must be nurtured in order to sustain change. Time and time again, principals, school librarians, and teacher leaders will be called upon to renew and reinvigorate the learning community's commitment to growth.

EMPOWERMENT AND TRANSFORMATION

Working within a collaborative culture of learning implies empowerment for all school stakeholders. Each member of the learning community must experience empowerment: "the process of becoming stronger and more confident, especially in controlling one's life and claiming one's rights" (https://en.oxforddictionaries .com). In a future ready learning environment, rather than "giving" power to others, administrators and educators claim their rights as professionals who co-lead. Classroom teachers, specialists, and school librarians engage in coteaching in order to improve their craft and are committed to helping everyone reach their full capacity. Empowered educators understand their roles as learning guides. They realize that empowered students who have voice, choice, and agency will be more eager to learn.

Empowered students are engaged, effective and critical readers, avid inquirers, and motivated knowledge creators. Empowered students develop agency and become self-directed learners; they are prepared for lifelong learning. The most effective way for school librarians to empower student learning is through classroom-library coplanning, coteaching, and coassessing outcomes. When school librarians bring their expertise to the collaboration table, they influence the curriculum, instructional strategies, and resources (including technology tools) that are available to all students in their schools.

Educators are agents in their own professional development through reciprocal mentorship. Through coteaching, educators hone their ability to effectively teach future ready students. Even when they are not coteaching with the librarian, classroom teachers and specialists apply the future ready learning strategies they learned through classroom-library coteaching. In this way, school librarians have the opportunity to impact the learning of all students in their schools. This is the way that empowered school librarian leaders best serve a future ready school.

School library programs led by future ready school librarians can transform entire communities. School librarians enter into partnerships to help others achieve their goals. As David Lankes writes in his book *Expect More: Demanding Better Libraries for Today's Complex World*: "The mission of the library is to improve society through facilitating knowledge creation in the community" (2012, 33). He goes on to discuss the importance of the word "improve," which along with "facilitate" implies proactive, collaborative, and transformational action (42–43). School librarians can serve as coleaders who help develop a collaborative culture of learning in which transformation and empowerment can thrive.

CHANGE IS CHALLENGING

If change were easy, then transforming learning communities would not be hard. Building the necessary trust, commitment, and teamwork for a successful change process is simply not easy. In their book *Switch: How to Change Things When Change Is Hard* (2010), Chip and Dan Heath offer a three-part process for successfully leading change. Figure 9.1 describes these essential components of successful change.

In Heath and Heath's view, change agents and aides have three challenges: "Direct the Rider," "Motivate the Elephant," and "Shape the Path." The "Rider," the rational side of followers' minds, gives confidence because it addresses people's needs for structure—for a plan. To direct the rider, leaders find out what's working and replicate it. Heath and Heath call these the "bright spots." The bright spots also help leaders lay out the critical steps that lead to the target outcome. That way followers are clear about the behavioral expectations for change.

The rider—the rational mind—may have an understanding of the change, but it lacks motivation (Heath and Heath 2010, 8). Change leaders simultaneously motivate their followers' emotions. Heath and Heath call this the "Elephant," the place where people's passions wait to be kindled. Followers need to have a sensory

FIGURE 9.1

How to Make a Switch

For things to change, somebody somewhere has to start acting differently.
Maybe it's you, maybe it's your team.
Picture that person (or people).

Each has an emotional "Elephant" side and a rational "Rider" side. You've got to reach both.
And you've also got to clear the way for them to succeed. In sort, you must do three things:

>DIRECT the Rider
FOLLOW THE BRIGHT SPOTS. Investigate what's working and clone it.
SCRIPT THE CRITICAL MOVES. Don't think big picture, think in terms of specific behaviors.
POINT TO THE DESTINATION. Change is easier when you know where you're going and why it's worth it.

>MOTIVATE the Elephant
FIND THE FEELING. Knowing something isn't enough to cause change. Make people feel something.
SHRINK THE CHANGE. Break down the change until it no longer spooks the Elephant.
GROW YOUR PEOPLE. Cultivate a sense of identity and instill the growth mindset.

>SHAPE the Path
TWEAK THE ENVIRONMENT. When the situation changes, the behavior changes. So change the situation.
BUILD HABITS. When behavior is habitual, it's "free" – it doesn't tax the Rider. Look for ways to encourage habits.
RALLY THE HERD. Behavior is contagious. Help it spread.

experience of the change; they must "feel" it. Leaders also divide the change into manageable steps so the emotional side is not overwhelmed. When working with the elephant, leaders appeal to followers' need to be part of a group that is moving forward together—part of the herd. Leaders and followers adopt a growth mindset in order for their passions to lead to action and the desired changes in behavior.

In Heath and Heath's view, the third component of leading change is to "Shape the Path." Leaders remove obstacles in the environment that prevent change or make it more difficult to achieve. The optimal environment provides a context for change. Support systems must be in place so that leaders and followers can develop new habits that promote confidence for the elephant and offer structure for the rider. Along with their change aides, change agents must "rally the herd." When the organization begins to move in the anticipated direction, leaders spread the word with the goal of replicating the change and making it contagious.

The challenges involved in building a collaborative culture of learning could be considered "big." Educator isolation has been a long-standing tradition in schooling. Many educators enter the profession for the autonomy of having their own students, their own curriculum, their own classroom or library—separate from their colleagues. The power structure of schools with individual educators as authorities in their disciplines and as authorities over students is also an aspect of traditional schooling. Breaking down the walls between educators, disciplines, and the power differential between educators and students is not an easy task.

"Big problems are rarely solved with commensurately big solutions. Instead, they are most often solved by a sequence of small solutions, sometimes over weeks, sometimes over decades" (Heath and Heath 2010, 44). Diffusing the components of future ready learning throughout the school through classroom-library coteaching can be an essential part of this sequence. Coteaching inquiry learning may be that one thing that puts the change into motion. Coteaching digital learning and traditional literacies may be that one thing. Whatever the innovation, building and sustaining a culture of collaboration provides the necessary foundation for change.

PRINCIPALS' RESPONSIBILITIES

As the embodiment of the school's culture, principals must create and sustain a caring and trusting learning environment. They must live, breathe, speak, and walk their talk. Principals' primary goal must be for all stakeholders in the learning community to reach their capacity. "Imagine so valuing the importance of developing people's capabilities that you design a culture that itself immersively sweeps every member of the organization into an ongoing developmental journey in the course of working every day" (Kegan and Lahey 2016, 5). Principals who are trusted leaders inspire others to embark on a transformational journey—together. They must create a "circle of safety" (Sinek 2014) in which faculty have the support and confidence they need to take risks.

Helping ready the faculty, staff, and parents for change is a principal's responsibility. Principals who practice strengths-based leadership understand that organizations can move forward if leaders and teams focus on strengths rather than on deficits. Research based on Gallup poll data notes three key findings. "The most effective leaders are always investing in strengths. The most effective leaders surround themselves with the right people and then maximize their teams. The most effective leaders understand their followers' needs" (Rath 2008, 2–4). Principals who know and develop their own strengths will create teams with complementary strengths. Practicing strengths-based leadership helps principals build capacity in their schools.

Principals can inspire faculty with their emphasis on and their own example of continuous learning; they "lead to learn." As learners and collaborators, principals facilitate "job-embedded, ongoing, coordinated learning opportunities that lead to increased student achievement" (Hall, Childs-Bowen, Pajardo, and Cunningham-Morris 2015, 4). All stakeholders in a collaborative culture school can follow the principal's lead and commit to growing their own capacity. As Simon Sinek (2014) notes, "leaders eat last." Sinek posits that leaders inspire because they willingly, even gladly, sacrifice their own safety and comfort for the good of others. When administrators are open about both the potential joy and discomfort inherent in learning and change, they help create a safe environment for risk-taking. The school culture they lead "should communicate and reinforce the value of all its members thinking interdependently" (Kallick and Zmuda 2017, 127). When principals work collaboratively with others, they model their expectation for how to best serve students and the entire learning community.

SCHOOL LIBRARIANS' RESPONSIBILITIES

Building connections to support a collaborative culture of learning is a core responsibility of school librarians. As the researchers Ross Todd, Carol Gordon, and Ya-Ling Lu found, school librarians working in collaborative school cultures gain the respect of their colleagues. In these schools, classroom teachers reported that "the school library conducts substantial, cost-effective, hands-on professional development through the cooperative design of learning experiences; school librarians have instructional expertise; and the school library offers a learning environment that is based on a complex model of teaching and learning that is exploratory and highly motivational" (Todd, Gordon, and Lu 2011, 26–27). School librarians must be seen as trustworthy and knowledgeable colleagues.

Particularly in their leader and instructional partner roles, school librarians are charged with supporting their principals' goals. With their responsibility for the entire learning community, school librarians maximize their impact through leading PD and through their service on committees and PLCs. They support job-embedded PD by coplanning, coimplementing, and coassessing instruction with fellow educators. Through coteaching, school librarians receive and provide informal coaching and feedback and practice reciprocal mentorship. They further the "circle of safety" that makes the faculty an effective team.

When the school community is engaged in building a collaborative culture of learning, school librarians who facilitate a shared learning space in the library learning commons can help determine the best ways to meet the needs of each and every library stakeholder. They co-curate and share resources. They codevelop learning plans and assessment strategies. School librarians are what George Couros calls "school teachers" because they are willing to share ideas and consider every student in the building their own (Couros 2015, 74). School librarians build and sustain relationships that can help cement the foundation of a culture of learners—young and older—who strive to make schools joyful, relevant, challenging, and effective learning environments for all.

CLASSROOM TEACHERS' RESPONSIBILITIES

In *Teaching in the Knowledge Society: Education in the Age of Insecurity,* Andy Hargreaves describes the knowledge society as a learning society with "brain power—the power to think, learn, and innovate" (2003, 18–19). He goes on to note that educators have a responsibility to "promote young people's opportunities in, engagements with, and inclusion within the high-skill world of knowledge, information, communication, and innovation. All children must be properly prepared for the knowledge society and its economy" (21). To accomplish these objectives, educators must attain a new professionalism in their roles as catalysts for learning.

Collegiality and teamwork are nonnegotiable requirements for faculty in schools that seek to become schools that learn.
#schoollibrarianleadership

Collegiality and teamwork are nonnegotiable requirements for faculty in schools that seek to become schools that learn. Future ready educators are open to change and take risks in order to build capacity. They develop collective intelligence in order to creatively and effectively solve problems. Educators are trustworthy and foster trust in others and in the change process. They include families as partners in the learning community. Educators must also develop and participate in personal learning networks to help them improve and reflect on their teaching. They must be willing to be "continually engaged in pursuing, upgrading, self-monitoring, and reviewing their own professional learning" (Hargreaves 2003, 24).

A collaborative culture of learning allows individual educators to capitalize on the strengths their colleagues possess while also building their own expertise. Educators take risks more easily with the support of instructional partners. They rely on the assistance of others in supporting, guiding, and facilitating student learning and success, and promoting student ownership in inquiry learning. By working collaboratively, educators are better prepared to help students work through the uncertainties, insecurities, and frustrations that are natural aspects of the learning process. Educators facilitate student learning most effectively with the support of a professional team working together in a collaborative culture.

STUDENTS' RESPONSIBILITIES

To be future ready, students must participate fully in their learning by taking "responsibility for actively pursuing information and ideas both in print and digitally, understanding those ideas and how they apply, drawing conclusions and developing new applications, and sharing these new understandings with others" (AASL 2009c, 48). Figure 9.2 shows the key commitments that students, school librarians, and school libraries are asked to make in order to be prepared for college, career, and life. These foundations and key commitments are from AASL's *National School Library Standards for Learners, School Librarians, and School Libraries.*

The competencies for today's learners shift primary control and responsibility from educators to students in order to help young people develop as independent learners. This shift toward student responsibility encourages students to practice and build dispositions such as "self-direction, adaptability, and a tolerance for ambiguity, in addition to critical skills like reading, communication, and collaboration. They experience and begin to get comfortable with the discomfort of learning" (Donhauser, Hersey, Stutzman, and Zane 2014, 11). Guiding their own learning results in empowered students who develop the necessary internal motivation and personal investment in their efforts that are essential for lifelong learning.

AASL Shared Foundations and Key Commitments

Shared Foundation	Key Commitments
I. Inquire	Build new knowledge by inquiring, thinking critically, identifying problems, and developing strategies for solving problems.
II. Include	Demonstrate an understanding of and commitment to inclusiveness and respect for diversity in the learning community.
III. Collaborate	Work effectively with others to broaden perspectives and work toward common goals.
IV. Curate	Make meaning for oneself and others by collecting, organizing, and sharing resources of personal relevance.
V. Explore	Discover and innovate a growth mindset developed through experience and reflection.
VI. Engage	Demonstrate safe, legal, and ethical creating and sharing of knowledge products independently while engaging in a community of practice and an interconnected world.

Excerpted from *National School Library Standards for Learners, School Librarians, and School Libraries* by the American Association of School Librarians, a division of the American Library Association, copyright © 2018 American Library Association. Available for download at www.standards.aasl.org. Used with permission.

In this way, students no longer perceive learning as a task assigned by a teacher. Instead, learning is driven by an internal need to know—one that is owned by the student and guided by a team of professional educators.

FAMILIES' RESPONSIBILITIES

School administrators and educators are responsible for creating opportunities for families to become partners in their children's education. School leaders must know their communities and be sensitive to the needs and circumstances of families. Conducting surveys or focus groups is one way to get a clearer picture of what types of communication and involvement will work best for families. Educators must offer multiple ways for families to participate in their children's learning and in the life of the school. Traditionally, families' main interaction with their children's schooling was through supervising homework. It is unlikely that this low level of involvement will increase families' understanding of future ready learning, however. It will not engender advocates for the school's transformation process.

In a school that learns, interactions between the school and families will be openly caring and robust. All oral and written communication between the classroom or school and families will be warm, welcoming, and inclusive. Every attempt will be made to communicate in the languages that are used in students' homes. School events, such as back-to-school night and open houses, will be scheduled at times that are convenient for most families. Making student performances and presentations a centerpiece of these events helps families understand the quality of learning and teaching within the school. Parents and caregivers will be invited into classrooms and the library to share their experiences and expertise. They will be encouraged to serve on planning teams and advisory boards that guide the school's policies and practices.

The school library, as the hub of learning in the school, may be an ideal contact point for many families. Like the front office staff, it is essential that the school librarian and library staff are approachable representatives of the school culture. Families may take advantage of family book and resource checkouts. They may access the virtual library. Some may volunteer to support library management, teaching, or fund-raising tasks. This level of engagement will give families a first-hand experience of the learning activities offered through the library program. School leaders may find that this is one of the most effective ways to increase families' knowledge about future ready learning. Involvement with the school library can lead families to become strong advocates for the librarian, library program, and future ready learning.

COMMUNITY'S RESPONSIBILITIES

Situating schooling in the community builds bridges between students' in-school lives and their current and future lives.

#buildingconnections4learning

Situating schooling in the community builds bridges between students' in-school lives and their current and future lives outside of school. In order to be successful, schools must value the other groups that affect students, and in turn these groups must value the connections they build with schools. Community-based educational experiences include working with preschools and day care centers, public libraries, museums, city/state/federal parks, scouting, music, and theater groups, religious organizations, businesses, and city/state/federal services. The school that learns strives to immerse students in intergenerational, interinstitutional learning. These connections give youth opportunities to learn with and from a wide variety of other groups in a wide variety of contexts.

There are a number of ways that schools can make sure that school board members and other elected officials, business owners and service organizations, and concerned community members know about the learning that is taking place in a future ready school. Similar to the invitations to families, involving community members in focus groups and surveys indicates a willingness to listen and respond to their ideas and concerns. They can be invited to serve on school committees or to attend school events. Community members may reciprocate and invite school representatives to become involved in their activities. This sets up an opportunity for coalition-building and for mutually beneficial advocacy.

Embedding the school library in the community increases advocacy opportunities while it spreads information about the school, the library program, and the work of the school librarian. School librarians can take the primary responsibility for reaching out to academic and public libraries in order to help students and families make lifelong literacy connections. Elementary school librarians may coteach preschool storytimes with child care agencies. Secondary librarians may collaborate with university and community college librarians to coplan and coimplement student visits to campus libraries. School librarians at all instructional levels may collaborate with public librarians to facilitate student and family involvement in public library initiatives; they may focus their efforts on summer reading, for instance, or collaborate year round by codeveloping and copresenting literacy learning opportunities. While it is the school and school librarian's responsibility to reach out into the community, it is the community's responsibility to respond to these overtures.

YOUR PLAN AND REALITY

In a successful change process, leaders plan for setbacks as well as successes. In the most innovative schools, moments of failure are regarded as opportunities for growth. Administrators, educators, and students expect risk-taking and experimentation to lead to both successes and setbacks. They welcome missteps as teachable and learnable moments (see figure 9.3).

FIGURE 9.3

Your Plan and Reality

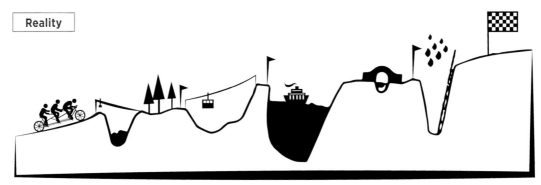

It is said that people learn more from mistakes and failures than they do from successes. In a school culture where stakeholders are supported in reaching their capacity, risk-taking will necessarily result in both successes and setbacks. Missteps give learners growth opportunities. Bumps in the road and detours on the path to success are valuable and should be analyzed and even celebrated in a school that learns. Revising strategies and trying again are part and parcel of learning and change.

"Having the freedom to fail is important to innovation. But even more important to the process are the traits of resiliency and grit" (Couros 2015, 37). The ups and downs on the road to future ready learning present students and educators with opportunities to develop the necessary dispositions for risk-taking and innovation. Sharing the journey means sharing the feelings associated with failure as well as success. With honesty and transparency, the entire school community can model resilience and grit throughout a change process. Students can then learn from their elders how to develop these dispositions as support for lifelong learning.

SUSTAINING A COLLABORATIVE LEARNING CULTURE

"Two things sustain change: one is a leader or leadership group that acts as a change agent; the other is a system or group of systems that supports change" (Schlechty 2001, 40). Today's principals and superintendents are focused on building capacity. School librarians are in a unique position to serve as change aides who support administrators' initiatives. When school librarians coplan, coteach, and coassess a lesson or unit of instruction, they diffuse innovations in teaching and learning throughout the school. With a future ready school librarian guiding the library program, it only "costs" adequate paraprofessional staff support and the willingness to take risks in order to embed professional learning in educators' daily practice.

The urgency of improving educators' teaching and students' learning is clear to site- and district-level school administrators who are responsible and held accountable for student achievement by families, school boards, state- and federal-level education agencies, and voters. Stakeholders agree that schools cannot let students fall behind in future ready learning. Developing literacies, practicing skills, and encouraging positive dispositions help students to be competitive in a global society and economy. Educators must be up-to-date with strategies to meet this broad range of learning objectives. They can achieve these objectives when they work in collaboration with their peers.

To borrow a slogan from the national school library advocacy campaign that grew out of the Dewitt Wallace-Reader's Digest Library Power Project in the 1990s: "Teaching is too difficult to do alone. Collaborate with your school librarian." This slogan frames the message that school librarians must spread in order to influence today's educational decision-makers. This was true at the dawn of the information age and it is even truer now in the age of innovation. Framing advocacy for school librarians in terms of what classroom teachers, specialists, and students need is a way to show principals and superintendents that they have

a partner in the library. School librarians can help administrators meet their goal for an effective teaching force.

Building a culture of collaboration is possible when all members of the learning community come together to agree on their purpose—their "why." Together, they enact a plan that includes both the "how" and "what" they do. Their plan is aligned with their values. Success requires strong leadership. It requires risk-taking, assessing missteps as well as celebrating successes, and committing to constant improvement. Leaders in such a community "expect themselves and others to be uncertain, inquiring, expectant of surprise, and perhaps a bit joyful about confronting the unknown" (Senge et al. 2012, 420). A collaborative culture nurtures trusting relationships. Trust is a condition where joy and learning can blossom.

School librarians can help administrators meet their goal for an effective teaching force. #buildingconnections4learning

AN EMPOWERED LEARNING CULTURE

Transformation in schools requires a systems thinking approach. It requires a circle of safety and a collaborative culture of learning (see figure 9.4), in which all stakeholders commit to work together. All pieces of an empowered learning culture affect the other parts. There are also openings in the puzzle for new connections to pieces that are not yet knowable. (Figure 9.4 is also available as a downloadable Web Extra.)

FIGURE 9.4

Empowered Collaborative Culture of Learning

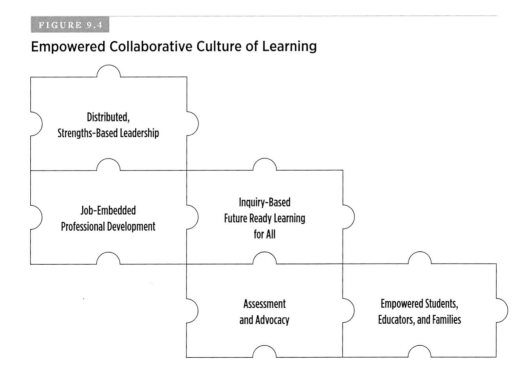

Transformation can begin and grow in a collaborative culture. "A team is not a group of people who work together. A team is a group of people who trust each other" (Sinek, Mead, and Docker 2017, 104). The relationships between leaders, educators, students, families, and the community are the foundation for any innovation. Beginning and ending with the plural pronoun "our," all members of the school learning community share responsibility; they all have a stake in student success. In a school that learns, students are referred to as "our students," the library as "our library," and the school as "our school." The codesigned and coimplemented curriculum is "ours." The resulting student learning outcomes are also "ours." In this culture of shared responsibility, everyone has a stake in making the school a successful learning environment for all students. In turn, educators, families, and community members share in "our success." A trusting collaborative culture creates a system that supports change.

"Courageous leadership and the perseverance to continually improve are critical to creating a better learning culture for all students and ultimately, to transform learning" (Sheninger and Murray 2017, 227). Becoming future ready requires individual as well as collective resilience on the part of all school stakeholders. They will continuously assess their progress and collaboratively determine their next steps. Future ready learning also requires ongoing advocacy for what works best for students. When all stakeholders work together, they can achieve the goals they set for future ready learning.

The Canadian author and educator Claude Thomas Bissell said it best:

> Risk more than others think is safe,
> Care more than others think is wise,
> Dream more than others think is practical,
> Expect more than others think is possible.

Risk and care more, dream big, and expect the impossible. Perhaps most importantly of all, build and sustain the connections that are needed for a collaborative culture of learning to thrive in your school. Then, take the next steps on a joyful and challenging learning journey—together.

BOOK STUDY GUIDE

I. Discussion Questions:

QUESTION #1: What do you do daily to build trust in a "circle of safety" in your school learning environment?

QUESTION #2: How do you involve students and families in creating your school culture and as partners in the change process?

QUESTION #3: What are your dreams in terms of future ready learning for students, educators, your school, and the community?

- *Individual Thinking*: Compose individual responses to the questions asked above.
- *Partner Sharing*: Share your individual responses to these questions with a colleague in your own school or another school.
- *Group Sharing*: As a small or whole group, discuss the feelings, ideas, hopes, and challenges that occurred to you as you responded to these questions or listened to your colleagues' responses.

II. Activities

Although these activities can be undertaken by individuals, they are designed for group work.

Activity 1

Are We There Yet?

Using the chart below based on figure 9.3, codevelop questions for the center column for each of the pieces of an empowered collaborative learning culture. Then complete the third column with evidence that answers each question. See the example for "Distributed, Strengths-Based Leadership."

Empowered Collaborative Learning Culture	Driving Questions	Evidence of Progress
Distributed, Strengths-Based Leadership	How does our principal distribute leadership responsibilities?	Faculty meeting agendas are developed collaboratively, and meeting facilitation rotates among PLCs.
Job-Embedded Professional Development		
Inquiry-Based Future Ready Learning for All		
Assessment and Advocacy		
Empowered Students, Educators, and Families		

This activity was inspired by a self-assessment, self-reflection chart developed by George Couros (2015).

Activity 2

Enabling Action for Coteaching

To build on Chip and Dan Heath's idea of "shaping the path," respond to the following statements that are related to enabling collaboration and coteaching. For statements 1 through 8, use a Likert scale from "strongly disagree" to "strongly agree" (include "do not know" as an option). Administrators may collect these data anonymously. Faculty can discuss responses to these statements in meetings or during conferences with principals. Administrators and educators may also use these statements as self-reflection prompts. This list was inspired by an "enabling action" diagnostic tool offered by Dan Cohen (2005, 132–33).

1. Our school structures make collaboration and coteaching possible.
2. Our administrators show their commitment to coplanning and coteaching by removing barriers and making job-embedded professional development a priority.
3. I have received sufficient training and support to be an effective collaborator/coteacher.
4. I have been given sufficient time to coplan during my contract hours.
5. I feel supported in my efforts to coteach with colleagues.
6. I have been supported in taking risks through coteaching.
7. I have been acknowledged for my coteaching efforts.
8. I have made improving my collaboration and coteaching skills a professional goal.
9. If there is one thing I could change about my collaboration and coteaching efforts, it would be:

Comments:

Activity 3

Identifying Short-Term Wins

To build on Chip and Dan Heath's idea of "bright spots," use the directions from Activity 2 to respond to the following statements related to creating short-term wins. This list was inspired by a "short-term wins" diagnostic tool offered by Dan Cohen (2005, 151–53).

1. I am actively seeking out opportunities to coplan and coteach.
2. Coteaching is improving my instructional practices.
3. Coteaching is improving students' learning as evidenced by their engagement.
4. Coteaching is improving students' learning as evidenced by their increased content knowledge.
5. Coteaching is improving students' learning as evidenced by their development of skills and dispositions.

6. Coteaching is improving our students' learning as evidenced by their ability to self-regulate and self-assess their learning.
7. I have improved my job satisfaction due to my coteaching efforts.
8. I have seen evidence that coteaching is benefiting my colleagues.
9. I am motivated to continue to develop as a collaborator and coteacher because . . .

Comments:

III. Reflection Prompts

Choose from these possible reflection prompts or compose one of your own.

1. Reflect on your thoughts, feelings, and concerns as you read this chapter and/or engaged in the discussion questions or activities.
2. Reflect on the challenges of sustaining change. What strategies are you using or will you use to refresh and reinvigorate yourself, your colleagues, and your entire learning community?
3. Especially for school librarians: Reflect on your role in sustaining a collaborative culture of learning in all grade levels, content areas, and across grade levels and disciplines. Share and discuss your reflection with your principal or district-level school library administrator.

NEXT STEPS

Since you have come to this page in the book, you and your team may be ready to continue the conversation on the book's website:

- http://schoollibrarianleadership.com

On this site, you can find resources such as:

- An interactive blog
- A downloadable one-page summary of each chapter for your files and to share with your colleagues
- A Twitter feed using these hashtags: #schoollibrarianleadership and #buildingconnections41earning
- A podcast series
- More handouts, graphic organizers, and other materials for your book study use
- *Maximizing School Librarian Leadership: Building Connections for Learning and Advocacy* testimonials, endorsements, and examples from the field
- More information about author Judi Moreillon

Web Extra resources are found on the ALA Editions website at alaeditions.org/webextras.

GLOSSARY

action research. Action research is a systematic inquiry conducted by educators or other school stakeholders. The purpose of action research is to gather local information about educators' effectiveness, students' learning outcomes, or how well the school itself is functioning. The goals of action research are to gain insight and develop reflective practice, improve student outcomes, and effect positive changes in the school environment (Mills 2010).

admit slip. An admit slip helps establish a purpose for reading or inquiring. It provides background information for students before they read the main text. An admit slip stimulates the reader's thinking by providing compelling facts or posing probing questions.

advocacy. Advocacy is an ongoing process of building partnerships and forming alliances so people will act together in support of a particular outcome or initiative.

andragogy. Andragogy is a theory of adult learning. It states that the adult learner is self-directed and should be autonomous during the learning event. Malcolm Knowles (1980) promoted the term and its principles in the United States.

anticipation guide. An anticipation guide is a preview. It helps learners prepare by providing background information or posing questions to help them focus their thinking about the ideas, information, or processes to be presented in the lesson.

authentic assessments. Authentic assessments measure how students apply their knowledge, skills, and dispositions as they participate in real-world tasks. Ideally, students have a voice in codeveloping authentic assessments. Educators often contrast these assessments with standardized or multiple-choice tests, which lack connection to actual contexts in which knowledge would be applied.

benchmarks. Benchmarks provide students and educators with formative assessments at specific points during the inquiry or other performance task. Students can use benchmarks to improve their learning outcomes; educators use them to improve their instruction.

blended learning. Blended learning involves educators providing students with online content and instruction as well as face-to-face instruction for small groups and individualized mentoring. In the online environment, students have control and responsibility for the "time, place, path, and pace of instruction" (Staker and Horn 2012, 3).

challenge-based learning. Challenge-based learning is another term used for "problem-based learning."

close reading. Close reading is an instructional intervention that involves readers in examining a difficult text thoroughly and methodically. Using think-alouds, educators model close-reading techniques, which are strategies designed to help readers gain or regain comprehension. The goal of close reading is for readers to uncover the deeper meanings in a text and arrive at a deeper understanding than they would have if they had only skimmed the surface of the text. In figure 4.3 of this book, sixteen "fix-up" options are recommended for readers' use in close-reading lessons.

cloud-based tools. Sometimes called Web 2.0 tools, cloud-based digital tools allow users to create products that are hosted on the Web. Web-based products can be embedded into webpages, blogs, wikis, and the like. Unlike software, the cloud-based digital tool itself is not downloaded to a computer, which means it can be accessed and edited from any Internet-connected computer at any time.

coding. Coding, or computer programming language, is a set of syntax rules that define how code should be written and formatted. Coding allows programmers to use binary input to make something happen.

collaboration. Collaboration is a way of working in which team members work together as equal partners to achieve a particular outcome or goal. Collaboration involves "working with a member of the teaching team to plan, implement, and evaluate a specialized instructional plan" (AASL 2016a). Collaboration requires effective ongoing communication, joint planning, individual and collective action, and commitment to a shared outcome.

collaborative learning. Students and educators enact collaborative learning when they apply interpersonal skills, individual knowledge and talents, and collective action to work together toward a goal. In effective collaborative learning, individuals and the group are held individually and collectively accountable for outcomes.

college, career, and community readiness (CCCR). Some states have adopted CCCR standards, although some do not include "community" in their CCR standards. Various schools and districts include these terms in their mission statements and specify outcomes related to CCCR. These may include literacies, skills and dispositions, the ability to transition from preK–12 schooling to postsecondary learning and life, and an understanding of the rights and responsibilities of citizenship.

community of practice. Through a sense of permanence and repeated contact, educators who form and sustain a professional community of practice develop shared beliefs, values, and practices (Wenger 1998). Sustained social interaction among group members results in a strong sense of "belonging" and "connection" among them. In the process, they develop a high level of trust.

constructivist approach. A constructivist approach to learning is based on the premise that learners build their own understandings and knowledge of the world through their experiences. As a result of new learning, they revise, modify, or change their schemas. Reflecting on their learning experiences helps learners crystallize new schemas.

content literacy. Content literacy is the ability to apply prior content knowledge, general literacy skills, and content-specific skills, such as graph skills in math or map skills in geography, in order to acquire new knowledge (McKenna and Robinson 1990).

cooperation. Compared with collaboration, cooperation tends to be more informal, short-term, and often lacks a focused planning effort. People who cooperate maintain their individual authority. They may not have a shared mission, but rather provide pieces of a puzzle without a commitment to the whole picture.

coordination. Coordination requires more communication than cooperation. It includes a shared mission and some planning and may be supported over a longer time period. Often one person will take the lead in coordinating activities and others will follow along in supporting roles. While there is more intensity in coordination than in cooperation, authority is still maintained by each individual.

coplanning. Coplanning by classroom teachers and school librarians occurs when equal partners work together to design instruction. Educators begin with the end in mind—students' attainment of learning objectives that show what students will know and will be able to do at the end of the learning activity. During coplanning, educators codesign assessment instruments and align students' learning tasks with objectives and assessments.

coteaching. In this book, coteaching is a strategy in which classroom teachers and school librarians work together as equal partners who coplan, coimplement, and coassess standards-based instruction. See chapter 2 for specific coteaching strategies.

coteaching approaches. Marilyn Friend and Lynn Cook identified five coteaching approaches (see figure 2.1). These coteaching models are best implemented after collaborative planning in which the educators take shared responsibility for instruction and student learning outcomes.

critical thinking. Critical thinking involves approaching ideas and issues with an open mind, considering multiple perspectives, resolving conflicting information, and arriving at a reasoned understanding or conclusion. The goal of critical thinking is for learners to analyze and evaluate an idea or issue and then be able to form a judgment based on evidence. By contrast, rote learning, which involves memorization, does not require or invite critical thinking.

crowdsourcing. To crowdsource a project, the organizer solicits information from a variety of people. Most crowdsourcing is done via the Web. A crowdsourced school libraries video will contain information from a variety of library programs.

crystallize. Crystallized intelligence relies on the ability to access the information stored in long-term memory. It affects a person's capacity to apply his or her skills, knowledge, and experience.

cultural literacy. Cultural literacy involves having an understanding, appreciation, and respect for other cultures as well as one's own. It is the ability to value the similarities and differences among cultural groups and understand how people's perspectives are shaped by their culture. Cultural literacy helps people communicate, builds empathy, and affirms diversity.

culture. Culture is a way of life. It is comprised of shared beliefs, values, knowledge, attitudes, language, behaviors, social interactions, and more. Cultures are created by people over time. Cultures are dynamic; they are not fixed. Cultures change as people's needs and norms change.

curation. School librarians who engage in curation collect, organize, and align resources with a curriculum. They engage in curation when they develop and codevelop print and online pathfinders that go beyond a list of titles or links to include annotations and additional information in order to support students' information-seeking activities.

deeper learning. The Hewlett Foundation identified six deeper learning competencies: 1. Master core academic content; 2. Think critically and solve complex problems; 3. Work collaboratively; 4. Communicate effectively; 5. Learn how to learn; 6. Develop academic mindsets (Hewlett Foundation 2013).

differentiated instruction. In teaching with differentiated instruction, educators plan for individuals or groups of learners to conduct and demonstrate their learning in different ways depending on students' learning styles or strengths, as long as they achieve the same learning outcomes. Two goals of differentiated instruction are to increase students' motivation and their success in learning targeted skills and strategies.

differentiated professional development. Just as individual students have different strengths, needs, and learning styles, so do faculty. When school librarians collaborate one-on-one or with a team of educators, they are able to provide adult learning support that meets the needs of individuals as well as groups.

diffusion of innovations. Everett Rogers (1995) described how innovations are introduced, spread, and sustained in organizations. He identified the various roles that individuals play in adopting innovations (see figure 2.3).

digital citizenship. Digital citizenship involves the strategies, skills, and dispositions that youth need in order to participate in online communication and share and use digital information responsibly and ethically. It can include issues such as privacy and safety as well as respect for intellectual property rights.

digital conversion. Digital conversion usually refers to the infusion of the school learning environment with digital devices, tools, and resources. It may or may not include a digital shift or digital transformation.

digital learning. Digital learning involves using technology to support and strengthen students' learning experiences. Digital learning involves more than just digital tools; it "emphasizes high-quality instruction and provides access to challenging content, feedback through formative assessment, opportunities for learning anytime and anywhere, and individualized instruction to ensure all students reach their full potential to succeed in college and a career" (Alliance for Excellent Education 2016a).

digital literacy. "Digital literacy is the ability to use information and communication technologies to find, understand, evaluate, create, and communicate digital information, an ability that requires both cognitive and technical skills" (ALA 2013). The technical skills involve the use of various information and communication technologies.

digital shift. Digital shift suggests a modification in instructional practices—a shift from print on paper to digital resources and tools.

digital transformation. When a school is engaged in a digital transformation, students and educators will participate in and facilitate learning experiences that could not have been as easily accomplished or even possible in a purely analog environment.

dispositions. Dispositions are character traits or tendencies that motivate behavior. While some dispositions are innate, some can be influenced through modeling and practice. Dispositions for future ready learners include curiosity, flexibility, adaptability, perseverance, risk-taking, and more (see figure 1.1).

distributed leadership. Distributed leadership means "that every employee, every community member, and every student has the opportunity to lead and is expected to lead—and that leadership is not solely reserved for those at the top" (Edwards 2015, 2).

domain. In the context of this book, a domain is a specific sphere of knowledge, such as history, mathematics, or science.

essential questions. Essential questions are key inquiries in a discipline. These are questions that "foster the kinds of inquiries, discussions, and reflections that help learners find meaning in their learning and achieve deeper thought and better quality in their work" (Wiggins and Wilbur 2015, 11).

evidence-based practice (EBP). This movement in school librarianship is founded on the need for school librarians to document their impact on student achievement through the use of empirical evidence. Educators base their instruction on research. They measure student outcomes by comparing pre- and post-assessment data. Educators then use the results to improve their practice. They share the results of EBP with students, colleagues, administrators, families, and others.

executive functions. Some of the behaviors associated with executive functions include motivation, perseverance, good study habits, and time-management skills.

exit slip. Educators use exit slips to assess student learning. Exit slips are collected at the end of a lesson, class period, or learning event. They can indicate students' acquisition of content knowledge, practice of skills, or development of dispositions. Educators can also invite students to share questions, uncertainties, or next-step ideas via exit slips.

flexible scheduling. With a flexible library schedule, individual students, small groups, and whole classes of students visit the library at the point of need. This is in contrast to a fixed schedule, in which classes are scheduled to visit the library on a fixed rotation.

flipped classroom. In a flipped classroom, students are given independent reading, viewing, or other assignments to do before they come to class. During class time, they may engage in exercises, projects, discussions, and more. One or more educators may work with individuals or small groups of students to teach or reinforce concepts connected with the assignment. Since most of these assignments are conducted electronically, students must have access to technology resources and tools outside the classroom for the flipped classroom approach to be effective.

formative assessments. Formative assessment can be informal based on educator observation, or it can be formal based on collecting data from various types of graphic organizers, composition drafts, or quizzes. Educators' goals are to use formative assessments to monitor student learning, provide feedback, and adjust instruction as needed.

frontloading. Frontloading is used at the beginning of a lesson. It can be a way to prepare students for the learning event by providing them with background knowledge. This could be in the form of content, vocabulary, or strategies that are new to students. Frontloading can also be used to access and assess students' prior knowledge or increase their motivation to engage with content or the learning process.

future ready learning. Future ready learning is a framework that includes the literacies, skills, and dispositions that students need to be successful in their schooling and economic, social, civic, and personal lives (see figure 1.1).

future ready students. Future ready students are in the process of learning and mastering the multiple literacies, skills, and dispositions that are involved in future ready learning.

genres. A genre is a particular category of book, one with a typical style, form, or content. Examples include realistic fiction, historical fiction, science fiction, fantasy, biography, and informational texts. When readers understand the characteristics of various genres, they can anticipate how authors present ideas and information.

graphic organizers. Graphic organizers are tools for learning. Unlike worksheets with one right answer for each blank, graphic organizers are open-ended and invite diverse responses from students. Organizers may take the form of Venn diagrams, category matrices or webs, and more. Graphic organizers are instructional scaffolds that support students in meeting the learning objectives.

growth mindset. The researcher Carol Dweck (2006) found that people who believe intelligence and talent are fixed will accept their fate and not take a proactive stance toward their own learning. By contrast, people who believe that intelligence and talent can be "grown" are open to learning new strategies and applying dedication and hard work to the task of developing their capacity for success.

Guided Inquiry Design (GID). Kuhlthau, Maniotes, and Caspari define guided inquiry as an approach to learning; they provide a GID framework with eight phases (see figure 3.3). Using this framework, students find and use a variety of sources of information and ideas to increase their understanding of a problem, topic, or issue. GID goes beyond the simple answering of questions and requires "investigation, exploration, search, quest, research, pursuit, and study" whereby students "connect their world with the curriculum" (2012, 2).

information and communication technology (ICT). The term "ICT" was originally used to refer to cable or other systems that linked telephone and computer networks. Today, ICT is used as a general term for electronic information and communication resources and tools that utilize multiple formats. It is the "technical" aspect of digital literacy.

information literacy. Information literacy can be defined as the ability to recognize when information is needed; to be able to find, evaluate, and use information to solve information problems; and to produce new knowledge.

innovation. "Innovation is a *way of thinking* that creates something *new* and *better*" (Couros 2015, 19). In his writings, George Couros stresses that "innovation is a process, not a product."

inquiry circles. Through small-group inquiry circles, students support one another in collaborative learning in various ways during the inquiry process. Students within the group may take various roles during conversations or while performing tasks. Inquiry circle members may discuss various questions, share inferences and interpretations of particular texts, or jointly monitor the inquiry process (Kuhlthau, Maniotes, and Caspari 2015, 32–36).

inquiry learning. Inquiry learning is an instructional framework that consists of a number of phases that begin with engaging students in the topic and end with the students presenting and reflecting on their new knowledge. While there are a number of inquiry learning processes that specify different phases in the process, in this book the term is defined by the Guided Inquiry Design framework.

interdependence. Interdependence is the mutual reliance between two or more individuals, groups, or components within one or more systems. Members in an interdependent relationship may be emotionally, intellectually, or morally dependent on and responsible to one another.

interdisciplinary approach. An interdisciplinary curriculum, or integrated studies curriculum, involves students applying processes and information from multiple subject domains during a single learning event or unit of study. For example, when students conduct an inquiry related to climate change, they may explore this topic using various disciplinary lenses such as geography, meteorology, or the political or social sciences, and they may be applying English language arts and mathematics skills in their learning process.

job-embedded professional development. This strategy for individual and collective instructional improvement is based on research that suggests that educators must apply their professional development learning in their actual teaching practice. In this book, job-embedded professional development results from classroom teacher and school librarian coteaching.

learning commons. This model for the use of the library's physical and virtual spaces, its resources, and the school librarian focuses the library program on knowledge-building by students and educators alike.

literacies. Literacies are cultural practices. They are the way people create meaning and communicate with others. Every discipline has its own set of literacy knowledge and practices that create and communicate meaning. In this book, reading and writing are referred to as "traditional literacies."

long-term memory. Unlike short-term memory, which has a limited capacity, long-term memory can store unlimited amounts of information indefinitely. Discipline-specific facts and concepts that are held in long-term memory serve as building blocks for new knowledge, creativity, and innovation.

makerspace. In schools, makerspaces provide a wide variety of hands-on opportunities for students to design, experiment, build, and invent. Makerspaces may contain tools, materials, and activities associated with science or computer labs, a woodshop, or an art room. In some makerspaces, there is a particular focus on science or engineering activities; these are more commonly known as STEM/STEAM labs. In other makerspaces, general tinkering is the norm.

marketing. Marketing involves service providers using various means, such as surveys and focus groups, to assess and meet constituents' needs.

media literacy. Media literacy involves accessing, analyzing, evaluating, and creating works in an interwoven system of media technologies, including print and online ones. Students who are media-literate are able to improve their communication skills and are more critical media consumers and effective and ethical media creators.

meme. A meme is an image, video, or piece of text that is copied or remixed. Memes spread rapidly on the Web.

mental models. Mental models are explanations of an individual's or group's thought processes that help them understand how things work in the real world.

metacognition. Metacognition is "thinking about thinking." It is the person's awareness or analysis of the cognitive processes she uses to think and to learn. Think-alouds are one way educators can demonstrate metacognition.

mini-lessons. Mini-lessons are short-term interventions conducted at the point of need. They are brief reviews of previously taught strategies. Educators may facilitate mini-lessons for individual students, small groups, or whole classes. These lessons are always embedded in a context where students will immediately apply them to the learning task at hand.

multidisciplinary curriculum. In this curriculum model, secondary disciplines, often the language arts, are used to support a discipline-focused curriculum. For example, writing across the curriculum is a multidisciplinary instructional practice. When students compose a narrative rationale for a science lab report, they are applying multiple disciplines in one activity.

multimodal texts. Multimodal texts combine various sign or symbol systems, such as alphabetic, oral, and visual, to make meaning. Multimodal texts are created in multiple formats and include a range of representation and communication modes including art, music, movement, drama, and various technologies.

nonlinguistic representations. There are many ways to represent information without using words. Some examples include graphs, mind maps, sketches, pictographs, scientific drawings or models, graphic organizers, concept maps, dramatizations, flow charts, and kinesthetic or computerized simulations.

notemaking. Recording information in one's own words is what distinguishes notemaking from notetaking. Notemaking requires that learners pass information through their prior knowledge and experience and determine what is important to record. Notetaking is essential for recording quotes, but notemaking more clearly indicates what the student has learned or understood from the text.

open education resources (OER). OER are teaching, learning, and research resources that are in the public domain or have been released by their creators under intellectual property licenses that permit free educational use and repurposing. OER can include textbooks, streaming videos, software, full courses, course materials, tests, or learning modules, and any other tools, materials, or techniques that are used to support access to knowledge (Hewlett Foundation 2014).

open library. An open library is one where students, classroom teachers, and families have access to the physical space and resources of the library throughout the school day. Library users visit the library on an as-needed basis. Individuals and multiple groups of students, educators, and families may be using the library space at the same time. The school librarian and principal make staffing decisions, such as hiring a full-time paraprofessional, so that the open library functions smoothly while the professional school librarian is teaching, or coplanning or coteaching with colleagues.

participatory culture. Cloud-based tools, social media, and other communication tools have launched a media-focused cultural context in which there are low barriers to widespread participation in the production and distribution of media. Participatory culture messages have the potential to reach global audiences (see Jenkins et al. 2009).

pathfinder. A pathfinder is a web page with reliable, preselected links and annotations. The most useful pathfinders also include additional information-seeking tips, such as web-searching guides. Pathfinders can provide a jumping-off point for students who are expected to identify their own resources. An Internet pathfinder is one way that school librarians curate resources.

performance-based assessment. In this book, a performance-based assessment measures students' application of the literacies, skills, and dispositions learned from a particular unit of study. The performance task challenges students to apply their knowledge and to use higher-order thinking skills.

performance task. These tasks are commonly associated with inquiry, problem-based learning, and project-based learning. In contrast to taking an objective test, a performance task requires students to apply their knowledge and skills to answer a question, solve a problem, or complete some other real-world task.

personalized learning. Personalized learning is organized for individual students to gain the literacies, skills, and dispositions they need to be successful. Whether in the classroom, online, or in the community, it can include hands-on and technology-enabled learning. Personalized learning is often centered on students' own interests. It can also include internships. Some educators equate personalized learning with student-centered learning.

portfolio. Portfolios are assessment tools that show a person's accomplishments over time. Students self-select the work to be included in their portfolios. In conferences with peers, educators, or parents, students can be prompted to reflect on the content, process, and meaning of the learning represented by each piece in the portfolio. "Learning portfolios" not only show best work or final products, but also show process and progress.

problem-based learning. In this learning framework, educators present a problem or dilemma for students to solve. In the literature, this framework is also called "challenge-based learning."

professional learning community (PLC). PLCs are ways that principals can organize the faculty for professional growth. PLCs develop a shared goal, make collective commitments, and take a problem-solving approach to meeting teaching and learning challenges. They are results-oriented; when PLCs are successful, student learning improves (DuFour 2001). Principals can organize PLCs by grade level, discipline, or other criteria that make sense in terms of addressing student and educator needs.

project-based learning. In this framework, students investigate real-world problems and challenges over an extended period of time. While the goal of project-based learning is for students to acquire deeper knowledge through their own extended efforts, educators often set the purpose, the type of the final product, and the audience for the project. In practice, project-based learning may result in a focus on the final product as much as or more than on the learning process itself.

public relations. Public relations, also known as promotion, is one-way communication in which people tell others who they are, what they do, and whom they serve.

question-answer relationship (QAR). QAR is a questioning strategy that helps students distinguish between locate-type questions and answers and think-type questions and answers. In QAR, students classify literal, inferential, or evaluative questions.

question the author (QtA). The goal of the QtA comprehension strategy is to increase readers' interaction and engagement with texts. Through questioning, readers learn to deconstruct the writer's craft and learn that through their interpretations, they share authority with the author.

reading comprehension strategies. There are seven core reading comprehension strategies that readers use to help them understand a text (Keene and Zimmermann, 1997; Moreillon 2007, 2012a, 2013; Zimmermann and Hutchins, 2003). Educators model these strategies, and students practice them with educator support. When readers are proficient, these strategies become skills they can select from and use at appropriate times to gain or regain comprehension and make sense of a text.

reciprocal mentorship. When educators work as equal partners and coplan, coteach, and coassess student learning, they serve as mentors for one another. One or more partners may have expertise in one or more areas, which they contribute to the shared learning of the team.

registers. In speaking and writing, registers refer to the level of informality or formality in which speakers and writers communicate their ideas. For example, a student talking or writing to a friend would not make the same word choices as when speaking or writing to an elder or to a prospective employer.

research-based instructional strategies. Researchers at Mid-Continent Research for Education and Learning conducted a meta-analysis of educational research studies to determine specific components of instruction that improve students' performance on standardized tests. They identified nine strategies that have a strong effect on student achievement, including identifying similarities and differences, summarizing and notetaking, nonlinguistic representations, cooperative learning, setting objectives and providing feedback, and questions, cues, and advanced organizers.

scaffolds. Scaffolds are structures or tools implemented by educators that support student learning. Scaffolds help learners reach a level of achievement that they may not be able to reach without the scaffold. A lesson plan format is a procedural scaffold. Outlines and graphic organizers are examples of instructional scaffolds.

schema. Schema theory suggests that knowledge is stored in abstract structures called schemas. People organize and retain information in their memories based on a hierarchy of characteristics. For instance, in my schema for my dog Pearl, I have an overarching concept of animal, then pet, then dog, then poodle, then finally the specific traits of this particular dog. When applied to reading comprehension, schema theory postulates that readers have preconceived concepts that influence their understanding of texts. This background knowledge is applied when texts are being read. Schemas change when new information supplants old information or is integrated into prior understandings.

shared writing. Shared writing involves educators acting as scribes while educators and students co-construct texts. Educators use think-alouds to demonstrate the process. The goal is to teach writing through writing.

sign or symbol systems. Sign systems are ways to express meaning and understanding. Readers can respond to literature and information using different modalities, including language, art, drama, music, and mathematics.

skills. In this book, the 4Cs identified by the Partnership for 21st Century Learning are the skills that future ready students must learn and practice: (1) creativity and innovation, (2) critical thinking and problem solving, (3) communication, and (4) collaboration (http://p21.org).

social media. Platforms such as Facebook, Twitter, Instagram, YouTube, Pinterest, and the like make communicating and sharing with a larger audience easy. Although many students are using these tools outside of school, access to them may be blocked by Internet filters in some schools.

standards. As a rule, standards are set at the state and national levels. They specify what students are expected to know and be able to do at specific points during their schooling.

STEM, STEAM, and STREAM. These acronyms represent various combinations of the following terms: science, technology, robotics or reading (and writing), engineering, the arts, and mathematics. Educational policy-makers who are concerned with developing a future ready workforce support STEM, STEAM, and STREAM initiatives.

strengths-based leadership. In this model, leaders know their own strengths and maximize the effectiveness of their organizations by building teams with complementary strengths. The focus on strengths, rather than deficits, also engenders a positive culture (see Rath 2008).

Stripling Model. Developed by Barbara Stripling (2003), there are six phases in this student-centered inquiry model: connect, wonder, investigate, construct, express, and reflect.

summative assessment. Educators use summative assessments to evaluate student learning at the end of an instructional unit. These assessments may take the form of inquiry learning products, written papers, or exams. They show the level of students' proficiency in meeting the targeted learning objectives. Standardized tests are also considered summative assessments.

systems thinking. According to the Waters Foundation, "systems thinking utilizes habits, tools and concepts to develop an understanding of the interdependent structures of dynamic systems. When individuals have a better understanding of systems, they are better able to identify the leverage points that lead to desired outcomes" (http://watersfoundation.org/systems-thinking/what/). Educators who understand how their teaching is supported or constrained by the system in which they work can learn how to collaborate with others to problem solve and make the system more supportive and effective. The goal of systems thinking in schools is to fine-tune, modify, or transform the system in order to benefit the entire learning community.

text. A text is the totality of a work that weaves together print and illustration, whether in paper or in electronic format. With digital resources, text may also include audio, moving images, or other information in addition to print.

text-dependent questioning protocol. There are four questions in this protocol: What does the text say? How does the text work? What does the text mean? What does the text inspire you to do? This strategy was developed by Douglas Fisher and Nancy Frey (2015).

text features. Text features help organize information. Tables of contents, indexes, time lines, glossaries, graphics (including illustrations, photographs, charts, maps, tables, and captions and labels), headings or titles, subheadings or subtitles, font variations, and other print elements are features often used in informational texts.

text set. Similar to a pathfinder, a text set is a set of materials that is provided by educators or created by students that helps learners investigate a topic, theme, problem, or dilemma. A text set is usually comprised of hard-copy printed materials and can be effectively combined with a web-based pathfinder of electronic resources.

text structures. Text structures are frameworks that can be used in both narrative and expository texts. Examples include description, cause and effect, comparison and contrast, problem and solution, and sequencing. In some cases, certain words signal particular structures. For instance, sequencing can be indicated by words such as *first, next, then,* and *finally.*

think-aloud strategy. Think-alouds are used by educators and students when they wish to orally share their thinking processes. In a how-to strategy lesson, educators use think-alouds in modeling. Think-alouds help others understand what's going on inside a person's head when he or she is learning. Think-alouds are a form of metacognition—thinking about thinking. When students understand their own thinking processes, they learn better.

think-pair-share. In this procedure, a question or problem is posed. Students think about a response or solution and turn to a partner to share their responses, and then the educators ask for volunteers to share their responses with the larger group or whole class.

third space. Students' experiences outside of school are the "first space," and state-mandated curricula are the "second space." The "third space" is a negotiated space where the first two overlap to make space for authentic learning. Students' authentic real-world questions are essential components of the third space.

WISE. The WISE inquiry model was developed by New York school librarians in the WSWHE BOCES School Library System. The model includes these phases: wonder, investigate, synthesize, express, and reflect.

writing process. There are five steps in the writing process: prewriting, writing, revision, editing, and publishing. These can be accomplished on paper, or students and educators can use various digital tools to facilitate this process.

zone of proximal development (ZPD). The ZPD is "the distance between the actual developmental level as determined by independent problem solving and the level of potential development as determined through problem solving under adult guidance, or in collaboration with more capable peers" (Vygotsky 1978, 86).

WORKS CITED

Alliance for Excellent Education (AEE). 2016a. "Digital Learning Day: What Do We Mean by Digital Learning?" www.digitallearningday.org/domain/54.

———. 2016b. "Future Ready Librarians." www.futureready.org/program-overview/librarians.

———. 2016c. "Future Ready Schools." www.futureready.org.

American Association of School Librarians (AASL). 1960. *Standards for School Library Programs.* Chicago: American Library Association.

———. 1969. *Standards for School Media Programs.* Chicago: American Library Association and National Education Association.

———. 2006. *Lessons Learned: Collaboration.* Chicago: American Association of School Librarians.

———. 2007. *Standards for the 21st-Century Learner.* Chicago: American Association of School Librarians. http://ala.org/aasl/standards.

———. 2009a. *Empowering Learners: Guidelines for School Library Programs.* Chicago: American Association of School Librarians.

———. 2009b. "Position Statement on the School Librarian's Role in Reading." www.ala.org/aasl/advocacy/resources/statements/reading-role.

———. 2009c. *Standards for the 21st-Century Learner in Action.* Chicago: American Library Association.

———. 2016a. "Position Statements: Definition for an Effective School Library Program." www.ala.org/aasl/advocacy/resources/statements.

———. 2016b. "Position Statements: Instructional Role of the School Librarian." www.ala.org/aasl/advocacy/resources/statements.

———. 2018. *National School Library Standards for Learners, School Librarians, and School Libraries.* Chicago: American Library Association.

American Association of School Librarians Advocacy Committee. "Advocacy Definitions." www.ala.org/aasl/advocacy/definitions.

American Association of School Librarians and Association for Educational Communications and Technology. 1988. *Information Power: Guidelines for School Library Media Programs.* Chicago: American Library Association.

———. 1998. *Information Power: Building Partnerships for Learning.* Chicago: American Library Association.

American Library Association. 2008. *Library Advocate's Handbook,* 3rd ed. www.ala.org/advocacy/advocacy-university/library-advocates-handbook.

———. 2013. *Digital Literacy, Libraries, and Public Policy: Report of the Office of Information Technology Policy's Digital Literacy Task Force.* www.districtdispatch.org/wp-content/uploads/2013/01/2012_OITP_digilitreport_1_22_13.pdf.

Azzam, Amy M. 2014. "Motivated to Learn: A Conversation with Daniel Pink." *Educational Leadership* 72 (1): 12–17.

Beck, Isabel L., Margaret G. McKeown, Cheryl Sandora, Linda Kucan, and Jo Worthy. 1996. "Questioning the Author: A Yearlong Classroom Implementation to Engage Students with Text." *The Elementary School Journal* 96 (4): 385–414.

Berger, Warren. 2014. *A More Beautiful Question: The Power of Inquiry to Spark Breakthrough Ideas*. New York: Bloomsbury.

Biancarosa, Gina, and Catherine E. Snow. 2006. *Reading Next—A Vision for Action and Research in Middle and High School Literacy: A Report to the Carnegie Corporation of New York*, 2nd ed. Washington, DC: Alliance for Excellence in Education.

Booth, Eric. 2013. "A Recipe for Artful Schooling." *Educational Leadership* 70 (5): 22–27.

Boyles, Nancy. 2012. "Closing in on Close Reading." *Educational Leadership* 70 (4): 36–41.

Buck Institute for Education, John Larmer, John Mergendoller, and Suzie Boss. 2015. *Setting the Standard for Project Based Learning: The Why, What, and How of Gold Standard PBL*. Alexandria, VA: Association for Supervision and Curriculum Development.

Buehl, Doug. 2009. *Classroom Strategies for Interactive Learning*. Newark, DE: International Reading Association.

Bullock, David. 2004. "Moving from Theory to Practice: An Examination of the Factors That Preservice Teachers Encounter as They Attempt to Gain Experience Teaching with Technology during Field Placement Experiences." *Journal of Technology and Teacher Education* 19 (4): 101–6.

Burgess, Shelley, and Beth Houf. 2017. *Lead Like a Pirate: How to Make School Amazing for Your Students and Staff*. San Diego, CA: Dave Burgess Consulting.

Chen, Milton. 2012. *Education Nation: Six Leading Edges of Innovation in Our Schools*. San Francisco: Jossey-Bass.

Church, Audrey P. 2008. "The Instructional Role of the Library Media Specialist as Perceived by Elementary School Principals." *School Library Media Research* 11: 1–36.

Cialdini, Robert B. 2008. *Influence: Science and Practice*, 5th ed. Boston: Allyn & Bacon.

Cohen, Dan S. 2005. *The Heart of Change Field Guide: Tools and Tactics for Leading Change in Your Organization*. Boston: Harvard Business School Press.

Collaborative for Academic, Social, and Emotional Learning. "CASEL: Educating Hearts. Inspiring Minds." www.casel.org.

Common Sense Education. "Digital Citizenship." www.commonsensemedia.org.

Couros, George. 2015. *The Innovator's Mindset: Empower Learning, Unleash Talent, and Lead in a Culture of Creativity*. San Diego, CA: Dave Burgess Consulting.

Donham, Jean. 2014. "College Ready—What Can We Learn from First-Year College Assignments? An Examination of Assignments at Iowa Colleges and Universities." *School Library Research* 17: 1–21.

Donhauser, Meg, Heather Hersey, Cathy Stutzman, and Marci Zane. 2014. "From Lesson Plan to Learning Plan: An Introduction to the Inquiry Learning Plan." *School Library Monthly* 31 (1): 11–13.

Drucker, Peter. 2006. *Managing the Non-Profit Organization: Practices and Principles*. New York: HarperCollins.

DuFour, Richard. 2001. "In the Right Context: The Effective Leader Concentrates on a Foundation of Programs, Procedures, Beliefs, Experiences, and Habits." *Journal of Staff Development* 22 (1): 14-17.

DuFour, Richard, and Robert Marzano. 2009. "How Teachers Learn: High-Leverage Strategies for Principal Leadership." *Educational Leadership* 66 (5): 62–68.

———. 2011. *Leaders of Learning: How District, School, and Classroom Leaders Improve Student Learning*. Bloomington, IN: Solution Tree.

Duke, Nell K., P. David Pearson, Stephanie L. Strachan, and Alison K. Billman. 2011. "Essential Elements of Fostering and Teaching Reading Comprehension." In *What Research Has to Say about Reading Instruction,* 4th ed., edited by S. Jay Samuels and Alan E. Farstrup, 51–93. Newark, DE: International Literacy Association.

Dweck, Carol. 2006. *Mindset: The New Psychology of Success.* New York: Random House.

Education Week. 2017. "Classroom Technology: Where Schools Stand." www.edweek.org/media/techcounts2017_release.pdf.

Edwards, Mark. 2014. *Every Child, Every Day: A Digital Conversion Model for Student Achievement.* Boston: Pearson.

———. 2015. *Thank You for Your Leadership: The Power of Distributed Leadership in a Digital Conversion Model.* Boston: Pearson.

Elias, Maurice J., Joseph J. Perrito, and Dominic C. Moceri. 2016. *The Other Side of the Report Card: Assessing Students' Social, Emotional, and Character Development.* Thousand Oaks, CA: Corwin.

Ewbank, Ann Dutton. 2010. "Values-Oriented Factors Leading to Retention of School Librarian Positions: A School District Case Study." *School Library Media Research* 13: 1–11.

Fawley, Nancy N. 2014. "Flipped Classrooms." *American Libraries* 45 (9/10): 19.

Feltman, Charles. 2009. *The Thin Book of Trust: An Essential Primer for Building Trust at Work.* Bend, OR: Thin Book.

Fisher, Douglas, and Nancy Frey. 2009. *Background Knowledge: The Missing Piece in the Comprehension Puzzle.* Portsmouth, NH: Heinemann.

———. 2015. "Fostering Critical Thinking about Texts." *Educational Leadership* 73 (1): 82–84.

Follett Learning. "Project Connect." www2.follettlearning.com/projectconnect/vision.cfm.

Friend, Marilyn, and Lynne Cook. 2012. *Interactions: Collaboration Skills for School Professionals,* 7th ed. Boston: Pearson.

Fullan, Michael. 2010. *All Systems Go.* Thousand Oaks, CA: Corwin.

Fullan, Michael, and Andy Hargreaves. 1996. *What's Worth Fighting for in Your School?* New York: Teachers College Press.

Future Ready Schools. 2016. "Future Ready Librarians." www.futureready.org/program-overview/librarians.

Gordon, Carol A. 2016. "Teacher-Librarians as Champions of Digital Equity." *Synergy* 14 (1). www.slav.vic.edu.au/synergy/volume-14-number-1-2016.html.

Grazer, Brian, and Charles Fishman. 2015. *A Curious Mind: The Secret to a Bigger Life.* New York: Simon & Schuster.

Green, Lucy Santos. 2014. "Through the Looking Glass: Examining Technology Integration in School Librarianship." *Knowledge Quest* 43 (1): 36–43.

Gruenert, Steve, and Todd Whitaker. 2017. *School Culture Recharged: Strategies to Energize Your Staff and Culture.* Alexandria, VA: Association for Supervision and Curriculum Development.

Guskey, Thomas. 2000. *Evaluating Professional Development*. Thousand Oaks, CA: Corwin.

Hall, Pete, Deborah Childs-Bowen, Phyllis Pajardo, and Ann Cunningham-Morris. 2015. *Leadership Matters: Building Principals' Capacity with the ASCD Principal Leadership Development Framework*. Alexandria, VA: Association for Supervision and Curriculum Development.

Harada, Violet. 2005. "Librarians and Teachers as Research Partners: Reshaping Practices Based on Assessment and Reflection." *School Libraries Worldwide* 11 (2): 49–72.

Hargreaves, Andy. 2003. *Teaching in the Knowledge Society: Education in the Age of Insecurity*. New York: Teachers College Press.

Hargreaves, Andy, and Michael Fullan. 2012. *Professional Capital: Transforming Teaching in Every School*. New York: Teachers College Press.

Harris, Judi. 1998. *Design Tools for the Internet-Supported Classroom*. Alexandria, VA: Association for Supervision and Curriculum Development.

Harvey, Stephanie, and Anne Goudvis. 2013. "Comprehension at the Core." *Reading Teacher* 66 (6): 432–39.

Haycock, Ken. 2007. "Collaboration: Critical Success Factors for Student Learning." *School Libraries Worldwide* 13 (1): 25–35.

———. 2011. "Advocacy Revisited: Newer Insights Based on Research and Evidence." Presented at the 7th Follett Lecture at the Dominican Graduate School of Library and Information Science, Dominican University, River Forest, IL.

———. 2017. "Leadership from the Middle: Building Influence for Change." In *The Many Faces of School Library Leadership*, 2nd ed., edited by Sharon Coatney and Violet H. Harada, 1–12. Santa Barbara, CA: Libraries Unlimited.

Heath, Chip, and Dan Heath. 2007. *Made to Stick: Why Some Ideas Survive and Others Die*. New York: Random House.

———. 2010. *Switch: How to Change Things When Change Is Hard*. New York: Broadway Books.

Hewlett Foundation. 2013. "Deeper Learning Competencies." www.hewlett.org/library/deeper-learning-defined.

———. 2014. "Open Educational Resources: Breaking the Lockbox on Education." www.hewlett.org/wp-content/uploads/2016/08/OER%20White%20Paper%20Nov%2022%202013%20Final_0.pdf.

International Society for Technology in Education (ISTE). 2016a. "ISTE Standards for Students." www.iste.org/standards/standards/for-students-2016.

———. 2016b. "Redefining Learning in a Technology-Driven World: A Report to Support Adoption of the ISTE Standards for Students." www.iste.org/docs/Standards-Resources/iste-standards_students-2016_research-validity-report_final.pdf?sfvrsn=0.0680021527232122.

———. 2017. "ISTE Standards for Educators." www.iste.org/standards/standards/for-educators.

Jenkins, Henry, Ravi Purushotma, Margaret Weigel, Katie Clinton, and Alice J. Robison. 2009. *Confronting the Challenges of Participatory Culture: Media Education for the 21st Century*. Chicago: John D. and Catherine T. MacArthur Foundation.

Johnston, Melissa P., and Lucy Santos Green. 2018. "Still Polishing the Diamond: School Library Research over the Last Decade. *School Library Research* 21: 1-63.

Kachel, Debra E., et al. 2011. *School Library Research Summarized: A Graduate Class Project*. Mansfield, PA: School of Library and Information Technologies Department, Mansfield University. www.sl-it.mansfield.edu/current-students/school-library-impact-studies-project.cfm.

Kallick, Bena, and Allison Zmuda. 2017. *Students at the Center: Personalized Learning with Habits of Mind*. Alexandria, VA: Association for Supervision and Curriculum Development.

Keene, Ellin Oliver, and Susan Zimmermann. 1997. *Mosaic of Thought: Teaching Comprehension in a Reader's Workshop*. Portsmouth, NH: Heinemann.

Kegan, Robert, and Lisa Laskow Lahey. 2016. *An Everyone Culture: Becoming a Deliberately Developmental Organization*. Boston: Harvard Business Review.

Khan, Salman. 2012. *The One World School House: Education Reimagined*. New York: Twelve.

Kimmel, Sue C. 2012. "Collaboration as School Reform: Are There Patterns in the Chaos of Planning with Teachers?" *School Library Research* 15: 1–15.

Knowles, Malcolm. 1980. *The Modern Practice of Adult Education: From Pedagogy to Andragogy*. Wilton, CT: Association.

———. 1990. *The Adult Learner: A Neglected Species,* 4th ed. Houston, TX: Gulf.

Kopcha, Theodore J. 2010. "A Systems-Based Approach to Technology Integration Using Mentoring and Communities of Practice." *Educational Technology Research and Development* 58 (2): 175–90.

Kotter, John P. 2012. *Leading Change*. Boston: Harvard Business Review.

Kuhlthau, Carol Collier. 2013. "Inquiry Inspires Original Research." *School Library Monthly* 30 (2): 5–8.

Kuhlthau, Carol C., Leslie K. Maniotes, and Ann K. Caspari. 2012. *Guided Inquiry Design: A Framework for Inquiry in Your School*. Santa Barbara, CA: Libraries Unlimited.

———. 2015. *Guided Inquiry: Learning in the 21st Century,* 2nd ed. Santa Barbara, CA: Libraries Unlimited.

Lakoff, George. 2014. *The ALL NEW Don't Think of an Elephant: Know Your Issues and Frame the Debate*. White River, VT: Chelsea Green.

Lance, Keith Curry. 2017. "School Library Impact Studies." www.keithcurrylance.com/school-library-impact-studies.

Lance, Keith Curry, and Debra E. Kachel. 2018. "Why School Librarians Matter: What Years of Research Tell Us." *Phi Delta Kappan Online*. www.kappanonline.org/lance-kachel-school-librarians-matter-years-research/.

Lance, Keith C., and Linda Hofshire. 2012. "Change in School Librarian Staffing Linked with Change in CSAP Reading Performance, 2005 to 2011." www.lrs.org/closer-look-studies/change-in-school-librarian-staffing-linked-with-change-in-csap-reading-performance-2005-to-2011–2/.

Lankes, R. David. 2012. *Expect More: Demanding Better Libraries for Today's Complex World*. CreateSpace Independent Publishing Platform.

Lemke, Jay L. 1998. "Metamedia Literacy: Transforming Meanings and Media." In *Handbook of Literacy and Technology: Transformations in a Post-Typographic World,* edited by David Reinking, Michael C. McKenna, Linda D. Labbo, and Ronald D. Kieffer, 283–302. Mahwah, NJ: L. Erlbaum Associates.

Leslie, Ian. 2014. *Curiosity: The Desire to Know and Why Your Future Depends on It*. New York: Basic Books.

Leu, Donald J., J. Gregory McVerry, W. Ian O'Byrne, Carita Kiili, Lisa Zawilinski, Heidi Everett-Cacopardo, Clint Kennedy, and Elena Forzani. 2011. "The New Literacies of Online Reading Comprehension: Expanding the Literacy and Learning Curriculum." *Journal of Adolescent & Adult Literacy* 55 (1): 5–14.

Levitov, Deborah. 2017. "The School Librarian as an Advocacy Leader." In *The Many Faces of School Library Leadership*, 2nd ed., edited by Sharon Coatney and Violet H. Harada, 31–46. Santa Barbara, CA: Libraries Unlimited.

Library Research Service. 2017. "School Library Impact Studies." www.lrs.org/data-tools/school-libraries/impact-studies.

Lilead Project. 2011. "Lilead Project: Empower, Engage, Equip." www.lileadproject.org.

Loertscher, David V. 2014. "Collaboration and Coteaching." *Teacher Librarian* 42 (2): 8–19.

Maniotes, Leslie K., and Carol C. Kuhlthau. 2014. "Making the Shift from Traditional Research Assignments to Guided Inquiry Learning." *Knowledge Quest* 43 (2): 8–17.

Martin, Ann M. 2013. *Empowering Leadership: Developing Behaviors for Success*. Chicago: American Library Association.

Marzano, Robert J. 2003. *What Works in Schools: Translating Research into Action*. Alexandria, VA: Association for Supervision and Curriculum Development.

McKenna, Michael C., and Richard D. Robinson. 1990. "Content Literacy: A Definition and Implications." *Journal of Reading* 34 (3): 184–86.

McKibben, Sarah. 2016. "Planning for Great Group Work." *Education Update* 58 (6): 2–3, 6.

McTighe, Jay, and Grant Wiggins. 2013. *Essential Questions: Opening Doors to Student Understanding*. Alexandria, VA: Association for Supervision and Curriculum Development.

Mills, Geoffrey E. 2010. *Action Research: A Guide for the Researcher*, 4th ed. Upper Saddle River, NJ: Pearson.

Moreillon, Judi. 2003. "A Case Study of University Faculty Development Utilizing Technology: People, Place, and Process." PhD diss., University of Arizona, Tucson.

———. 2007. *Collaborative Strategies for Teaching Reading Comprehension: Maximizing Your Impact*. Chicago: American Library Association.

———. 2008. "Two Heads Are Better Than One: Influencing Preservice Classroom Teachers' Understanding and Practice of Classroom-Library Collaboration." *School Library Media Research* 11: 1–26.

———. 2012a. *Coteaching Reading Comprehension Strategies in Secondary School Libraries: Maximizing Your Impact*. Chicago: American Library Association.

———. 2012b. "Job-Embedded Professional Development: An Orchard of Opportunity." In *Growing Schools: School Librarians as Professional Developers*, edited by Debbie Abilock, Kristin Fontichiaro, and Violet Harada, 141–56. Santa Barbara, CA: Libraries Unlimited.

———. 2013. *Coteaching Reading Comprehension Strategies in Elementary School Libraries: Maximizing Your Impact*. Chicago: American Library Association.

———. 2014. "Inquiry Learning and Reading Comprehension Strategy Instruction: Processes That Go Hand in Hand." *Knowledge Quest* 43 (2): E1–4. www.ala.org/aasl/sites/ala.org.aasl/files/content/NovDec14_OE1_Moreillon.pdf.

———. 2016. "Assessment Is Not an Option: Gathering Evidence of Effectiveness."
School Library Connection 1 (7): 28–30.

———. 2017a. "Literacy Leadership and the School Librarian: Reading and Writing—
Foundational Skills for Multiple Literacies." In *The Many Faces of School Library
Leadership*, 2nd ed., edited by Sharon Coatney and Violet H. Harada, 86–108. Santa
Barbara, CA: Libraries Unlimited.

———. 2017b. "The Learning Commons: A Strategic Opportunity for Teacher
Librarian Leadership." *Teacher Librarian* 44 (3): 21–25.

Moreillon, Judi, and Susan D. Ballard, eds. 2013. *Best of KQ: Instructional Partnerships:
A Pathway to Leadership.* Chicago: American Association of School Librarians.

Moreillon, Judi, Michelle Luhtala, and Christina Russo. 2011. "Learning That Sticks:
Engaged Educators + Engaged Learners." *School Library Monthly* 28 (1): 17–20.

National Assessment of Educational Progress. 2015. "Nation's Report Card:
Mathematics & Reading." www.nationsreportcard.gov/reading_math_2015.

National Council for the Social Studies (NCSS). 2013. "The College, Career, and Civic
Life (C3) Framework for Social Studies State Standards: Guidance for Enhancing
the Rigor of K–12 Civics, Economics, Geography, and History." www.socialstudies
.org/c3.

National Research Council. 2000. *How People Learn: Brain, Mind, Experience, and School,*
2nd ed. Washington, DC: National Academies Press.

New Media Consortium and Consortium for School Networking. 2017. *The NMC/CoSN
Horizon Report: 2017 K–12 Edition.* www.cdn.nmc.org/media/2017-nmc-cosn
-horizon-report-k12-EN.pdf.

NGSS Lead States. 2013. "Next Generation Science Standards: For States, by States."
www.nextgenscience.org.

Organisation of Economic Cooperation and Development (OECD). 2015. "Students,
Computers, and Learning: Making the Connection." www.oecd.org/publications/
students-computers-and-learning-9789264239555-en.htm.

Ouzts, Dan T. 1998. "Enhancing Literacy Using the Question-Answer Relationship."
Social Studies and the Young Learner 10 (4): 26–29.

Parrott, Deborah J., and Karin J. Keith. 2015. "Three Heads Are Better Than One."
Teacher Librarian 42 (5): 12–18.

Partnership for 21st Century Learning (P21). www.p21.org.

Pearce, Terry. 2013. *Leading Out Loud: A Guide for Engaging Others in Creating the Future,*
3rd ed. San Francisco: Jossey-Bass.

Polselli, Robert. 2002. "Combining Web-Based Training and Mentorship to Improve
Technology Integration in the K–12 Classroom." *Journal of Technology and Teacher
Education* 10 (2): 247–72.

Rath, Tom. 2008. *Strengths-Based Leadership: Great Leaders, Teams, and Why People
Follow.* New York: Gallup.

Reinsborough, Patrick, and Doyle Canning. 2010. *Re:Imagining Change: How to Use
Story-Based Strategy to Win Campaigns, Build Movements, and Change the World.*
Oakland, CA: PM.

Resnick, Lauren. 1999. "Making America Smarter." *Education Week* 18 (40): 38–40.

Ribble, Mike. 2015. *Digital Citizenship in Schools: Nine Elements All Students Should Know,*
3rd ed. Arlington, VA: International Society for Technology in Education.

Ritchhart, Ron. 2015. *Creating Cultures of Thinking: The 8 Forces We Must Master to Truly Transform Our Schools*. San Francisco: Jossey-Bass.

Robbins, Pam. 2015. *Peer Coaching to Enrich Professional Practice, School Culture, and Student Learning*. Alexandria, VA: Association for Supervision and Curriculum Development.

Robinson, Ken. 2006. "Do Schools Kill Creativity?" TED Talk. www.ted.com/talks/ken _robinson_says_schools_kill_creativity.

———. 2013. *Finding Your Element: How to Discover Your Talents and Passions and Transform Your Life*. New York: Viking.

Robinson, Ken, and Lou Aronica. 2015. *Creative Schools: The Grassroots Revolution That's Transforming Education*. New York: Viking.

Rogers, Everett. 1995. *Diffusion of Innovations*, 4th ed. New York: Free.

Rothstein, Dan, and Luz Santana. 2015. *Make Just One Change: Teach Students to Ask Their Own Questions*. Cambridge, MA: Harvard Education Press.

Rothstein, Dan, Luz Santana, and Andrew P. Minigan. 2015. "Making Questions Flow." *Educational Leadership* 73 (1): 70–75.

Routman, Regie. 2014. *Read, Write, Lead: Breakthrough Strategies for Schoolwide Literacy Success*. Alexandria, VA: Association for Supervision and Curriculum Development.

Ruppert, Sandra S. 2006. *Critical Evidence: How the Arts Support Student Achievement*. www.nasaa-arts.org/Publications/critical-evidence.pdf.

Schlechty, Phil. 2001. *Shaking Up the Schoolhouse: How to Support and Sustain Educational Innovation*. San Francisco: Jossey-Bass.

Schmoker, Mike. 2006. *Results Now: How We Can Achieve Unprecedented Improvements in Teaching and Learning*. Alexandria, VA: Association for Supervision and Curriculum Development.

Scholastic. 2016. *School Libraries Work! A Compendium of Research Supporting the Effectiveness of School Libraries*. New York: Scholastic Library.

Senge, Peter M. 1990. *The Fifth Discipline: The Art and Practice of a Learning Organization*. New York: Doubleday.

Senge, Peter, Nelda Cambron-McCabe, Timothy Lucas, Bryan Smith, Janis Dutton, and Art Kleiner. 2012. *Schools That Learn: A Fifth Discipline Fieldbook for Educators, Parents, and Everyone Who Cares about Education*. New York: Crown Business.

Shannon, Donna M. 2009. "Principals' Perspectives of School Librarians." *School Libraries Worldwide* 15 (2): 1–22.

Sheninger, Eric C., and Thomas C. Murray. 2017. *Learning Transformed: 8 Keys to Designing Tomorrow's Schools, Today*. Alexandria, VA: Association for Supervision and Curriculum Development.

Short, Kathy G., and Carolyn Burke. 1991. *Creating Curriculum: Teachers and Students as a Community of Learners*. Portsmouth, NH: Heinemann.

Simmons, Annette. 2007. *Whoever Tells the Best Story Wins: How to Use Your Own Stories to Communicate with Power and Impact*. New York: AMACON.

Sinek, Simon. 2009. *Start with Why: How Great Leaders Inspire Everyone to Take Action*. New York: Penguin.

———. 2014. *Leaders Eat Last: Why Some Teams Come Together and Others Don't*. New York: Portfolio/Penguin.

Sinek, Simon, David Mead, and Peter Docker. 2017. *Find Your Why: A Practical Guide for Discovering Purpose for You and Your Team.* New York: Penguin.

Snipes, Phyllis Robinson. 2017. "Developing a Meaningful Self-Assessment/Evaluation Instrument in Georgia." *School Library Connection.* ABC-CLIO.

Snow, Catherine E. 2013. "Cold versus Warm Close Reading: Building Students' Stamina for Struggling with Text." *Reading Today* 30 (6): 18–19.

Staker, Heather, and Michael B. Horn. 2012. "Classifying K–12 Blended Learning." San Mateo, CA: Innosight Institute. www.eric.ed.gov/?id=ED535180.

Stiggins, Rick J. 2011. *An Introduction to Student-Involved Assessment for Learning,* 6th ed. Upper Saddle River, NJ: Pearson.

Stripling, Barbara. 2003. "Inquiry-Based Learning." In *Curriculum Connections through the Library,* edited by Barbara K. Stripling and Sandra Hughes-Hassell, 3–39. Westport, CT: Libraries Unlimited.

Swan, Bonnie, and Juli Dixon. 2006. "The Effects of Mentor-Supported Technology Professional Development on Middle School Mathematics Teachers' Attitudes and Practice." *Contemporary Issues in Technology and Teacher Education* 6 (1): 67–86.

Sztabnik, Brian. 2015. "A New Definition of Rigor." www.edutopia.org/blog/a-new -definition-of-rigor-brian-sztabnik.

Todd, Ross J. 2007. "Evidence-Based Practice in School Libraries: From Advocacy to Action." In *School Reform and the School Library Media Specialist,* edited by Sandra Hughes-Hassell and Violet H. Harada, 57–78. Westport, CT: Libraries Unlimited.

———. 2009. "School Librarianship and Evidence-Based Practice: Progress, Perspectives, and Challenges." *Evidence Based Library and Information Practice* 4 (2): 78–96. ejournals.library.ualberta.ca/index.php/EBLIP/article/view/4637/5318.

Todd, Ross J., Carol A. Gordon, and Ya-Ling Lu. 2011. *One Common Goal: Student Learning: Report of Findings and Recommendations of the New Jersey Library Study, Phase 2.* Center for International Scholarship in School Libraries. www.cissl .rutgers.edu.

———. 2012. "Clone the School Librarian: Evidence of the Role of the School Librarian in Professional Development." In *Growing Schools: Librarians as Professional Developers,* edited by Debbie Abilock, Kristin Fontichario, and Violet H. Harada, xxi–xxiii. Santa Barbara, CA: Libraries Unlimited.

Tough, Paul. 2012. *How Children Succeed: Grit, Curiosity, and the Hidden Power of Character.* Boston: Houghton Mifflin.

Trilling, Bernie, and Charles Fadel. 2012. *21st Century Skills: Learning for Life in Our Times.* San Francisco: Jossey-Bass.

Turkle, Sherry. 2015. *Reclaiming Conversation: The Power of Talk in the Digital Age.* New York: Penguin.

U.S. Department of Education. 2015. Every Student Succeeds Act. www.ed.gov/ essa?src=rn.

Vygotsky, Lev. 1978. *Mind in Society: The Development of Higher Psychological Processes.* Cambridge, MA: Harvard University Press.

Wagner, Tony. 2008. "Rigor Redefined." *Educational Leadership* 66 (2): 20–25.

Wagner, Tony, and Ted Dintersmith. 2015. *Most Likely to Succeed: Preparing Our Kids for the Innovation Era.* New York: Scribner.

Weeks, Ann C. 2016. "From Library Power to the Lilead Fellows Program: Creating New Expectations for School Libraries and Librarian Leaders." *Teacher Librarian* 44 (1): 12–15.

Wenger, Etienne. 1998. *Communities of Practice: Learning, Meaning, and Identity.* New York: Cambridge University Press.

Wiggins, Grant, and Jay McTighe. 2005. *Understanding by Design,* 2nd ed. Alexandria, VA: Association for Supervision and Curriculum Development.

Wiggins, Grant, and Denise Wilbur. 2015. "How to Make Your Questions Essential." *Educational Leadership* 73 (1): 11–15.

Wilhelm, Jeffrey D., Tanya N. Baker, and Julie Dube. 2001. *Strategic Reading: Guiding Students to Lifelong Literacy 6–12.* Portsmouth, NH: Heinemann.

Wilkinson, Ian A. G., and Eun Hye Son. 2011. "A Dialogic Turn in Research on Learning and Teaching to Comprehend." In *Handbook of Reading Research, Volume 4,* edited by Michael I. Kamil, P. David Pearson, Elizabeth B. Moje, and Peter P. Afflerbach, 359–86. New York: Routledge.

Wineburg, Sam, and Pam Grossman, eds. 2000. *Interdisciplinary Curriculum: Challenges to Implementation.* New York: Teachers College Press.

Woolman, Michael. 2000. *Ways of Knowing: An Introduction to the Theory of Knowledge.* Camberwell, Australia: IBID.

WSWHE BOCES School Library System. 2011. *WISE: Inquiry Model Teacher's Guide.* New York: WSWHE BOCES.

Zimmermann, Susan, and Chryse Hutchins. 2003. *7 Keys to Comprehension: How to Help Your Kids Read It and Get It!* New York: Three Rivers.

Zmuda, Allison, and Violet H. Harada. 2008. "The Learning Specialist: Clarifying the Role of Library Media Specialists." In *Librarians as Learning Specialists: Meeting the Learning Imperative for the 21st Century,* edited by Allison Zmuda and Violet H. Harada, 23–43. Westport, CT: Libraries Unlimited.

INDEX

A

AASL
  See American Association of School Librarians
"AASL Standards Framework for Learners" (AASL), 78
action research
  definition of, 167
  in educator portfolio, 121–122
activities
  for assessment, 126–127
  for connections for learning, 16–17
  for connections in collaborative culture, 161–163
  for deeper learning, 87–88
  for digital learning, 106–107
  for inquiry learning, 51–53
  introduction to, xvi
  for job-embedded professional development, 34–35
  for leadership/advocacy, 144–145
  for literacy learning, 71–72
administrators
  collaborative learning culture, sustaining, 158–159
  collaborative school culture and, 9–11
  leadership/advocacy by, 129–130
  See also principals
admit slip, 167
advocacy
  assessment and, 125
  book study guide, 143–145
  for deeper learning, 85–86
  definition of, 167
  for inquiry learning, 50
  outreach, 138–139
  plan, sample, 140–142
  promotion/marketing and, 137–138
  public relations/advocacy tools, 133–134
  scenario, 139–140
  school librarians as technology stewards, 104
  School Librarians' Public Relations, Marketing, and Advocacy Checklist, 136
  for school library program, 135–137
  of school library to community, 156
  stance, 142–143
  strategies for, 15
  team, principles of influence, 131–133
  for traditional literacy learning, 57, 69–70
AECT (Association for Educational Communications and Technology), 8
agency
  student agency in digital learning, 95
  student self-assessment and, 112
ALA
  See American Library Association
Alliance for Excellent Education (AEE)
  on digital learning, 92, 170
  Future Ready Librarians initiative launched by, x

Future Ready Schools project, 99–100
  mission of/URL for, 93
  on responsibilities of school librarians, 13
alliances, 130–131
alternative teaching, 24
American Association of School Librarians (AASL)
  on advocacy, 135
  advocacy program guidelines/support, 143
  belief about learners, 148
  on classroom-library collaboration, 8
  on collaboration, 168
  on coteaching, 23
  deeper learning competencies, 78
  on digital learning at school library, 91
  on inquiry learning, 38, 39
  on intellectual freedom, 58
  on literacy, 55
  marketing/advocacy tools of, 137
  "Position Statement on the School Librarian's Role in Reading," 58–59
  on reading, 70
  on roles of school librarians, 12–13
  school librarian self-assessment criteria, 121
  school librarians as technology stewards, 95, 104
  "School Library Evaluation Checklist," 119
  on shared foundations/key commitments, 155
  on students' responsibilities, 154
American Library Association (ALA)
  advocacy campaigns of, 134
  on advocacy network, 137
  "Developing Your Action Plan Worksheet," 142
  on digital literacy, 170
  Digital Literacy Task Force, 91–92
  reading advocacy by school librarians, 57–58
andragogy
  definition of, 167
  job-embedded PD meets criteria for, 20
anticipation guide, 167
Arizona Technology Integration Matrix, 98
Aronica, Lou
  Creative Schools: The Grassroots Revolution That's Transforming Education, 4
  on environment for learning, 41
  vision for schooling, 7
arts/humanities, 75–76
ASCD (Association for Supervision and Curriculum Development), 9
assessment
  advocacy and, 125
  book study guide, 125–127
  of coplanning/coteaching, 32
  educator evaluation/self-assessment, 119–121
  educator portfolios, 121–122
  of educator professional learning, 123–125
  educator self-reflection, 122
  formative assessments, 112